A Magical Universe

The Best of *Magical Blend* Magazine

Jerry Snider
Michael Peter Langevin

Illustrations and Cover Design
by Matthew Courtway

Swan•Raven & Co.
An imprint of:
Blue Water Publishing, Inc.
P. O. Box 190
Mill Spring, NC 28756

Library of Congress Cataloging-in-Publication Data
Snider, Jerry, 1952-
Langevin, Michael, 1952-
A Magical Universe: The Best of Magical Blend Magazine

Matthew Courtway.
p.   cm.
ISBN 0-926524-39-9
1. Occultism.
2. New Age movement.
3. Science.
I. Langevin, Michael Peter, 1952-   .
II. Magical blend magazine.
III. Title.
BF1411.S67 1996 133—dc21 96-46576
CIP

Cover Artwork:
Matthew Courtway
Manuscript editors:
Jerry Snider, Michael Langevin, David Merritt, Pam Meyer and Brian Crissey

Special thanks to Larry Chavis, past and present Magical Blend staff members,
and the many friends who have given so much to this project over the years.

Printed in the United States of America.

Address all inquiries to:
Swan•Raven & Co.
an imprint of Blue Water Publishing, Inc.
P. O. Box 190
Mill Spring, NC 28756
U.S.A.

Blue Water Publishing, Inc., is committed
to use 100% recycled paper and organic inks
whenever possible.

Magical Universe

Contents

A Magical Universe

A Magical Universe

Introduction

Snider: What is the Magical Universe?

If you don't already know, I can't help you, for at heart it is an experience, and until you have had that experience and recognize it for what it is, you will not believe what others say about it. Fortunately few are so impoverished. Most of us have had glimpses into the Magical Universe, and most of those glimpses change our lives in some small way, forever. If you have ever fallen head-over-heels in love, you have been there. And if even once you have been touched by grace, you don't need a description from me.

Not that the Magical Universe is always benign. Far from it. There are bogeymen galore, but they seem to serve a purpose, getting us to face our fears if nothing else. Some people are convinced that any encounter with the Magical Universe is an invitation to pure evil, but I suspect this is a case of quantum semi-consciousness—you know, the observer affecting (or should I say infecting) the observed. In most cases, the link to the Magical Universe appears to be passion, and if your overriding passion is a dark one, darkness you will find there. But this, I think, is an aberration, since eyewitness accounts of the Magical Universe are invariably painted in images of light: gods and demigods outlined by the flickering light of the stars; the Otherworldly glow of faery encampments; the ETs' luminous crafts; the Virgin Mary's blinding orb; the angel's halo, the White Light at the end of the NDE tunnel; and, yes, the light bulb of inspiration over the artist's or inventor's head.

The Magical Universe is nothing if not diverse. It reflects images the way a prism reflects light, offering a rainbow of colors with which to paint your conceptualization of it. Perhaps that's why every culture and every tradition recognizes its own window into the Magical Universe but rarely appreciates the neighbor's view. It's as if we become so enchanted with, say, green, we feel compelled to give green our undivided attention, and feel like an unfaithful lover if we shift our gaze to yellow. Such is the nature of enchantment. Any peek into the Magical Universe is the ultimate peek, the peak peek. But is green a better color than yellow? It depends upon perspective. Try to give the magical universe an identity, and you will be right, but in being right you will miss out on all the other colors, which are also reflections of the same Light.

Encounters with the Magical Universe are fleeting. Although they often have a lasting effect, the experience itself fades quickly. But having once seen the Magical Universe, one wants to see it again. We are creatures of habit and naturally try to get back by the same route we took the first time. This is a problem, since there is no reliable path to the Magical Universe. Trying to get back by the same route you took the first time usually results in getting hopelessly lost, or so say the popular myths of encounters with the Magical Universe. The creative genius who becomes lost in madness, the spiritual seeker who ends up a heartless religious fanatic; the everyday Joe whose brush with the paranormal becomes an obsession, these are all testaments to habit-bound humans turning a miraculous encounter into a crippling addiction. There are plenty of burnt-out alcoholics and addicts whose nightmares began with an encounter with the Magical Universe. There are also love junkies, religious hopheads and true-believers of all stripes strung out on various addictive ideologies, all trying in vain to get yet another glimpse of the Magical Universe. These are the walking wounded. You could say they have been blinded by the Light. Whatever stirs passion, it seems, stirs trouble. Perhaps that's why throughout human history the power of the Magical Universe has been stepped down through myth and ritual into socially acceptable channels.

A full-on encounter with the Magical Universe can be just too much to bear. As creatures of habit, we humans see what we have been taught to see, and we have been taught to see in a way that protects the framework of our society. A single glimpse into the Magical Universe can rip the fabric of the known and ordinary. And while it may open us up to whole new worlds, those vistas are often at the expense of the world we believe we know and in which we feel safe.

I suspect that the reason so many people view the Magical Universe with so much fear has something to do with confusing safety for security. Security is based on repetition. Repetition is how we keep the Magical Universe at a safe distance. Repetition creates the illusion of reality. The Magical Universe has little respect for security. If anything, it regards it as a pathology. Religious tradition would no doubt argue this observation, but the fact that every religious tradition ultimately splinters itself into competing doctrines of exoteric dogma and direct experience suggests that tradition is a human attempt to tap the power of the Magical Universe without opening ourselves up to chaos. Direct encounters with the Magical Universe invariably upset the applecart of normalcy; this suggests that novelty, not tradition, is the name of the game. And while novelty can be euphorically liberating, too much of it can be overwhelming. A world in which everything is novel is an insane world; witness our own late 20th century asylum, where novelty has become an obsession.

Many critics lay the blame for this at the media's doorstep and complain that MTV's hugely successful rapid-fire collage of images has infected not only entertainment but also the news. These critics blame the endless and often meaningless barrage of disjointed information for a generation unable to concentrate. I suspect misinterpretation of the data. It seems more likely that what we are seeing, instead, represents an important lesson from the Magical Universe on the growing importance of pattern recognition and holistic thinking. Our modern Western culture has become adept at linear thinking. We have learned it well, to the core. It has become part of our genetic makeup. It is not likely to go away, but then neither are the problems resulting from an over-reliance on it. Over the last few decades we have seen, time and again, that traditional linear attempts to correct one problem only seem to create more problems. Linear thinking takes time, and as more and more of us are discovering, there is not enough time to process the information we are being fed. If there is one thing we have in abundance today it is information, and rather than becoming lost in it, we are at a stage where learning how to use it has become critical. Although our cultural obsession with novelty has helped to weaken moribund traditions and institutions and often makes us feel adrift in our own culture, ultimately it may engender a new way of thinking that can encompass paradox and diversity—a way of thinking that can finally help us to get out of our own way.

Does this mean we are moving closer to the Magical Universe? Some say yes. The New Age movement is built on the premise that the Magical Universe is closing in on us, and points to the relentless novelty of modern life as proof. While much media attention has focused on the New Age movement, all the attention has failed to capture any cohesive picture of it. Most reports, if not downright derisive, are cautiously neutral. The collective phenomenon is treated like an alien virus from outer space. I find this odd since the historical roots of the New Age movement are easy to trace.

Paradoxically, the New Age movement is an offspring of World War II. First, the global nature of the conflict brought cultures and traditions together on a face-to-face, individual level at an unprecedented scale. Second, the emphasis on technological warfare fueled a belief in technology as salvation, a belief which flourished in the postwar years. Thanks to the advances of modern technology, as well as modern merchandising, "New and improved" has become the mantra for postwar industrial bliss. For over four decades, television has focused its attention on convincing us that neither our old toothpaste, soap powder or car is any longer good enough. Why, then, were social critics so surprised when the generations that grew up on television began to question other less tangible products society had been selling us, namely ideas. We became enthralled with new music, new art and new spirituality. While tradition offered comfort, it rarely evoked passion, and the promise of new and improved is always passion, which, as we've noted, is a key to the Magical Universe.

Not only did technology breed a dissatisfaction with moribund tradition, it made available for inspection other cultures' traditions, which, though old, seemed new to us. These ancient traditions stressed harmony with the Earth and encouraged us to see life all around us. It prompted us to consider our planet as a single organism, a living world of energy that pervades not only the animal kingdom but also the vegetable and mineral kingdoms as well, infusing all with its own form of consciousness. Even now, as the cultures that spawned these traditions are being displaced by the onslaught of technology, theoretical physics is, to its own surprise, discovering profound truth in these ancient myths.

While the media chooses to imagine the New Age movement as a bunch of born-again Druids, it is much more than that. It is a gestalt of all the influences that have been shaping our culture for generations, come together in a bewildering complexity that stresses process over identity and spirit over form. It is a child of change, growing more and more at home in the nexus of novelty. It is not a movement in the political sense, but in an organic sense. It is a new way of processing ideas and scanning them for relevance. Certainly there is a lot of foolishness that falls under the New Age banner, and many of its current enchantments may turn out to be irrelevant, but that is the process of hybridization. We won't know for sure what the flower looks like until it blooms, and the New Age is still a sprout.

Many see New Age flamboyance as an exercise in ego. Ego has taken its deserved knocks in recent years. We are still reeling from the excesses of the so-called "Me Generation." So far we have concentrated on the negative aspect of an egocentric population. Perhaps it is time to consider it from a different angle. The much-maligned human ego has a purpose—to provide perspective. After all, wherever you look, what you see depends upon where you stand. Some people get very attached to their views, and that's fine, but learning to stand in different places and look from different eyes provides a much more compelling picture. Remember a time when you were in love and then fell out of love, when the faery glow of romance turned into the bright unflattering light of day. Which was the true experience? The answer depends upon which perspective you choose.

In the final analysis we need our perspectives. Which one we choose is a matter of choice and comfort. It doesn't matter—they all have wondrous views, but like using a pinhole to view an eclipse, we are, it seems, just not meant to look into the Light directly. Ultimately the Magical Universe we are capable of glimpsing is always but a projection of something much more. For those who think they can take up permanent residence in the Magical Universe, this is a frustrating, and sometimes impossible to face, fact of life, but it needn't be, since we have many perspectives to choose from. After all, change perspective and you change everything; a dim memory of a foray into the Magical Universe becomes a fresh chance to journey there anew, for it is not a place, it is an encounter, and one does not follow a map to an encounter. An encounter happens not just in space, but also in time. To encounter the Magical Universe requires being in the right place at the right time. A quest can get you moving, and synchronicities can point the way, but ultimately you do not find the Magical Universe, it finds you; which brings us to this book and to the magazine in which this material originally appeared.

Magical Blend magazine published its first issue in 1980. There were a few "New Age" magazines before it, and many more were to follow in its wake, but *Magical Blend* was, and is, different. For one thing, its canvas has always been both larger and brighter than its competitors, perhaps because it has never limited itself to the two mandatory requirements of modern media—a focused marketing strategy and a one-sentence sound-bite identity. Instead, for 17 consecutive years we have sought our identity through an old-fashioned device borrowed from the movie Citizen Kane—a Statement of Purpose, which first appeared in issue eight and has appeared in every issue since: *The transformative journey. Magical Blend accepts the premise that society is undergoing a fundamental transformation. A new world view is being born, and whether this birth is to be an easy or difficult one will depend largely upon the individual. It is our aim to chart the course this transformation is taking and to assist the individual to cope with and contribute to the birthing process. We believe that people's thoughts influence their reality; if this is true then the world we live in is a combination of our highest hopes, our deepest fears and the whole range of experience that falls between. Our goal is to embrace the hopes, transform the fears and discover the magical behind the mundane. In this way, we hope to act as a catalyst to encourage the individual to achieve his or her highest level of spiritual awareness. We endorse no one pathway to spiritual growth, but attempt to explore many alternative possibilities to help transform the planet.*

As co-editor of the magazine for its 17-year run, I have often returned to that Statement of Purpose for guidance, although I must admit I have also always felt slightly uncomfortable with it, for it sounded too high and mighty. How was I supposed to "help transform the planet"? I had no doubt that simply chronicling the shape-shifting of the world was challenge enough, and I preferred more distance from the "spiritual," a word people interpret without even trying. To me, our thrust has been to capture a feeling for the spirit of the times, and since this spirit informs a dazzling array of spiritual outlooks, I prefer the line about seeing the magical in the mundane. Overall, the most telling aspect of the Statement of Purpose is its framing of the magazine not as a package but as a process, a quest. It's been an honor over the years to participate in that quest, and now to pass the process on in a slightly different form.

Darshan is a Hindu concept in which the novice, simply by being in the presence of the master, experiences a blessing. That has been the aim of *Magical Blend* from the beginning. The articles and interviews in this book represent a diversity of subjects and viewpoints. Some derive from long-established traditions, while others represent a maverick approach, a fresh perspective inspired by the unique times in which we live. Some you will resonate with and some you will not; that is the nature of perspective. They are not meant to provide enlightenment, but to provoke encounters with the Light. Hopefully they will spark your own recognition of a time and place in which the Magical Universe miraculously appeared to you. When this happens, you will know you are on the right track. Although great truths sometimes appear in blinding flashes, more often than not they emanate through the cracks of mundane reality as the glimmering light of the Magical Universe.

Trying to fit the material in this book into sections proved to be a frustrating experience. Although certain broad categories seemed obvious, the pieces themselves weren't easily confined. They wanted to spill over into other categories, or create their own. Such is the nature of novelty. The categories we came up with are best seen as prisms through which the Light of the Magical Universe is reflected. They are not separate elements, but part of the fabric of the whole. A reading of the material makes it apparent that technology and creativity need not be distinct from spirituality. And any encounter with the Magical Universe, through whatever means, by its very nature alters reality. Furthermore, any attempt to track these elements separately will always lead you to the same place—the here and now we call the "real world." But the real world is different to different people. In modern Western societies, "real" is generally equated with the material, but the Balinese and the Australian Aborigine societies put the emphasis on the spiritual world. It probably doesn't matter where you start, the trick lies in the balance where the two worlds come together, material becomes animated and spirit becomes grounded. Such an encounter opens the way to the Magical Universe.

Culture is an amalgam of the forces that shape it, and if the New Age movement is correct in its belief that the Magical Universe is encroaching upon the material world, then any look at the changing face of culture is a look into the heart of the Magical Universe. The five areas presented here—Creativity, Alternate Realities, Technology, Spirituality, and Culture—offer the promise of bringing us face to face with the Magical Universe, but they are not it; they are only reflections. So don't get caught up in the sections. Think of them as a place to pause and switch perspective. Think of them as pinholes through which to observe a remarkable convergence of magical energies, one view at a time.

Creativity

Creativity

The creative impulse attempts to reach into the Magical Universe and bring back something of value. In this age of mass media merchandising, it is easy to forget that contact with the Magical Universe is its own reward. For years, we've had the good fortune to talk to some of the most creative artists on Earth, and when asked about their work, seldom do they feel compelled to talk about sales or influence. Instead they often sound like mystics describing the bliss of the creative experience. Consider Robin Williams' remark that "no drug in the world is as exhilarating as creativity."

An encounter with the Magical Universe is rarely as easy as the great artists make it seem. A common misperception of successful creative artists is that they are more fulfilled than the rest of us, that they are repositories of great insight that pours forth on command. But the material in this section stresses emptiness over fullness. A trip to the Void, it seems, may be a prerequisite for true creativity. Even for an accomplished artist, the muse does not descend from on high by invitation, but must be wrestled to the ground, a fact of creative life that prompted Julia Cameron to remark, "For most people, the only thing spiritual about creativity is its resemblance to crucifixion."

A hallmark of creative genius is the ability to see the world with new eyes and new ears, the willingness to enter the Void with few expectations. Perhaps that is why so many of these artists describe themselves as "outsiders" who never really fit in with their fellows.

Quieting the ego is a prerequisite for passage into the Magical Universe. While suffering is one way, there are others. For example, Julia Cameron's "how to" approach to creativity is more of a "how not to" approach—how not to become sabotaged by your own limiting beliefs, fear, jealousy, guilt, addiction and other inhibiting forces that block self-expression. Keeping the internal critic out of the way during the initial stages of creative play is imperative. Jerry Garcia observed that part of the "magic" of the Grateful Dead, "is that we've always avoided defining it…. It's process, and I believe that if you can open the door to process, it tells you how to do it and it works. Being stale is death, that's why we never play anything exactly the same way twice."

When one reaches out with the heart, one connects with the Magical Universe. The mystic knows it, and so does the creative genius. Perhaps that's why their messages sound so much alike.

Creativity
The Creative Outlook

───────────◯───────────

Robin Williams: Karma Comedy

with Penny King

He goes through life in a positive way. He experiences premonitions of the future, he meditates, uses creative visualization and believes in reincarnation. He's not pretentious, but sensitive, spontaneous, creative, very adaptable and extremely energetic. He has so much energy it's hard to keep up with him. He visualizes things and describes them immediately and succinctly. By using his different voices, expressions and sound effects he helps his audience to easily visualize the same ideas which are part of his reality. He's Robin Williams, comic genius of our time.

Have you ever had any psychic experiences in your lifetime?

Robin Williams: Not really psychic experiences or anything that could be classified as a vision, but I've had a lot of experience where I'd see things in the future that came true. I meditate and sometimes use creative visualization.

Do you use crystals when you visualize?

Robin Williams: I collect them. I have a huge crystal ball which someone gave me, after I gave them $2000. I think that has some power to it. It's a very strange old piece. It has fractures within it and looks incredible from all different angles. It sits on a little pedestal and rotates.

Do you believe in reincarnation?

Robin Williams: I think so. Yes. A friend just died recently, a wonderful comedian named Andy Kaufman. I think if anybody would be reincarnated it would be him. A wonderful quote I heard at the funeral was that whenever someone dies you think of it as a boat taking them away, and we're the people on the shore saying good-bye. But you have to think there's someone on another shore saying, "Hello, who's that?" I think of the positive aspects. When my son was born I saw that little babies, when they're born, are not little babies. They're little old men. Little old men who have just been through a major trauma, so they're like (in a little old man's voice) "Pardon me, is there a tit nearby? Excuse me, please. Don't cut that! Oh! I guess I'll have to live off those two people. Those are my parents? Fabulous. Oh. I've got to be a baby. Ahh! Is that better? Ahh!" You look at a child and they don't look like babies when they're first born. They're little old men. My baby looked like Gandhi. "Who can make the world change? The Gandhi man can." A friend also had a theory that souls wait in a holding pattern like that in an airport, and as soon as there's conception, a voice like that on an intercom says, "Thank you. Next. We have a Caucasian male. Thank you." And down he goes. I do believe in reincarnation, heavily. I believe people have seen past lives. I haven't really examined my past lives. I have a feeling that one of them had to have been a Shakespearean actor in the time of Shakespeare because "I have this strange need to over enunciate for no reason."(in the voice of Richard Burton) Sometimes I think if you look, you have awareness of different civilizations or a tendency towards things, and you think you might have been there before.

Do you think you have a purpose for here and now?

Robin Williams: Yes. To collect unemployment. No, a purpose? I think just to make people happy. I really enjoy that. That and sell vibrators door to door.

What does it feel like being up on stage knowing you have power over all the people?

Robin Williams: It's a fine line. It's dancing. Dancing on hot coals. It's fun and also keeps your feet moving. It's not control. I don't want to try and control anybody. I just want people to have an interesting time. Think, if they can. Enjoy it. And try and stimulate certain thought processes. For me, I love the transformations, playing, improvising, working off it. For me the high of it is when I find new thoughts. There's no drug in the world as exhilarating as creativity. Einstein must have been going "I am so loaded right now. I just found this concept. These things work. I don't know why."

What kind of thoughts are you trying to stimulate?

Robin Williams: Awareness of certain things. It's a fine line between preaching to people and playing with them. Comedy also allows you to say certain things so that while people are laughing they can digest them quicker. Like someone saying, "Oh, he was talking about war. So strange, I was laughing." You can play with that. You can get certain things by people. The wonderful thing that was open when I took up doing this is that it's an open world. You can talk about evolution, you have all of history to play with plus a little bit of the future if you want to play with that. It's wonderful. That's what's exciting.

Comedy has been a transformative tool in society. Do you consciously make an effort to help the world in this transformation?

Robin Williams: It's always been the purpose of comedy to make fun of things that people hold near and dear, or to make fun of the pompous. It was the fool in the middle ages that would say, "The king! Ha! Ha! The king's a queen!" The comedian would take the wind out of the king so he wouldn't take himself so seriously. For me comedy is a tool. It helps. It's therapeutic for me. I use it as a release. You first start with yourself, making fun of yourself, then the world is open to you. I think the first comedy was somebody running in with his hair on fire going "Ha! Ha! You crazy guy, come over here. How many Neolithics does it take to light a fire?" Sometimes comedy can be cruel. Like Infertility saying, "Not tonight. It's my pyramid." It's been around for a long time. It's a transformation. Comedy can be positive and negative. It can be mocking and cruel. That's the danger. I don't ever want to do that. It's a fine line. There's a positive energy for the whole society.

Eventually my son will be calling: "Dad?" "Zack?" "Yeah, Pop, I'm on Alpha Centauri. I want you to meet my wife." "Is that the one with the gills?" "Yeah, Dad." My own father has seen transformations; He was born in 1903 and the things he's seen have been amazing, and the things that I'll see will be amazing. It'll be wonderful. I just don't want the one major fear in the back of everybody's mind right now of "Will there be the Big One?" That's the fear.

If everybody's talking about the world holocaust in that aspect, what about something worldly to do with the weather and nature?

Robin Williams: Every time there's an earthquake I think it's just nature going, "Get those condominiums off my back" There's a possibility, too, while we're worried about this nuclear holocaust we're also depleting the ozone layer, raising the temperature of the planet, slowly but surely melting the ice caps, transferring the rotation. There are many dangers. But the one positive thing is that there is somewhere in the back of man's subconscious an incredible ability to transform.

Arthur Koestler wrote a book on the animal mind versus the rational mind. The animal mind hasn't caught up to the rational mind to keep the rational mind from doing what happens in the case of genocide where the rational mind justifies killing off other people. This is the rational mind over-riding the mammal instinct that would not allow you to hurt a fellow human being. But the rational mind takes over and you wipe out an entire race. This is what Koestler says—that somehow by advocating the use of some drug we could connect the two minds so that maybe we could grow up and meet somewhere in-between. We've evolved one mind quicker than the other. It's a dangerous time. I do believe there's potential. I believe some of the ways to prevent it are through information. I have hope but I also have incredible fears right now.

A Pentagon official once said in time of nuclear war, the people who would actually push the button probably have never seen the death of a person. He said the only hope, and it's a very strange thought, is if they put the button to launch the nuclear weapons behind a man's heart. You'd have to actually kill the man, cut out his heart with a rusty knife at that, and then press the button. It's only hope now is a chance for understanding, because many people don't have an understanding of the Russians. And I know that the Russians aren't getting a lot of information about us. It just builds up. It's a scary thing. Hopefully we can try to bridge it.

How do the Russians conceive comedy?

Robin Williams: The Russians themselves have an incredible sense of humor. It's almost like in the Russian dictionary under irony it says "see irony." The Russian sense of humor is like when I was talking to a Russian friend he said, "Wouldn't it have been great if they could have combined Andropov's funeral and the Winter Olympics: 'Carry the casket to the downhill bobsled run.' They play with it. They need that. They have that joke, "Knock, knock. Who's there? KGB. KGB who? We ask the questions!" When they have men in black suits that can follow you, come into your house, do anything at all times, you make fun of them. Their Polish jokes are KGB jokes: "How many KGB's does it take to screw in a light bulb? One. If it's willing to transmit." Humor is a necessary part of their survival. The Russians are deep people. They have soul in the black sense of the word, because soul comes from pain and suffering transformed in living. They dance, they drink. They function within that. If they ever let the lid off the Russian people in the creative sense you'll see another renaissance. They've had writers like Tolstoy, music by Tschaikovsky, incredibly complex beautiful people and they're just waiting to be opened up again. They have boundless creative energy that's just being stifled. That's their sense of consciousness.

Do you have any comments on comedy and the Eastern philosophies?

Robin Williams: (in a guru voice) You mean comic consciousness. I think comedy is like Zen. People go (in Californese) "Wow, explain it." "If I do, then it would not be funny." I think when it really works you don't know why you laugh but it just happens. A lot of Zen monks were like traveling stand up comedians.

They used to have people ask what is the meaning of life? Their way of answering was like (in a Chico Marx voice) "Hey, what are you worried about? We're all going to the big void. Hey, take a break. Rusty, say, what is a satori? Satori? I ain't even got there yet. Hey, stand back. You're out of your mind."

Great thinkers like Mozart said he didn't know where the music came from; he was just a channel. If you allow yourself to be open enough and free enough then things come. You just have to accept that. Also, I think comedy's like Zen because when they'd ask the Buddhist monks (again in a guru voice) "What is Zen. What is about this karma?" They would say, "I cannot tell you. If you must ask, then you don't know." And if you try to analyze comedy, if you pick apart the humor, then in the end it becomes not funny.

(Magical Blend issue #12)

Special thanks to the video crew at San Diego City College for making this interview possible.

Creativity
The Creative Outlook

Jerry Garcia: Spiritual Music

with David Brown and Rebecca McClen Novick

When you've had a street named after you then you can congratulate yourself on a certain notoriety (although you will probably be dead), but when you've had an ice cream named after you, well, that's an honor that dreams are made of.

After thirty years of playing with one of the most successful bands in the history of rock 'n' roll, Jerry Garcia finds himself, at the age of fifty-one, at the zenith of his popularity. His almost mythical status got an extra boost when he journeyed to the Jaws of Death and back after falling into a diabetic coma, and he has reached a point in his career where if he were half asleep and out of tune, the audience would still hang on every note with a reverent sigh.

An Old Testament prophet mixed with your favorite uncle and dash of garden gnome, Jerry Garcia spoke to us at the Grateful Dead's homey headquarters in San Rafael. As the interview evolved it became clear that now, with the ages of acid-tests, afros and junk bonds behind him, one of this man's favorite pastimes is contemplating the inner shenanigans of the Universe.

How did you get started in music?

Jerry Garcia: My father was a professional musician, my mother was an amateur. I grew up in a musical household and took piano lessons as far back as I can remember. There was never a time in my life when music wasn't a part of me.

The first time I decided that music was something I wanted to do, apart from just being surrounded by it, was when I was about fifteen. I developed this deep craving to play the electric guitar. I fell in love with rock 'n' roll. I wanted to make that sound so badly. So I got a pawn shop electric guitar and a little amplifier and I started without the benefit of anybody else around me who played the guitar, or any books.

My stepfather put it in an open tuning of some kind and I taught myself how to play by ear. I did that for about a year until I ran into a kid at school who knew three chords on the guitar and also the correct way to tune it. That's when I started to play around at it, then I picked things up. I never took lessons or anything.

Who particularly inspired you?

Jerry Garcia: Actually no particular musician inspired me, apart from maybe Chuck Berry. But all of the music from the fifties inspired me. I didn't really start to get serious about music until I was eighteen and I heard my first bluegrass music. I heard Earl Scruggs play five-string banjo and I thought that's something I have to be able to do. I fell in love with the sound and I started earnestly trying to do exactly what I was hearing. That became the basis for everything else—that was my model.

How do you compare your early days to now?

Jerry Garcia: Well, in some ways it's better and in some ways it's not. The thing that was fun about those days was that nothing was expected of us. We didn't have to play. We weren't required to perform. People came to acid-tests for the acid-test, not for us.

So there were times when we would play two or three tunes or even a couple of notes and just stop. We'd say, to hell with it, we don't feel like playing! It was great to have that kind of freedom because before that we were playing five sets a night, fifty minutes on, ten minutes off every hour. We were doing that six nights a week and then usually we'd have another afternoon gig and another nighttime gig on Sunday. So we were playing a lot. Also, we weren't required to play anything even acceptable. We could play what ever we wanted. As far as a way to break out from an intensely formal kind of experience it was just what we needed, because we were looking to break out.

And you're still able to maintain that free-form style to a certain extent even though now you're more restricted by scheduling and order?

Jerry Garcia: Well, also we're required to be competent, but we've improved a lot. Now when we play, the worst playing we do isn't too bad. So the lowest level has come way up, and statistically the odds have improved in our favor.

What do you think it is about The Grateful Dead that has allowed you such lasting popularity?

Jerry Garcia: I wish I knew.

Do you think you can define it?

Jerry Garcia: I don't know whether I want to, particularly. Part of its magic is that we've always avoided defining any part of it, and the effect seems to be that in not defining it, it becomes everything. I prefer that over anything that I might think of.

Do you feel at all disillusioned at the rate of social evolution? In the '60s, many thought that massive social change was just around the corner.

Jerry Garcia: I never was that optimistic. I never thought that things were going to get magically better. I thought that we were experiencing a lucky vacation from the rest of consensual reality to try stuff out. We were privileged in a sense. I didn't have anything invested in the idea that the world was going to change. Our world certainly changed. Our part of it did what it was supposed to do, and it's continuing to do it, continuing to evolve. It's a process. I believe that if you open the door to the process, it tells you how to do it and it works. It's a life strategy that I think anyone can employ.

How do you feel about the fact that many people have interpreted your music as the inspiration for a whole lifestyle—the Deadhead culture?

Jerry Garcia: Well, a little silly! You always feel your own work is never quite what it should be. There's always a dissonance between what you wish was happening and what is actually happening. That's the nature of creativity, that there's a certain level of disappointment in there. So, on one level it's amusing that people make so much stuff out of this and on another level, I believe it's their right to do that, because in a way the music belongs to them. When we're done with it, we don't care what happens to it. If people choose to mythologize it, it certainly doesn't hurt us.

How do you feel about your divine-like status in the eyes of so many of your fans?

Jerry Garcia: These things are all illusions. Fame is an illusion. I know what I do and I know about how well I do it, and I know what I wish I could do. Those things you mentioned don't enter my life. I don't buy into any of that stuff. I can't imagine who would. Look at David Koresh. If you start believing any of that kind of stuff about yourself, where does it leave you?

So what is the relationship dynamic between you and the audience when you're on stage?

Jerry Garcia: When things are working right, you gain levels. It's like *bardos.* The first level is simply your fundamental relationship to your instrument. When that starts to get comfortable the next level is your relationship to the other musicians. When you're hearing what you want to and things seem to be working the way you want them to, then it includes the audience. When it gets to that level, it's seamless. It's no longer an effort; it flows and it's wide open.

Sometimes however, when I feel that's happening, the music is really boring. It's too perfect. What I like most is to be playing with total access, where anything that I try to play or want to make happen, I can execute flawlessly—for me that's the high-water mark. But perfection is always boring.

I've heard that musicians using computer synthesizers are complaining that the sound produced is so perfect that it's uninteresting, and that manufacturers are now looking to program in human error.

Jerry Garcia: Right. I think the audience enjoys it more when it's a little more of a struggle.

What do you think is missing?

Jerry Garcia: Tension.

Tension between what and what?

Jerry Garcia: The tension between trying to create something and creating something, between succeeding and failing. Tension is a part of what makes music work—tension and release, or if you prefer, dissonance and resonance, or suspension and completion.

Do you feel sometimes at your shows that you're guiding people?

Jerry Garcia: I don't feel like I'm guiding anybody. I feel like I'm sort of stumbling along and a lot of people are watching me or stumbling with me or allowing me to stumble for them. I don't feel like, here we are,

I'm the guide and come on you guys, follow me. I do that, but I don't feel that I'm particularly better at it than anybody else.

For example, here's something that used to happen all the time. The band would check into a hotel. We'd get our room key and then we'd go to the elevator. Well, a lot of times we didn't have a clue where the elevator was. So, what used to happen was that everybody would follow me, thinking that I would know. I'd be walking around thinking, "Why the fuck is everybody following me?" So if nobody else does it, I'll start something—it's a knack.

A lot of people are looking for someone to follow.

Jerry Garcia: Yeah. I don't mind being that person, but it doesn't mean that I'm good at it or that I know where I'm going or anything else. It doesn't require competence. it only requires the gesture.

Is there any planning involved in choosing songs in a certain sequence to take people on a journey?

Jerry Garcia: Sometimes we plan, but more often than not we find that when we do, we change our plans. Sometimes we talk down a skeleton of the second set, to give ourselves some form—but it depends. The important thing is that it not be dull and that the experience of playing doesn't get boring. Being stale is death. So we do whatever we can to keep it spontaneous and amusing for ourselves.

You play more live shows than any other band I know of. How do you manage to keep that spontaneity? Is this a natural talent you've always had or is it something you've had to work to achieve?

Jerry Garcia: Part of it is that we're just constitutionally unable to repeat anything exactly. Every one in the band is so pathologically anti-authoritarian that the idea of doing something exactly the same way is an anathema—it will never happen. So that's our strong suit—the fact that we aren't consistent. It used to be that sometimes we'd reach wonderful levels or else we played really horribly, terribly badly. Now we've got to be competent at our worst.

I'm curious about how psychedelics influenced not only your music but your whole philosophy of life.

Jerry Garcia: Psychedelics were probably the single most significant experience in my life. Otherwise I think I would be going along believing that this visible reality here is all there is. Psychedelics didn't give me any answers. What I have is a lot of questions. One thing I'm certain of is that the mind is an incredible thing and there are levels of organizations of consciousness that are way beyond what people are fooling with in day-to-day reality.

When you project into the future how do you see your music evolving?

Jerry Garcia: I have no idea. I was never able to predict it in the past; I certainly don't feel confident to predict it now.

Did you ever imagine it would get this far?

Jerry Garcia: Oh God no! It exceeded my best expectations fifteen or twenty years ago. We're way past the best I could come up with.

How did you come up with the name The Grateful Dead?

Jerry Garcia: We called ourselves the Warlocks, and we found out that some other band already had that name, so we were trying to come up with a new one. I picked up a dictionary and literally the first thing I saw when I looked down at the page was "The Grateful Dead." It was a little creepy, but I thought it was a striking combination of words.

Nobody in the band liked it; I didn't like it either, but it got around that that was one of the candidates for our new name and everybody else said, "Yeah that's great." It turned out to be tremendously lucky. It's just repellent enough to filter curious onlookers and just quirky enough that parents don't like it.

What's your concept of God, if you have one?

Jerry Garcia: I was raised a Catholic so it's very hard for me to get out of that way of thinking. Fundamentally I'm a Christian in that I believe that to love your enemy is a good idea somehow. Also, I feel that I'm enclosed within a Christian framework so huge that I don't believe it's possible to escape it, it's so much a part of the Western point of view. So I admit it, and I also believe that real Christianity is okay. I just don't like the exclusivity clause.

But as far as God goes, I think that there is a higher order of intelligence something along the lines of whatever it is that makes DNA work. Whatever it is that keeps our bodies functioning and our cells changing, the organizing principle—what ever it is that created all these wonderful life forms that we're surrounded by in such incredible detail.

There's definitely a huge, vast wisdom of some kind at work here. Whether it's personal—whether there's a point of view in there, or whether we're the point of view—I think is up for discussion. I don't believe in a supernatural being.

What about your personal experience of what you may have described as God?

Jerry Garcia: I've been spoken to by a higher order of intelligence—I thought it was God. It was a very personal God in that it had exactly the same sense of humor that I have. I interpret that as being the next level of consciousness, but maybe there's a hierarchical set of consciousnesses. My experience is that there is one smarter than me, that can talk to me, and there's also the biological one that I spoke about.

You became very ill a few years ago and came very close to death. I'm interested in how that experience affected your attitude about life.

Jerry Garcia: It's still working on me. I made a decision somewhere along the line to survive, but I didn't have a near-death experience in the classical sense. I came out of it feeling fragile, but I'm not afraid of death.

Were you afraid of death before?

Jerry Garcia: I can't say that I was, actually. But it did make me want to focus more attention on the quality of life. So I feel like now I have to get serious about being healthful. If I'm going to be alive I want to feel well. I never had to think about it too much before, but finally mortality started to catch up with me.

You say that you didn't have a near-death experience, but did anything happen that gave you any unusual insight?

Jerry Garcia: Well, I had some very weird experiences. My main experience was one of furious activity and tremendous struggle in a sort of futuristic, spaceship vehicle with insectoid presences. After I came out of my coma, I had this image of myself as these little hunks of protoplasm that were stuck together kind of like stamps with perforations between them that you could snap off. They were run through with neoprene tubing, and there were these insects that looked like cockroaches which were like message units that were kind of like my bloodstream. That was my image of my physical self and this particular feeling lasted a long time. It was really strange.

Did it affect what you think might happen after death?

Jerry Garcia: No. It just gave me a greater admiration for the incredible baroque possibilities of mentation. The mind is so incredibly weird. The whole process of going into coma was very interesting too. It was a slow onset—it took about a week—and during this time I started feeling like the vegetable kingdom was speaking to me.

It was communicating in comic dialect in iambic pentameter. So there were these Italian accents and German accents and it got to be this vast gabbling. Potatoes and radishes and trees were all speaking to me. It was really strange. It finally just reached hysteria and that's when I passed out and woke up in the hospital.

And when you came out of your coma, did you come out of it in stages?

Jerry Garcia: I was pretty scrambled. It was as though in my whole library of information, all the books had fallen off the shelves and all the pages had fallen out of the books. I would speak to people and know what I meant to say, but different words would come out. So I had to learn everything over again. I had to learn how to walk, play the guitar, everything.

Did you always have faith that you would access your memory again? Did it scare you that you might have lost it forever?

Jerry Garcia: I didn't care. When your memory's gone, you don't care because you don't remember when you had one.

What do you think happens to consciousness after death?

Jerry Garcia: It probably dies with the body. Why would it exist apart from the body?

People have had experiences of feeling like they're out of their body.

Jerry Garcia: That's true. But unfortunately the only ones who have gone past that are still dead. I don't know what consciousness is, apart from a physical being. I once slipped out of my body accidentally. I was at home watching television and I slid out through the soles of my feet. All of a sudden I was hovering up by the ceiling looking down at myself. So I know that I can disembody myself somehow from my physical self, but more than that I have no way of knowing.

So you don't believe in reincarnation, in the recycling of consciousness?

Jerry Garcia: It may happen in a very large way. It may be that part of all the DNA-coding, the specific memory, returns. There's definitely information in my mind that did not come from this lifetime. Not only is there some, but there's tons of it! Enormous, vast reservoirs.

What does the term "consciousness" mean to you?

Jerry Garcia: I go along with the notion that the universe wants consciousness in it, that it's part of the evolutionary motion of the universe and that we represent the universe's consciousness. Why it wants it, I don't know, but it seems to want it.

Here's the reason I believe this. If the point of an organism is survival, why go any further than sharks or simple-minded predators that survive perfectly beautifully? Why continue throwing out possibilities? So my sense is that conceivably there is some purpose or design. Why monkeys with big heads? Because that's the most convenient consciousness carrier, perhaps.

Have you ever felt like you've been in communication with beings of a higher intelligence than humans?

Jerry Garcia: I've had direct communication with something which is higher than me. I don't know what it is, it may be another part of my mind. There's no way for me to filter it out because it's in my head. It's the thing that's able to take bits and pieces of things and give me large messages. To me, they are messages as clear as someone speaking in my ear, they're that well expressed and they have all the detail that goes along with it.

Sometimes it comes in the form of an actual voice and sometimes it comes in the form of a hugeness, a huge presence that uses all of the available sensory material to express an idea. And when I get the idea it's like "Duh! Oh, I get it!" And it's accompanied by that hollow mocking laughter: "You stupid fuck! You finally got it, huh? Geez it's about time." For me, enlightenment works that way, but it's definitely a higher order of self-organization that communicates stuff.

My psychedelic experiences were sequential. They started at a place and they went through a series of progressive learning steps. When they stopped happening it was like, this is the end of the message—now you're just playing around. That was when psychedelics stopped having the relevance they originally had. It lasted for about a year I'd say.

What do you think a Dead show in Virtual Reality would be like?

Jerry Garcia: Deadheads would want to be part of the band, I would imagine. I think it would be fun if they could be, because it would make them see the experience differently. But I think they would be disappointed if they saw our version of it.

Why do you think that?

Jerry Garcia: I don't know why. Remember, I don't know what The Grateful Dead are like. I've never seen them, so I don't know what it is that the people in the audience experience that they value so highly.

You facilitate the potential for an experience. People have full-on religious experiences at your shows; they pass out, speak in tongues, and are even picked up by flying saucers. Are you aware of the impact you have on people's minds?

Jerry Garcia: Not like that. I've made an effort to not be aware of it because it's perilously close to fascism. If I started to think about controlling that power or somehow trying to fiddle around with it then it would become fascism.

Have you ever been tempted to dabble in the power?

Jerry Garcia: Oh yeah. For the first eighteen years or so, I had a lot of doubts about The Grateful Dead. I thought that maybe this is a bad thing to be doing, because I was aware of the power. So I did a lot of things to sabotage it. I thought fuck this! I won't be a part of this. I dragged my feet as much as possible but it still kept happening! So in that way I was able to filter myself out of it and think well, it's not me. Phew! What a relief!

Have you heard of the Spinners? They wear long dresses and do this whirling dervish dance at Dead shows.

Jerry Garcia: They're kind of like our Sufis. I think it's really neat that there's a place where they can be comfortable enough to do something with such abandon. It's nice to provide that. That's one of the things I'm really proud of The Grateful Dead for, because it's kind of like free turf.

It doesn't bother you that they use you as their religious focus?

Jerry Garcia: Well, I'll put up with it until they come to me with the cross and nails.

What are your priorities now? Are they very different from what they were twenty years ago?

Jerry Garcia: Not very. Basically, I'm trying to stay out of trouble. I'm trying to play well. For me, playing music is a learning experience and it's satisfying to me to still be learning stuff. Also, my objective is to have as much fun as I possibly can. That's a key ingredient.

Do you feel there is a New Age, or to use Terence McKenna's term, an "Archaic Revival" coming about?

Jerry Garcia: Sure, I'll go along with that—I love that stuff. I'm a Terence McKenna fan. I prefer to believe that we're winding up rather than winding down. And this idea of the year 2012 when everything tops out, well, I would love to be here for it. I'll buy into that belief—I don't want to miss it! It's like the millennium. At this point it's a matter of personal pride. We have to survive, the band has to be able to play till at least the turn of the millennium.

What do you think that the future of the human race depends upon?

Jerry Garcia: Getting off this lame fucking trip, this egocentric bullshit. There's entirely too many monkeys on this mudball and that's going to be a real problem. People have to get smart. I've always thought that the thing to do is something really chaotic and crazy like head off into space. That's something that would keep everyone real busy and would also distribute more bodies out there.

Otherwise we end up staying here and killing each other and damaging the planet. I've gotten into scuba diving so I've developed a great affection for the ocean. I just don't want to see it get worse than it is. I'd like to think we could get smart enough sometime soon to make things better than they are instead of worse.

Are you optimistic about the future of life on earth?

Jerry Garcia: I think the earth doesn't have any real problems in the long run. I think we're just another disturbance. I don't think even we can really fuck up the earth.

How did you get involved in helping to save the rainforest?

Jerry Garcia: Well, I remember we started hearing about these things twenty-five to thirty years ago. The clock kept ticking by and nothing was really happening. So we thought maybe we should call attention to this. Then there was the matter of finding out who the true players were, because there are a lot of bullshitters in the environmental movement, there are a lot of frauds.

You have to really go into it to find out who's really doing stuff and also who has the right perspective. So for us it was about a two-year process of finding the players and then getting them to agree to work together so we could do something that would matter. I think everybody wants to do stuff about these problems. We didn't want to just call attention to how powerless everybody is, instead we wanted to do some things that were really hands on, using direct action, and it's worked out quite well.

Can you tell us about any current projects that you're involved in?

Jerry Garcia: I'm involved in an interesting project with a little symphony orchestra down the Peninsula called The Redwood Symphony. I'm getting about five or six musicians to write pieces for me and this orchestra. Danny Elfman is one, David Byrne seems to want to do one and so do my friends John Kahn, Bob Bralove, and David Grisman. The interesting part about it for me is that my oldest daughter plays first violin with this orchestra. So it'll be kind of fun to be involved in a project where she and I play together.

That sounds wonderful. What are some of the basic music messages?

Jerry Garcia: We've always avoided putting any kind of message in there, but I find myself more comfortable with committing to emotional truths as life goes on. I'm not an actor so I can't get on stage and sing a song that doesn't have some emotional reality for me. Sometimes it's only something about the sound of the lyrics, it may not be the sense of it at all, but there has to be something in there that's real for me.

My writing partner, Robert Hunter, is really good about writing into my beliefs—he understands the way I think and he knows me well enough to know what I'll do and what I won't do. He knows that I'm always going to be battling with my intelligence about whether I can sing this lyric or if I'm going to feel like an idiot singing it. It has to resonate in some way.

How have you managed to remain so unaffected by your fame?

Jerry Garcia: If you were me, you'd be modest too. Deadheads are very kind. When they enter my private life they almost always say, I just want to thank you for the music, I don't want to bother you. When I feel that I really don't want to know about it, I just tell them. I treat everybody who speaks to me with respect. I've never been hurt by anybody or threatened in any way so I have no cause to be afraid of this kind of stuff. It just isn't part of my life most of the time.

Besides, I'm kind of like a good-old-celebrity. People think they know me. It's not like, "Oh gosh! look who it is!" It's more like, "Hi, how ya doin'?" I'm a comfortable celebrity. It's very hard to take the fame seriously and I don't think anybody wants me to. What's it good for? The best thing about it is that you get to meet famous people and you get to play with wonderful musicians.

If you hadn't been a musician what might you have been?

Jerry Garcia: I'd be an artist. I was an art student and that was where I was going in my life before music sort of seduced me.

What inspired you to design a line of ties?

Jerry Garcia: I don't really have any control over them, they're just extracted from my artwork. I don't design ties, for God's sake!

How do you feel about the importance of humor?

Jerry Garcia: Humor is incredibly important. It's fundamental. You have to be able to laugh at yourself and your place in the universe.

What do you think happens when you lose your sense of humor?

Jerry Garcia: Well, at the very least you won't have much fun. Humor characterizes consciousness. For me, life would be so empty without humor. It would be unbearable, it would be like life without music.

(Magical Blend issue #41)

David Jay Brown and Rebecca McClen Novick are the authors of two collections of interviews with renowned thinkers: Mavericks of the Mind *and* Voices from the Edge *(both by Crossing Press, 1-800-777-1048.)*

Creativity
Overcoming Creative Blocks

Julia Cameron: The Artist's Way

with Jerry Snider

Besides having worked in Hollywood as a film and television writer, director and producer of independent features and documentaries, Julia Cameron is an award-winning journalist who has written for such diverse publications as the *Washington Post, New York Times, Rolling Stone,* and *Vogue.* Her book, *The Artist's Way* (Jeremy P. Tarcher/Perigee Books) is a twelve week, step-by-step course on creativity developed from over a decade of teaching workshops, including a recent stint as writer-in residence at Northwestern University. What makes Julia Cameron's approach unusual is that, rather than approach creativity from a how-to approach, she guides the frustrated artist through what perhaps can best be described as a how-not-to strategy—how not to be sabotaged by limiting beliefs, fear, jealousy, guilt, addictions and other inhibiting forces that block self-expression. Considering the need at every level of society for creative problem solving, we asked Julia Cameron to give us some tips on how to release the artist within.

How would you describe your book, The Artist's Way, *and what made you write it?*

Julia Cameron: I think of it as being the tools that after decades of practicing my craft I've discovered and tossed over my shoulder sort of like, "This works, try this one."

I've been writing for two and a half decades. I have been a journalist for a great deal of that time for the *New York Times, Washington Post, Rolling Stone,* etc., etc. I have also been a playwright, a working poet, a short story writer, and a film maker. So I've been a working artist for a long, long time.

For a decade now, I have also taught a spiritual workshop aimed at freeing people's creativity. I have taught artists and nonartists, painters and film makers, home makers and lawyers—anyone interested in living more creatively through practicing an art; even more broadly, any one interested in practicing the art of creative living. I teach people to let themselves be creative.

Which means teaching people to overcome their own creative blocks.

Julia Cameron: What people need to understand is that in any life they are going to sustain injuries. It's the same thing for one's creative life. Blocks to creativity often begin very early in life, often from well-meaning parents and teachers. As a result, people internalize a lot of damage. What *The Artist's Way* aims at doing is going back and finding those pain points and releasing the toxins. It's a little bit like pulling out the accumulated porcupine spines.

When I was reading the book, my first impression was "Gee, it seems like she's addressing some really severely blocked people." Then I stopped to think about it and I had to admit that, like it or not, a lot of it did apply to me. I was more blocked than I realized. As I mulled this over, I started to think about a cultural paradox concerning creativity. I mean the US is famous for its creative contributions to the world and yet at the same time, we seem to have a culture that blocks creativity.

Julia Cameron: I do think our culture is very repressive creatively. Yes, historically we've had many examples of genius, but one of the problems in our culture is that we accolade genius but we do not reward process. We have become extremely product-oriented. We are attuned to result rather than to the reward of the act itself. The development of media as we now have it has been enormously destructive to creativity. We have become, whether we like it or not, a *People* magazine culture judging our own creativity against the PR-handled external of somebody else's success.

James Colley tells the story of knocking on Picasso's door and being met by a servant who told him, "Picasso will see you or not see you." He didn't say, "Picasso's up stairs vomiting because he doesn't think he can draw today." He didn't say, "Picasso's upstairs having another one of his eternal fights with his mistress so he won't have to draw today."

Picasso was one of the first artists to merchandise himself and to present himself like the Wizard of Oz. And that's the relationship that we now have with successful artists, due to the media. I don't think you can underestimate how much that skews the process. People have had

their creativity flattened, leveled, and made far more competitive because of the way the press machine works.

The Artist's Way *stresses the link between creativity and spirituality—
a link you apparently don't think most people understand since you write,
"For most people, the only thing spiritual about creativity is its resemblance
to crucifixion."*

Julia Cameron: I don't separate creativity and spirituality. I think that
what we are talking about when we talk about creativity is exactly the
same thing that people discuss when they try to articulate a mystical
experience. A creative act is difficult because creativity is essentially a
matter of faith. When we talk about the still small voice in spiritual life,
this is the same thing that the artist is moving on when he or she is ex-
pressive.

*Let's talk about some of the exercises you teach to get the creative juices
flowing.*

Julia Cameron: The primary tool is called "morning pages." The morning pages consist of three pages of longhand writing. They are strictly
stream of consciousness. These daily morning meanderings are not
meant to be art. They are a form of meditation. They are simply the act
of moving the hand across the page and writing down *whatever* comes
to mind. Nothing is too petty, too silly, too stupid, or too weird to be
included. Most people, after they have done them a while, find that the
morning pages put them into a light trance state or a creative state.

Although occasionally colorful, the morning pages are often negative. As people begin to do them, they will experience a very powerful
inner voice which will say things like, "This is all whining. This is all
drivel. It's stupid and pointless." That's the voice of the critic, which is
typically a very amplified voice for most of us. But as you continue doing the morning pages, you find that the voice of the critic becomes
miniaturized. Instead of accepting this voice as the gospel, you begin to
see the critic as a wet-blanket character, and as you learn to muffle the
negative voice, you find that the creative voice becomes amplified.
What happens with the morning pages is that you learn to risk clarifying for yourself how you're really feeling. This involves a small personal risk. And done on a daily basis, these small increments of risk
prepare you for the larger risk that any creative endeavor involves.

This exercise also clears internal space, because what you're doing
is essentially writing down "cloud thoughts"—those little thoughts

that just skitter across the mind. What happens is that, as you drain off these stray thoughts, you will begin to experience the first green shoots of original creative thought. Perhaps you won't even notice it while you're writing, but later you'll look back and realize that your novel began with some impulse generated by the morning pages.

Maybe we ought to clarify that it's not just creative writing these exercises are meant to enhance, but creativity in general.

Julia Cameron: Right. The morning pages work for painters, for sculptors, for poets, for actors, for lawyers, for housewives—for anyone who wants to try anything creative. One of the interesting things about the morning pages is that they very quickly prioritize your life. For example, after three or four weeks of sitting down in the morning and grousing about having to do every dish in the house, you begin to realize that this genuinely annoys you. Finally, you turn to your significant other and say, "Jim, it's your turn on the dishes." And suddenly you have an extra forty-five minutes in your day for your creative pursuits. The morning pages are very deceptive because they're so simple, but they're also powerful.

One other thing that I should mention is that the morning pages are not to be reread for the first week you're doing them. Also, they are not, under any circumstances, to be shown to someone else, because as you know the first rule of magic has to do with containment and incubation. So we draw a sacred circle, as it were, around them.

Another tool you write about is called the 'artist date.' Could you elaborate?

Julia Cameron: An artist date is a block of perhaps two hours weekly, especially set aside and committed to nurturing your creative consciousness, your inner artist. Basically you are taking your creative consciousness out on some kind of adventure, alone just the two of you, no significant other, no babysitting, just a very focused, deliberate pushing of the envelope. Creativity involves a two-part process.

I find it interesting that while most people are terrific at doing morning pages, they tend to sabotage themselves in regard to the artist date. When I'm teaching, it will often take me six weeks into the course to get everyone doing an artist date. Most of us become extremely anorexic along anything that smacks of self-pleasure, and that's what the artist date is all about. The idea is to have some fun and to do it alone. And also to do something you might not ordinarily let your self do. So it doesn't mean taking yourself to the opera unless you're absolutely mad for opera. It may mean that you have noticed the Athenian candle store and never walked into it. It may mean that you've been meaning to go to the new Vietnamese restaurant. It may mean that you're going to let yourself go sit in the park and do nothing for a little bit. It doesn't have to be elaborate. I like it to be sensual though. One thing it's not, however, is going to the park and reading a book, because that still keeps you deprived of your sensory input.

In the book, you mention that if you're feeling particularly blocked creatively, you might want to refrain from reading any thing for a week.

Julia Cameron: Right. Reading deprivation is one of the most potent tools in the kit. We take in words each day, almost like little pills. What happens when you stop taking in opinions of others on a daily basis in large doses is that you begin to be able to hear your own inner silence and a welling-up of things you didn't know you thought or felt or wanted to express.

You make the point that most of us want to intellectualize everything, and that keeps us from actually getting involved in the process. Let's talk about process.

Julia Cameron: I think that most of us are much more comfortable with the idea that the universe is not paying a lot of attention than we are with the possibility that the universe might actually be superbly interactive. I have found that when we clearly notify our inner selves and, if you will, the universe, of our interests, there is an acceleration to opportunity. There's a wonderful spiritual line—"Whatever you believe you can do, begin it, because action has magic, grace, and power in it." When we commit, the universe moves also. I think that each of us is in possession of a great deal more power than we care to acknowledge. I'll give an example. One of the people working with the course wrote a film script and wanted to get it to Tom Cruise. A week later at a health club in Chicago, he sat next to Cruise's cousin on an exercise bike. These kinds of lucky, significant coincidences happen all the time. And I think that we are extremely reluctant to acknowledge them because implicit in acknowledging them is the fact that we probably could do most of the things that we're telling ourselves we can't do.

You write, "Creativity is oxygen for our soul. Cutting off our creativity makes us savage and we act like we're being choked." That almost sounds like a good description of the weirdness we see presented daily on the evening news.

Julia Cameron: That's true. I think people underestimate the power of creativity. If we deny it, it will emerge despite ourselves. For example, if you are a blocked writer you may find that you write more letters than other people, or perhaps your creativity is being channeled into gardening. So even though you may repress it, it will show up. Sometimes when creativity is really repressed it can feel geyser-like when it's unleashed. That's why the book is very, very specific and careful to explain to people that creativity is a trackable process and that there are certain weeks when they're going to be uncomfortable, but that those periods of discomfort will pass. People will say, "I feel like I'm going crazy" and I will say, "Well, going sane feels just like going crazy."

I'd like to address the indirectness of some of the exercises you present in The Artist's Way. *A lot of them don't seem to be directly connected to creativity, but are instead very personal, very practical exercises like listing twenty things one enjoys doing. Another is to bake something. In other words, they're creative acts that we don't associate with creativity.*

Julia Cameron: I think one thing that the book ends up doing is broadening people's notion of creativity so that they're able to have much more creative satisfaction across the board. The tools are a little shrewd. They're Zen tools, if you will. They tell you to face north and as you face north, something starts to happen in the south. And a lot of creativity is actually grounded in just that type of mystery. I also want to say that we tend to make creativity too mysterious; we tend to think of it as something that's very far removed from our daily life, when it's not. So the book points out things like how people get great ideas when they're doing the dishes and it explains why.

Okay, let's get practical. What can I do in the next fifteen minutes that will help me become more creative?

Julia Cameron: I guess I would ask you to consider what's holding you back. I think that people are afraid to move into their creativity. They wonder: "What if I'm not really creative? What if I unlock myself and I do some creative work and it's bad?" Even worse, "What if I have a show and my work is out there and everyone knows it's bad except for me?" I would like you to consider the possibility that it could be a lot more tragic than that. What if you're really creative, what if you're really good, what if you were meant to use this gift and the real tragedy is that you don't have the courage to do it?

We have this mythology that tells us there's such a thing as a real artist. And a real artist is different than the rest of us. A real artist is someone who was born knowing he is a real artist and he has never experienced doubt or fear. And as near as I can tell, this mythological tribe of real artists doesn't exist. All artists experience doubt. All artists experience fear. The good news is that we can all learn how to live with the fear and live through the fear. By connecting with your creativity you connect with a whole, something that is a completeness within yourself.

Over any extended period of time, being an artist requires enthusiasm more than discipline. Enthusiasm is not an emotional state. It is a spiritual commitment, a loving surrender to our creative process. Enthusiasm (from the Greek, "filled with God") is an ongoing energy supply tapped into the flow of life itself. Enthusiasm is grounded in play, not work. Far from being a brain-numbed soldier, our artist is actually our child within, our inner playmate. As with all playmates, it is joy, not duty, that makes for a lasting bond.

(Magical Blend issue #42)

Alternate Realities

Alternate Realities

If there's one thing that defines an encounter with the Magical Universe, it's a sense that the terrain of reality has in some sense shifted. Such a shift can be profound, as when one ingests a psychedelic substance, or it can be so subtle as to be barely noticed. In discussing bardos, or the various states one trans-verses after death, The Tibetan Book of the Dead *advises that in the begin-ning these states may be so familiar, that the recently deceased only gradually becomes aware that something is amiss. Dreams, too, often begin with such a close approximation of the everyday world that the dreamer at first has diffi-culty distinguishing the dream from the waking world.*

It may be that the dream world represents our most reliable threshold to the Magical Universe. Not only is it the one alternate reality we have all expe-rienced, but allusions to it and comparisons with it also abound in the litera-ture of mysticism, spiritual illumination, paranormal experiences, psychotic breaks, creative genius and drug-induced hallucinations. Modern psychology has labeled the realm of the dreamer the subconscious. But what is this subcon-scious? For the most part, it remains a vague term, useful for describing en-counters with the Magical Universe, but of not much help in understanding the terrain in which these encounters take place. Psychiatrist Stanislav Grof, who in this section recounts his thirty years of research into the effects of LSD on the human psyche, describes the subconscious as the frontier between the personal and the transpersonal and states that "intimate knowledge of transpersonal realms is absolutely essential, not only for understanding the psychedelic process, but for any serious approach to such phenomena as sha-manism, religion, mysticism, rites of passage, mythology, parapsychology and schizophrenia." He also notes that "virtually all of the world's cultures, other than our own Western industrial civilization, have held these states in very high esteem and spent a lot of time developing some powerful techniques for getting into them."

Over the years, Magical Blend *has examined a number of these tech-niques, from chanting to drumming to lucid dreaming to meditation to myth-ological perspectives to transpersonal psychology, but invariably the most popular discussions center around shamanism, encounters with UFOs and psychedelic substances.*

Tribal and pre-industrial societies not only recognized different levels of reality, but they also handed down in story and lore occasions when these re-alities overlapped. Not surprisingly, many of these stories sound remarkably familiar to modern encounters with UFOs and extraterrestrials. Jacques Vallée, a serious researcher into the UFO phenomenon, observes that in most reports of alien encounters and UFOs, researchers come up against the "Oz Factor," a point where consensus reality no longer fits the described experiences. While the "Oz Factor" may be a term coined for UFO investigations, it also describes the skepticism surrounding stories of shamanic flights into other realities as well as just about any encounter with strange spirits from another dimension, be they leprechauns, angels or demons—all of which are roundly dismissed by modern science.

Aldous Huxley suggested that "reality" may be simply too vast for the human brain to comprehend. As a result, the species has evolved screening mechanisms to make sense of the world, letting in just as much or as little reality as we can safely handle. If this is true, then it seems that language is one of the prime filtering mechanisms we have developed. Any attempt to describe reality depends on language, which itself depends on linear thinking. Linear thinking is also the hallmark of the modern scientific method, which has not only provided the framework for our modern understanding of reality, but has also given us a fair amount of control over our everyday consensus world. But it may be that the Magical Universe simply cannot be understood through traditional linear thinking. When the "Oz Factor" enters into the picture, encounters with the Magical Universe get dismissed out of hand. But as Jacques Vallée notes, in taking this view modern science is actually distancing itself from its own intellectual vanguard—quantum physics, which no longer considers the existence of other dimensions as a marginal idea, at least on a quantum level.

Today quantum physics has become the bridge for understanding encounters with the Magical Universe, perhaps because it stresses holistic thinking over linear thinking. While linear thinking, which traces the thread of cause and effect, can shed a great deal of light on the quantum universe, it ultimately fails to describe the tapestry of which it is but a thread. As theoretical physicists keep discovering, attempting to apply cause and effect to the quantum universe always seems to result in the same "Oz Factor" that haunts investigations into UFOs, shamanism and other aspects of the paranormal.

The great Truth of the ancient alchemists was expressed in the dictum, "As above, so below." Attempts to map the Magical Universe through the techniques of quantum physics merely turns this dictum around, insisting that if the smallest components of matter cannot be understood using traditional linear thinking, then neither can the greatest. Quantifying, classifying and categorizing may be an indispensable intellectual endeavor, but the intellect is but one thread of human understanding; it is not the entire cloth.

Perhaps that's why the cutting edge of investigation into the UFO phenomenon boldly goes one step beyond mere technical explanation. Instead, it *sees in the UFO phenomenon a modern technological face to an ancient lineage of Otherworldly encounters. Whether these encounters are with faeries, angels or aliens, one thing seems certain—they are distinctly not human. What are they then, visitors from another dimension or merely projections of the human psyche? The fact that such encounters have changed the course of innumerable lives gives them a* de facto *reality, but does that reality exist only in the mind, or does it extend through the entire fabric of the Magical Universe? This is a question that lies at the heart of serious investigation into the curious effect psychedelics have on the human psyche.*

Before thirty years of research into LSD was shelved in the late sixties, Stanislav Grof conducted more than 4,000 psychedelic sessions in which he traced encounters with archetypal human beings, visits to mythological realms, past incarnation memories, extrasensory perception and out-of-body experiences. Grof believes this research was gradually pushing psychology into serious consideration of what had previously been dismissed as the paranormal. Unfortunately, though the "war on drugs" has yet to stop the use of drugs, it has virtually put an end to scientific research, although there are exceptions. Alexander Shulgin is one of these. For three decades now, Shulgin and his wife, Anne, have been manipulating molecules to discover how they alter consciousness. By flipping chemical switches in the brain to illuminate unseen landscapes, the Shulgins see their work as an important exploration into the "terra incognita" of the human psyche.

Ultimately any attempt to describe reality depends as much upon the workings of the human brain as it does on anything "out there." Trying to separate the two is probably a mistake. Holistic thinking requires that we consider the two together. Just as two eyes give depth to visual perception, perhaps these two lenses of interior and exterior realities are required to provide a working understanding of the dreamlike realm of the Magical Universe.

Alternate Realities
Psychedelics

Sasha and Ann Shulgin: Ecstasy, A Love Drug

with Faustin Bray

In the chemical computer that we call a brain, a flipped switch can illuminate very strange landscapes. Shamans, searchers, saints and sinners have been exploring these chemically revealed vistas since time began. Only recently, however, have we actually begun to invent them.

For three decades Sasha Shulgin has been manipulating molecules to discover how they alter consciousness. For the past 11 years, he has been collaborating with his wife Ann. Now, concerned that their work may be lost or repressed in the wake of the current "war on drugs," the Shulgins have decided to share their insights into the hallucinogenic dreamtime of designer drugs in a book provocatively titled, *PIHKAL (Phenethylamines I Have Known and Loved)*.

Weighing in at 978 pages, *PIHKAL* is as heavy and convoluted as the issue of drugs itself. Howard Rheinbold, in the *Whole Earth Review*, has called it "part autobiography, part metaphysical guidebook, and part cookbook." Faustin Bray, who was finally granted an interview after 12 years of requests, calls it a love story—"love of chemistry, love of the compounds created, love of their research group companions, love of each other, and love of the grail of a 'unified reality.'"

However you describe it, *PIHKAL* is sure to create controversy, a fact not lost on the Shulgins. In a culture that sees "drugs" and "drug abuse" as synonymous, and where white-coated scientists are busy slicing and dicing the brain to see what makes it tick, Sasha and Ann Shulgin are attempting to "redirect the question from the brain to the mind." By flipping chemical switches in the brain to illuminate unseen landscapes, the Shulgins see their work as an important exploration into the "terra incognita" of the psyche.

In 1983 you made a moving speech at the Psychedelic Conference 2, at the University of Santa Barbara explaining your life's devotion to researching and developing particular compounds. The major feeling that I got from that talk was that you were searching for a chemical that created an empathic connection between individuals in problematic conditions. In other words, you seemed to be hoping for peaceful solutions—a magic pill.

Sasha: Well, a person doesn't go out and design a specific drug for a specific purpose. That would require skills that no one has. You design something that might have some action, and observe what it actually does. If it has some property that, as you see it, has value, then it becomes a research tool. Then that value may influence the design of something else. If you find that the molecular change produces some toxic effect that is not desirable, or that it goes into areas that are not valid for research, then that change is something you may exclude from the next design. But with every structural change, no matter how small, you have a new molecule; one that is unique and totally unpredictable.

The process is an endless turning over of stones to see what is underneath. Usually nothing, but occasionally, there is a beautiful scarab beetle. Perhaps there is the rare genius who has some divine insight as to which stone to turn, but in my case I simply turn over as many as I can, and carefully look under each. So, in the finding of new compounds, it's not a matter of saying, "Hey, here's a neat one! I'll bet that it will do such and such." You methodically find out what each one does, and sometimes it turns out it's a total waste of time. There are many stones out there with no beetles under them.

Ann: I think what Sasha was saying in Santa Barbara was that what these materials basically do is give a clue as to what the ingredients of the entire human psyche are, 90% of which we don't consciously know. Drugs are only one way of doing it. No matter how it's done, whether with meditation or hypnotherapy or whatever, it is essential we start understanding that *terra incognita*, to start being less afraid of finding out what's there—what drives us, what are the destructive impulses, the nurturing impulses. That is what is at the bottom of this research.

Big business and science are looking into brain chemistry for all sorts of reasons.

Sasha: Yes, but I feel that the wrong questions are being asked and the wrong process is being used. Some researcher will make a radio-labeled chemical—an antidepressant, a hallucinogen, etc.—and get it into an experimental rat. After a period of time the rat is decapitated. The brain is removed, finely sliced, and put onto photographic film.

The pictures of various parts of the brain are then shown on a slide at a seminar with the statement that this is how these drugs work. In reality, all you can say is this is where these drugs go in a rat.

I don't believe the study of chemicals that influence our mental process can ever be understood just from animal studies. You can determine the toxicity of the chemical in an animal for that animal but you can't extrapolate to any other animal. With the hallucinogenic phenethylamines there can be a hundred-fold difference in toxicity just between rats and mice. Which would you prefer to use to extrapolate to man?

I'm trying to redirect the question from the brain to the mind, and I use the only species that can express joy or doubt or paranoia or what have you.

Where is the mind located?

Sasha: I have no idea, but it is in there somewhere. My hope is to develop tools that can probe the way the mind works. I think the mind, to most research pharmacologists and psychopharmacologists, is about as scary a thing as the unconscious is to most psychologists. It's an area you just don't want to talk or think about. There is a desperate search by brain chemists to find that one lesion, that one chemical imbalance, that makes the schizophrenic different than the normal. It has not been found, but the hope is always to find some obvious abnormality because it allows me to explain the difference between *him* and *me*. It allows one to say that I am OK, and he is sick. We don't want to be able to relate to a guy who goes into a restaurant in Texas and shoots 26 people and then himself. So, first we hope he's on drugs so that we can blame the drugs. Usually, these people who explode are not on drugs. So, in *post mortem* we look at the brain hoping to find a tumor of some unusual structure, but we rarely find anything strange. Instead, we are left with that very grim conclusion that he is as you are, as I am. We begin to realize that inside of each of us there's a capability of doing exactly what horrifies us. I have stayed that impulse to destroy. Why did he not? You'll not answer that by looking at radioactive distribution in rat brains. I don't know if you'll get the answer with the tools I've been working with either, but I think it's a more promising direction for searching.

Ann: I think that when you begin exploring your own psyche, you are, at the same time, exploring the human psyche at large. So, the more you explore your own mind—and that's all you can explore—the more you begin to understand what the human species is and what its potentials are. The entire culture is scared to death of the unconscious. We're fascinated by ax murderers and mass murderers. When people go to horror movies to see heads rolling in the dust, what they're doing is connecting with what the ancient Indians called "Kali"—the personification of bliss through destruction. They are exploring their own unacknowledged destructive capabilities by seeing it on the screen.

People who are afraid of the unconscious say, "Don't psychologize. Don't get into this kind of thing. You'll just get messed up." What they don't understand is that the angels and devils are all in the same unconscious. You cannot have it all good because we are not made up of all good. We are the Kali and the Christ, all of us.

The closer you get to understanding these archetypes and these forces, the more you begin to empathize with, and have compassion for, the rest of the human race. Maybe eventually we will begin to get a clue as to how the destructive part could be turned around. To do that we will necessarily have to understand how to exercise the negative, the dark side, in a way that does not threaten to destroy the species. We have to try and mold our society in such a way that the anger, the resentments, and the negativity can find expression in a way which does not threaten the entire tribe, and eventually the human race. We have a long way to go, and these chemical tools are just beginning steps, and, again, they are not the only tools.

Do you think you're getting some answers to those big questions?

Sasha: Unfortunately, my main art is in the creation of the tools.

It is said that they enhance one's visual acuity, and appreciation of beauty. How would you define beauty?

Sasha: I guess it is what I appreciate.

But there are many occasions that one appreciates something for other than its beauty.

Sasha: If you enhance the seeing of color, it is not the colors that have changed. You are merely making yourself aware of a greater variety of inputs that are there all the time. The person who is unrestrictedly aware of this mass of input all the time, is what we call a schizophrenic; where there is no limitation, and no priority given to what one takes in from one's environment, there is confusion.

We need filters?

Sasha: Yes, this is one of the hazards in psychedelic experience. You can lose the capability of assigning risks and benefits to various inputs. You may very well respond to the beauty of red and green lights, and fail to interpret them appropriately when walking across the street. The idea of a filter is a very desirable one for self-preservation. Otherwise you might be overwhelmed by the surrounding environment and possibly find yourself with a very compromised experience.

Let's talk about fun, the noble pursuit of fun.

Sasha: Well, I don't want to say that the goal of this research is to invent things that produce fun, but on the other hand it would be ridiculous to disavow the fact that there is pleasure experienced with these chemicals. But we as a culture are so invested in the dark Calvinistic philosophy which states, "Thou shalt not enjoy." If you laugh, God will smite you. You'll find that if there's a collective depression or paranoia, it is because a lot of people out there dare not feel much pleasure for fear of some retribution.

Ann: When you explore these territories with psychedelics eventually you come to an experience of total sorrow. It feels like a place of death, and you have to learn your way in and your way out. When you do get through and you do survive, you have a much deeper feeling of what that area of darkness and despair is. It's the same as when somebody who survives a heart attack tells their friends how the experience made them appreciate being alive. It is understanding that the only really good prayer is to say "Thank you for life." It is the recognition of the fact that you are alive and intact. For all its sadness and miseries, life is extremely precious, and that joy is something you owe yourself and the greater consciousness. One of the most tragic things about this culture and one of the hardest programs to outgrow, is that we've been taught by certain religions and certain people that if you are too happy for too long there is going to be a crash. In other words there is a vengeful God or gods out there who are going to punish you if you enjoy yourself. I don't believe that. Obviously tragedies happen all the time. They are part of the ups and downs and the general process of living. But you can't avoid them by avoiding joy. Joy, pleasure, and even moments of total euphoria are necessary. If you don't experience them, you are not truly allowing yourself to live; you are cutting short the full potential of your own psyche.

Sasha: Your mention of the joy of an altered state reminded me of a recent conversation. I was talking to a person who was adamantly against any changes in states of mind and he said, "If you don't like where you are, you should find out where you are failing in life." So, I asked him what it felt like to be awake 24 hours a day. When he realized that I was referring to his dream states as altered states of consciousness, he acknowledged that he indeed had two sides to his own world as well, and that maybe he could learn from each of them.

You both have children. How do you feel about these tools and children or when it is appropriate, or when it isn't.

Sasha: I have very strong feelings against the use of tools to explore the structure of the consciousness or the unconscious in children, where there is not yet an integration and a completeness of that young person's psychic structure.

How can you judge that?

Sasha: By observation and judgment. You know, it may be that psychedelics remove a boundary that children don't even have. I saw one example where LSD had been inadvertently consumed. The parents had sugar cubes in their refrigerator and the child swallowed some of them and thus consumed an unknown amount of LSD. The child was acting in a very childlike way. He was responding to stimuli that the parents could not see, but then children very often respond to stimuli that parents can't see. I don't think the behavior was particularly abnormal. So it may well be that as infants we are in that altered, expanded place at all times. Our learning process may be one of closing down to some degree. When PCP was used as an anesthetic, children responded to it far better than adults. In the recovery room they would have visual goings on and they would follow camels across the ceiling. To kids this need not be a problem. "Far out! There are camels going across the ceiling!" But adults would have a much more difficult time because they know intellectually that there are no camels on the ceiling. So, while I think these are powerful tools for learning and self realization for adults, for a small child they can be virtually without effect. It is in the adolescent in-between area that I think some very destructive things can occur because the adolescent is not yet a complete tapestry, so to speak. He cannot assimilate the complex inputs, both positive and negative, that occur during a psychedelic experience.

Ann: I believe that one of the things that is necessary for a person to be able to use psychedelics at all, successfully, is for him to have gotten to the stage in his life where his sense of self, of identity, has been developed quite strongly.

One of the most important aspects of this entire area of exploration, no matter how it is done, is to make conscious as much of the unconscious mind as possible. The more we do that, the more we can understand with *all* of the intellect as well as the gut. You can't do that when things remain unconscious.

I've told my son, who intends to be a psychologist, that if he's going through a very difficult experience he can store the experience while he is suffering it. He can activate the observing part of himself, so that it learns; it notes what the reactions are, what thoughts and emotions come up. Later, as a therapist to other people, he will have an empathy that can only come from having experienced, in some form, what that other person is suffering. It will make him a much better healer because he has felt it himself.

A lot of people want to make this entire realm only spiritual. They see the body and the body's reactions as a lower place. It is not as good, or as high, or as fine as the non-physical. My own feeling is that this is just plain nonsense. The mind and the psyche and the body should be together. This is one of the reasons that Sasha does not like compounds which divorce one part of yourself from the rest. I feel the same way about it. My warning bell goes off if I cannot truly and deeply feel emotions. If I am emotionally flat, then that's one drug I will not take again because it means that something is being cut off.

In your book, PIHKAL, *you address the idea of approaching the mental and physical changes of increased maturity while using these tools over the years. Can you tell how your research has impacted your mental agility?*

Sasha: Well I personally believe that as you learn more from around you, you learn more about yourself. You discover what's strong and what's weak in your own unconscious. This is one of the most powerful aspects of these tools; they provide you with access to the unconscious, an area not readily gotten to. It is there where roam the beasts that we are scared of. We don't know why we're scared of them, and many of our actions are in direct response to these fears of the unknown.

Is there some way that on a really essential level we can approach our general basic fear of death with a pill?

Ann: How about Huxley's death?

Sasha: As Huxley was dying, he chose to use LSD, perhaps to ease the transition. I would not subscribe to that myself, because I feel that you could obscure the essence of another learning experience. The death process is a very definite change of the state of consciousness, and I feel that, in our culture, the accepted practice of medicine often calls for an excessive use of narcotics, which can muck up the process with amnesia and with a form of unnaturalness.

On the other hand, learning to become at peace with altered states could be instructive and valuable. Death is strictly another altered state. It's another transition, and there is no reason for it to be feared. I think one of the reasons that people fear death is the fact that they have not resolved life. The best course is to resolve as many of the conflicts as possible while you are alive. One thing I've suggested on occasion, when talking to people, is to look at their fear as a form of excitement. There is excitement in not knowing what's around the corner, at being unable to predict. Suddenly it's the same phenomenon, but instead of living in fear, you can live in excitement. You'll still have the unknown ahead of you, but you'll be seeing a different face of it.

Is there a particular direction that you intend to go with your future research?

Sasha: I just want to keep turning over rocks and finding what's there. I want to keep learning.

Ann: And publish the results.

Sasha: Yes, and publish the results.

Audio and video recordings of the Shulgins, other like-minded authorities, and the Shulgins' book, PIHKAL, are available from SOUND PHOTOSYNTHE-SIS catalog: P.O. Box 2111, Mill Valley, CA 94942. Phone: (415)-383-6712.

Alternate Realities

Psychedelics

Stanislav Grof: Beyond LSD

with Jerry Snider

The sensationalism surrounding the widespread use of LSD in the late sixties resulted in legislative overkill that virtually ended psychotherapeutic LSD research. Thirty years of studies were put on the shelf, with little attention paid to their findings. Of course LSD itself did not disappear. It is still widely available and still widely used, but serious investigation into its unique effect on the human psyche was all but abandoned. What did the research show? And was it just LSD that frightened the authorities, or was there something more? Could it be that LSD research was abandoned in part because it was forcing psychology into areas it feared to tread, opening up the paranormal to legitimate scientific investigation?

Stanislav Grof, MD, began his research into the psychotherapeutic uses of LSD in 1960 at the Psychiatric Research Institute in Prague, Czechoslovakia. Over the years, he conducted more than 4,000 psychedelic sessions. What he found were some highly unusual experiences—including encounters with archetypal beings, visits to mythological realms of various cultures, past incarnation memories, extrasensory perception and episodes of out-of-body states—that could not be described by the narrow and superficial conceptual model used in academic psychology. Convinced that such experiences were not simply drug-induced, but rather represented natural and normal manifestations of the deeper dynamics of the human psyche, Grof saw the need for a much larger cartography of the psyche than had previously been allowed. This, he felt, would not only require revision of our ideas about the human mind, but revision of traditional beliefs about the nature of reality.

Dr. Grof is the founding president of the International Transpersonal Association and has taught and lectured in academic and workshop settings worldwide. He is the author of numerous books, including *LSD Psychotherapy* (Hunter House, Alameda, CA), on which this interview is based. His latest book is *The Holotropic Mind.*

LSD has been both demonized and lionized. What do you think is the single greatest misconception about LSD?

Stanislav Grof: I would say these two reactions reflect the basic misconception, that LSD is either good or bad. It is neither. By itself, LSD has no intrinsic healing potential, nor does it have any intrinsic destructive potential. The outcome depends on who is doing it, with whom, for what purpose and under what circumstances. Yet everything that happens under the influence of LSD tends to be credited or blamed on the drug itself.

Years ago, during the initial flurry of bad publicity over LSD, I had a very interesting discussion with Humphrey Osmond, one of the early pioneers of LSD research. He pointed out the ridiculous turn the debate had taken by pointing out that LSD is just a tool. He said if the worth of some other tool, a knife for instance, was discussed in the same way LSD was, you'd have a policeman saying it was bad, while pushing statistics of people killed with knives in back alleys. A surgeon would see it as good, pointing out the healing possibilities of the knife. A housewife might talk about cutting salami. An artist might talk about wood carving. As you can see, what is being said says less about the knife than about how it is used. We don't make the mistake of blaming or crediting the knife with how it's used, but with LSD it's all kind of thrown together.

You have concluded from your studies that LSD psychotherapy is least effective with two groups, excessively compulsive people and spiritually highly developed people. Why is this?

Stanislav Grof: The defenses are strongest with excessively compulsive people, whereas the spiritual master may have already experienced all those states where psychedelics would take them.

So LSD psychotherapy is most successful with basically intelligent, normal acting people who, like most of us, have a couple of significant emotional blocks?

Stanislav Grof: Yes. They can function well. They have a family and a good job. They're very successful and, at the same time, have difficulties seeing any deeper meaning in life. There's a kind of "So what?" attitude, like, "I'm making a lot of money and I have a family. So what?" What they're lacking is a feeling of deep connection to existence and a kind of zest in life.

Aldous Huxley likened the brain to a valve that allows us to take in only as much "reality" as we can handle. He felt that psychedelics open this valve and let a larger reality flow in. You write, "a person who has taken LSD does not have an 'LSD experience,' but takes a journey into deep recesses of his or her own psyche." What is the terrain of the experience? Where do psychedelics takes us that everyday reality doesn't?

Stanislav Grof: First of all, it's not limited to psychedelics. I include psychedelics in a much larger category of nonordinary states. Psychedelics are one way to access these states, but so are certain kinds of breath work, rebirthing, sensory isolation, primal therapy, drumming, chanting and so on.

As far as the topography is concerned, what I discovered during 20 years of clinical research is that when somebody was beginning with psychedelics and using relatively small dosages, the first thing that surfaced was a lot of biographical material. These experiences stayed, by and large, in the context that has been defined by traditional psychology, which is limited to biology, postnatal biography and the Freudian individual unconscious. But as the sessions continued and the dosage increased, we found patterns of experiences for which the traditional psychological context doesn't have any conceptual framework, patterns like sequences of psychological death and rebirth, encounters with archetypal beings, visits to mythological realms of various cultures, past incarnation memories, extrasensory perception, episodes of out-of-body states and experiences of cosmic consciousness.

What is absolutely amazing is that traditional academic psychology and psychiatry have not admitted any evidence from the study of nonordinary states, whether this evidence is coming from history, comparative religion or anthropology. Virtually all of the world's cultures, other than our Western industrial civilization, have held these states in very high esteem and have spent a lot of time trying to develop some powerful techniques for getting into them. Our society, on the other hand, has not only pathologized them but also outlawed the tools and the context. They have, in effect, discounted the entire spiritual history of humanity. That's why I think work with nonordinary states, including LSD therapy, is one of the most fascinating areas in psychology and psychiatry. It is something that can really bring completely new discoveries and can facilitate what we call a paradigm shift.

In your work with psychedelics and nonordinary states, you discovered a series of four stages that correspond both to shamanic death/rebirth rites and the stages of natal development. Could you explain these perinatal matrices?

Stanislav Grof: Perinatal experiences are quite regularly accompanied by a complex of physical symptoms that can best be interpreted as a derivative of biological birth. I found they provide clues to the understanding of many otherwise puzzling aspects of LSD experiences.

The experiences come in four patterns. It doesn't necessarily follow the order of one, two, three, four, which is the order of the progress of biological delivery. But there are patterns of experience that can be associated with the different stages.

The first perinatal matrix is related to primal union with the mother, to the original state of intrauterine existence during which the mother and the child form a symbiotic unity. The elements of undisturbed intrauterine existence can be experienced in LSD sessions in a concrete biological form, or in the form of its spiritual counterpart, the experience of cosmic unity. With eyes closed, the phenomenon of cosmic unity is experienced as oceanic ecstasy. With the eyes open, it results in an experience of merging with the environment and a sense of unity with perceived objects.

LSD subjects confronted with the second perinatal matrix frequently relate it to the very onset of biological delivery. In this situation the original equilibrium of the intrauterine existence is disturbed, first by alarming chemical signals and later by muscular spasms. Individuals in this matrix report an experience of "no exit." Subjects feel encaged or trapped in a monstrous claustrophobic situation, which is typically absolutely unbearable. While under the influence of this matrix, the individual cannot see the possibility of any end to his or her torments.

The third experiential matrix is associated with the second clinical stage of biological delivery. In this stage, the uterine contractions continue, but the cervix stands wide open and makes possible gradual and difficult propulsion through the birth canal. LSD subjects confronted with this matrix may experience a realistic reliving of various aspects of the struggle through the birth canal. Or it may be experienced as an atmosphere of titanic fight, sadomasochistic orgies, intense sexual sensations, scatological involvement and the element of purifying fire occurring in various combinations. This stage constitutes the death-rebirth struggle. While matrix two, the no-exit situation, involves sheer suffering, the experience of the death-rebirth struggle represents the borderline between agony and ecstasy and the fusion of both.

The fourth perinatal matrix seems to be meaningfully related to the third clinical stage of delivery. In this final phase, the agonizing process of the intense struggle culminates; the propulsion through the birth canal is completed and the extreme intensification of tension and suffering is followed by a sudden relief and relaxation. The symbolic counterpart of this final stage of delivery is the death-rebirth experience. Physical and emotional agony culminates in a feeling of utter and total annihilation on all imaginable levels. The experience is usually described as "ego death"; it seems to entail an instantaneous and merciless destruction of all the previous reference points in the life of the individual.

After the subject has experienced the limits of total annihilation and "hit the cosmic bottom," he or she is struck by visions of blinding white or golden light. The claustrophobic and compressed world of the birth struggle suddenly opens up and expands into infinity. The general atmosphere is one of liberation, salvation, redemption, love and forgiveness. There is often a strong tendency to share and engage in service and charitable activities. The universe is perceived as indescribably beautiful and radiant.

How do these matrices fit into the transpersonal?

Stanislav Grof: Perinatal experiences seem to represent a frontier between the personal and the transindividual, as is reflected by their deep association with biological birth and death. The transpersonal realm then reflects the connections between the individual and the cosmos. Intimate knowledge of the transpersonal realms is absolutely essential, not only for the understanding of the psychedelic process but for any serious approach to such phenomena as shamanism, religion, mysticism, rites of passage, mythology, parapsychology and schizophrenia.

Is that what happens with a bad trip, you get caught in one of these matrices and don't understand the framework?

Stanislav Grof: Yes. We have a kind of superficial model of the psyche, where unless somebody was seriously abused or battered, there are supposed to be no difficult elements in the unconscious. Then we are surprised when something like Nazism or Communism comes along, or the things happening in Uganda or Somalia, or what happens during the uprisings in prisons, where emotional suffering is unbelievable and destructive, and self-destructive behaviors emerge. And there's simply no explanatory system because the traditional model of the psyche has nothing to offer.

So you see these same four perinatal matrices working themselves out in culture and history, as well as individual lives?

Stanislav Grof: In my book *Beyond the Brain,* there's an epilogue showing the connections between these matrices and some social/political phenomena. For example, in a totalitarian regime, people seem to get stuck in the second matrix. It's as if they find themselves stuck in the womb. There's usually a lot imagery of defecation. Then, when the process moves to the third matrix, you get a lot of these historical images related to revolution.

Lloyd Demause, the New York psychoanalyst/journalist who has studied a number of situations prior to outbreaks of major wars and revolutions, gives examples of how leaders, who were trying to mobilize the nation to war or revolution, all used figures of speech or metaphors related to biological birth. For example, "The enemy is closing in; it is strangling us; it's squeezing the last air out of our lungs." The solution to the political struggle is also presented in terms of birth imagery: "There is light on the other side of the tunnel; I will lead you to life; we all are going to breathe freely again," and so on.

The development of the atomic bomb included six or seven secret codes that used birth symbolism. For example, the plane that carried the Hiroshima bomb was named after the pilot's mother, Enola Gay, and they painted a nickname on the bomb, which was Little Boy. The agreed-upon code that was wired to Washington when Little Boy was dropped was "The baby was born."

What about our current cultural period? The social climate today has a feeling of hopelessness, of being trapped. People have lost faith in most of our institutions, especially our political institutions. In our urban populations, the rampant crime keeps people feeling trapped. Are we in any single classic stage?

Stanislav Grof: Yes. Many people who have these inner experiences take a larger look and see that we have now enacted in our world a lot of the elements you would encounter internally when you are in a transformation process. For example, you would encounter tremendous unleashing of aggression. You would confront destructive and self-destructive tendencies within yourself if you have an inner experience. There is also a liberation of repressed sexuality. This has been happening for years. Just about every aspect of sexual behavior has been openly presented in the media. There are all kinds of very unusual sexual experiments such as S&M parlors, sexual slave markets—all these things have sprung up. So the sexual impulse is sort of being released and acted out, and also the aggressive. There is an increase not only in criminality but in terrorism as well, all over the world. Then you have satanic elements emerging from the collective unconscious. The deep levels of the psyche are now being ventilated.

What can we do as a society to confront the problems these behaviors bring about?

Stanislav Grof: I think the problem is that instead of confronting the core issues experientially, where it would become transformative, we are acting them out in society. An essential kind of imperative in work with nonordinary states is to create a safe framework in which people can confront it internally. In acting it out, you may kill someone. So what seems to be happening now is that we are in a race, where if we continue projecting and acting out all these tendencies, we are on a trend that is very clearly destructive, and it's unlikely that we will make it as a species. If, on the other hand, that process could be internalized, it might end up in a major evolutionary jump in consciousness.

Many people feel the crisis we are facing is a crisis in consciousness. It has a lot to do with the fact that we lost spirituality. The religions are very seriously undermined, but I believe religions are part of the problem, not part of the solution. A lot of the world's conflicts, at least on the surface, are actually religiously motivated. Look at what's happening in the Middle East or India. What we need instead of religion is spirituality, where you actually connect experientially to the transpersonal dimensions of existence. You have a personal experience rather than going to church and listening to somebody talk about the spiritual experiences of people who lived two thousand years ago.

I know you believe that experimentation with LSD should be supervised, but since people are going to use it regardless of its legal status or wise usage, what advice do you have for people who are trying to make these discoveries on their own?

Stanislav Grof: What's most important, at least on a societal level, is the need to recognize that there is an extremely powerful drive in human nature for transcendence. The need for a transcendental experience is stronger than sex. If you study history, you find that every other culture, except the industrial civilization, honored it. They had rituals and technologies for people to access transcendental experiences in a socially-sanctioned framework, in the context of rituals, ceremonies and so on. Psychedelics have that potential. A nonordinary state has the potential to take you to the transcendental place. In other words, the motivation for those experiences is extremely strong. This is what is manifesting in the drug scene. So I believe the only way you can really counteract this taking of drugs—I'm talking here about heroin and alcohol, cocaine, crack and so on—is to offer the means to have a genuine experience. I see drug addiction and alcoholism as a very unfortunate and misguided effort to reach transcendence. It is coming from a transcendental need, and the only way you can counteract it is to open up channels to a pure, clean spiritual experience.

If it's true that there is this powerful transcendental pull in people, some kind of silly program like "Just Say No" is simply ridiculous. If I say the drive is more powerful than sex, you can compare it with a situation in the sexual realm. What success would you have with a program trying to eliminate masturbation through a campaign of "Just Say No?" The only way you can influence masturbation is to open up the way to adult sexuality, because behind it is a very powerful drive. To the extent that there is a transcendental drive behind drug taking, the only way to influence it is to open the way to mature spirituality.

Alternate Realities
UFOs

Ken Carey: Extraterrestrials

There seem to be two extremes of viewpoint surrounding the whole subject of extraterrestrial intelligence, each of which tends to alienate the other. The first extreme comes from those who expect extraterrestrials to come here and "save us" from the effects of human ignorance. It is held by people who appear all too willing to abnegate responsibility for themselves and their worlds, waiting—as some Christians wait—for the descent of problem-solvers from the sky. This view denies both our roles as co-creators and our immediate responsibility for self and environment. The other extreme, often held by people reacting to the former view, denies the existence of extraterrestrial intelligence altogether. It regards those of us who are interested in them as dreamers and escapists.

I think the easiest way to clear up both these misperceptions is to use an analogy—childbirth. When a mother is about to give birth to a child, she alone has full responsibility. She provides 100% of the labor required to deliver the child. But the intelligent mother does not turn away the midwife! She knows that a loving and experienced midwife can be of inestimable help in facilitating optimal conditions for a healthy and natural birth. The midwife reminds the mother to keep breathing deeply. She reminds the mother of the large perspective when the immediacy of the contractions might otherwise cause her to forget.

Similarly, as humankind approaches the dawn of the Third Millennium, we are facing a sort of collective birth—a fundamental transformation of meta-historical proportions. A universal species is emerging from the womb of human history. We would do well, I think, to welcome those who come to assist us through this momentous event. They are here to help us keep perspective, to remind us of our larger vision and purpose when things may seem darkest, when economic, social or environmental contractions loom overly large.

During the past decade I have had numerous encounters with entities that fall into the general classification of extraterrestrial. These encounters have convinced me that there are many different types of extraterrestrials, different tribes, species, classes—whatever you want to call them. In the course of recording my 1979 book, *The Starseed Transmissions,* I stopped at one point, and I asked the being with whom I was blending, "You're extraterrestrial aren't you?"

This is the conversation that followed.

"Yes, to a large extent we have been extraterrestrial, though our present interaction with you and with others of your species is the beginning of the end of that condition for us."

Out of curiosity, I asked the entities what they looked like. "I would like to see you," I said. "Do you sometimes appear to people?"

"Yes, we do sometimes project appearances. We do occasionally materialize in order to be seen, but materialization requires a great deal of energy, and since you are able to communicate with us telepathically, we would rather not waste the energy that would be required to coalesce a physical manifestation for you."

"I understand that," I said. "But I am still curious. Suppose you did coalesce physically, suppose you did create a physical manifestation, what would you look like?"

"When there is a need," the entity replied, "to bring our presence to the attention of some human who is unable to sense us telepathically, as you are now, we reach into that individual's consciousness and animate whatever image that person holds that most nearly corresponds to the reality of who we are. We choose from their conceptions and animate those that are the closest to our nature. In other words, we dress in their images, putting them on like you might put on a suit of clothing.

"In Europe, during the Middle Ages, we most often appeared as angels; to Native Americans, as great winged beings of light. In this contemporary, industrial civilization, your nearest approximating images are often 'highly-advanced technological' or extraterrestrial. So these are the forms that we assume when it is necessary to alert someone to our presence through some outer means.

"However, our preference has always been to alert people to our presence through inner means. For, in truth, we come not as separate beings outside of yourselves, but as the reality of your own forgotten spirits. We are your eternal selves, the aspect of you that never forgot its unity with the Creator, the aspect that created your very bodies, that aspect of you that historically has been denied access to your consciousness. We come bringing tidings of great joy, to show you that you share the very being of God and are indeed the specks designed to express the Creator's intentions on this world. We come to awaken you to your true reality.

"Whenever this can be accomplished without the wasted energy and the frequent misunderstandings that accompany external physical manifestations, we always prefer the telepathic methods."

"That's good," I thought, feeling rather proud of myself, "I am among those who didn't need to be alerted through an external manifestation."

It was as if the entity laughed.

"That's what you think, Ken! We have been trying to get your attention for a long time! You have forgotten the many times we have manifested externally before you. We have washed these occasions from your memory because we knew you were likely to become distracted with appearances. The inner, the spiritual communion between us, is the reality; that is what is important. With you, as with many, it has taken numerous external manifestations to bring you to a point where you could blend with us in consciousness as you are now doing. We have worked with you for quite some time to bring you to this present level of receptivity.

"Do you remember that evening, back in the summer of 1977, when Sherry called you out to see an unusual light moving across the Sky?"

I did remember the incident then, though I had forgotten.

Our second floor bedroom ends in a small east-facing porch looking out over a pasture. About 11:00 one evening, I was just getting into bed when my wife, Sherry, who was out on the porch taking a last look at the night sky, suddenly called to me in an urgent tone, "Ken, come here quick! You've got to see this!"

I went out on the porch and could not believe my eyes. There was an object that appeared about the size of a full moon, a cylindrical object, very white, like the color of the moon. It was moving slowly across the sky, leaving an immense fiery trail behind it. We had it in view for several minutes before it finally disappeared behind some trees.

I had never really forgotten this, but for some reason I had not remembered that I remembered.

That night, after I was asleep, they came to the house. In fact, they came to me every night after that for several months. I grew to look forward to their coming because it was such a pleasant experience. Initially, I would feel them as I was drifting off to sleep, a cool light flowing down through the top of my head.

As I lay in bed with my eyes closed on those nights, I could both see and feel what appeared to be a sort of multicolored river of living, liquid energy flowing from the top of my head downward throughout my body. It must have been flowing through my nervous system and the hemispheres of my brain. I could see it branching treelike into arteries and tributaries. Red, blue, green and yellow it flowed, a soothing, refreshing sensation. Then a voice would begin speaking to me and my class would begin. These classes became so much a matter of course during the months that followed that they never stood out in my memory. I think now I know why.

1977 was a year of intense physical activity for me. It was an idealistic cycle of my life during which I attempted to live without a motorized vehicle. That may not be too difficult if you are living in a city with the availability of public transportation and perhaps a bicycle, but we lived 12 miles from the nearest town and 15 miles away from my place of employment. Every morning I would leave the house at 6:30 and walk my ten-speed bicycle down the mile-long dirt road to the pavement.

I would then pedal 14 miles to work and spend the day in hard physical labor, usually framing a building or laying concrete blocks. At the end of the day, I would pedal my bicycle 14 miles back again and walk the remaining mile of dirt road. I came home utterly exhausted. Sleep was a very necessary thing for me. I think now in retrospect, it may have been partially because of my exhaustion and the subsequent depth of my sleep that his communication was somehow made possible. I often remember the voice trailing off as I would sit up in bed, resuming again where it left off as I lay back down. Most nights I was too tired and sleepy to pay it much conscious attention, but there were exceptions. In the course of the above conversation, I began to remember one of those exceptions. I don't know how I could have forgotten it. It occurred one evening as I was lying in bed drifting off to sleep. The voice had just asked me if I knew who they were. I answered that I had assumed they were extraterrestrials.

"Would you like to work with us?" the voice asked.

"Yes," I replied with enthusiasm, "More than anything in the world!"

"All right then, can you handle this?"

Suddenly I was sitting at my desk, the 12-volt light was on over my head. My hand held a pen, poised over a blank sheet of paper. I looked around in amazement. A second ago the room had been dark and I had been in bed, conversing as usual with my eyes closed.

"What do you mean, 'Can I handle this?'" I asked in puzzlement.

"Well, can you handle this?" The voice returned. Instantly the room was dark again, and I was back in bed.

Intrigued, I asked if they wouldn't mind running that by me one more time.

"Done," was the instant reply. Immediately I was at my desk again with the light on and pen and paper once more in front of me.

"This is amazing," I said, "Is it real?"

"Of course it's real."

"But how do you do it!"

"Never mind how we do it. Can you handle it?"

"I love it!" I said. "Let's do it some more."

"No," the entity replied. "There is no need to do it any more."

I found myself back in bed. The lessons resumed. I guessed that I had been put through a sort of trust exercise. As time passed, my ego began to realize that these things were benevolent, that they could be trusted. It learned that it could let go of its incessant need to control and understand and actually come through the relationship with these entities better off than before: recharged and understanding more. No doubt this experience and others like it helped to lay the inner groundwork that allowed *The Starseed Transmissions* to appear a year or so later.

For over a decade I have avoided sharing accounts of this nature because I have always considered them more or less irrelevant. Excessive focus on mere "phenomena" can be a deadly distraction—at best of only peripheral relevance. The message that these spirit-beings are now bringing to the Earth is far more important than the little dramas associated with their coming. While tales of extraterrestrial encounters may be interesting, the number of encounters is increasing at such a rate that one could easily get sidetracked keeping up with the many proliferating accounts and entirely miss the whole point. The vital thing is not how these beings appear, but who they are, why they are here and what they have to say.

My book, *Return of the Bird Tribes*, elaborates on the identification given in *The Starseed Transmissions*. It describes these entities as a category of spirit beings, synonymous with what many today are calling the "higher selves." They are our own eternal spirits before and after our association with the physical plane, undistorted by what they call "the spell of matter." They are the beings responsible for the creation of our human forms.

Now, identifying these beings as the entities who began the creation of the human species and who have now come to blend with us in the completion of that creation, I have run into some controversy from those who insist that "God" created the first human beings. Well, as I understand it, God did create the first humans. I have no argument with that. However, God created the first humans through the instrumentality of a family (or tribe) of god beings. In that act "God" is plural. Even the Biblical creation story uses the plural in the twenty-sixth verse of the first chapter of Genesis when God says, "Let us make man in our image, after our likeness." That these Original Creators of Life (as Iroquois tradition refers to them) should be among those we now regard as extraterrestrial is right in keeping with many of our early creation mythologies.

Among the numerous tribes of extraterrestrials, there are two primary categories. The first, the category referred to in the above Genesis verse, is the Bird Tribes, or higher selves of humankind. The emphasis of their work right now is the communicative process that will lead to their eventual incarnations in human form. They are our own eternal selves. We awaken into awareness of our true nature in them, but, of course, for those awake, there is no further us/them dichotomy.

The second category consists of those beings who have come to help during this transition, but who have no intention of dressing in material form. They have come at this time primarily to radiate emotional stability. Indications are that well-meaning extraterrestrial beings have journeyed to this Earth from all over this galaxy—and in a few cases from distant galaxies, to assist us as midwives at this time of birth. Some of them, like the creatures Whitley Strieber describes in his book, *Communion*, are still learning about us, still trying to determine just how they can be of assistance. Many of them find humans almost totally incomprehensible, so they inadvertently blunder a bit in trying to understand how they can best serve.

It helps to understand that all of human history has been a process of education. For tens of thousands of years, populations of the Earth have been in preparation for this time that is now upon us. Our human egos have been learning but one essential lesson, a lesson that can be stated in a few simple words: Fear motivation leads to pain, suffering and death. Love motivation leads to the blossoming of creative potential, to peace between people and nations. The entire historical educational process is reaching a point of culmination, coinciding, as near as I can sense it, with the last 25 years of the Great Mayan cycle, a cycle which stretches all the way from 3114 BC to the winter solstice of the year 2011 AD.

As the 5,125-year Mayan cycle draws to a close, the most significant trend among humankind is a gradual turning away from external sources of spiritual guidance and a reorientation—on the part of the individual—to the in-dwelling spirit of God. Looking to the external world for behavioral cues and definitions of self creates a distorted world full of images and endlessly rebounding reflections; it cuts us off from the inner directives of our own eternal spirits.

Reorienting to the directives our higher selves (each of which is consciously united with every other higher self in the God source) produces a shift at the very core of our self understanding. The shift is so fundamental (and so profound!) that is very much like a birth. It can be thought of as the birth of our eternal consciousness on the physical plane. Such births are now occurring in rapidly growing numbers. Their numbers will increase dramatically as the Great Cycle culminates. The collective phenomenon is nothing less than the birth of a universal species. Think of it! A once fragmented humankind, a body of many warring members, coming into harmony, flexing its muscles, opening its eyes, breathing as one, feeling a single heart beat, a single pulse.

This is so different from our historical views that we truly have to let go of all prior forms of understanding in order for the new meta-personal understanding to show us the immensity of this phenomenon.

Within any given human culture, forms of understanding are wrapped in words, and frozen in linguistic descriptions. Historically we have identified with these forms of understanding. Yet reality cannot possibly be portrayed in such inadequate terms. Forms of understanding, even the best of them, are no more than clothing: something that we put on and express through. They have a place, but there is a distinction between them and the experiential understanding that, in an awakened state, animates them and makes them of value.

All of this is just to say that we cannot now afford to divide ourselves on the basis of how we prefer to describe all this. We have divided ourselves enough! It is time to emphasize the great common denominator that unites the races, tribes, and cultures of Earth—the single being of the Creator who through all our higher selves is seeking to awaken in the physical dimension of this blessed planet.

We are all facing the common challenge of moving entirely beyond even the very best that our egos may understand into the actual experience of blending with our eternal selves. Each one of us is an eternal being with an experience base stretching back to the creation of the first stars, the first gasses, the first matter worlds. We have a common past and a common future, both rooted in the infinite Presence of God.

We truly understand these things when we understand through our spirits. The ego can gain a certain amount of preliminary knowledge, and this can be of some value in preparing it for the awesome news that our spirits bring, but it is important not to confuse this preparatory and often second-hand knowledge with the real thing. The real knowledge comes when we allow the eternal beings that we are to flood our curiosity, to fill our bodies, minds and hearts and to dissolve the last traces of doubt and uncertainty that have kept us defined in the arbitrary patterns of history.

It makes no difference if we call them extraterrestrials, angels or higher selves. They are here to help us awaken. And it is vital that we do so.

(Magical Blend issue #24)

Alternate Realities
UFOs

Jacques Vallée: From Other Dimensions

with Michael Peter Langevin and Richard Daab

When two different realities clash, the easiest way to douse the fires of intellectual curiosity is by making the improbable seem impossible. One such crossroads of realities—the field of UFO research—seems particularly inclined to turn the initial *aha* into a subsequent *ha-ha*. A scene from the movie *Close Encounters* deftly illustrates this point: The U.S. Air Force, having created an elaborate hoax to divert attention from the imminent arrival of extraterrestrials, finds its bogus explanation beginning to unravel. Locals gathered at a town meeting aren't buying the bull. Then, just as things look bad for the government boys, they are saved by the bell when a scruffy local suddenly announces, "I saw Bigfoot once!" With that one remark, the possibility of alien contact is no longer taken seriously. Disinformation prevails because its unbelievability is eclipsed by an even odder statement.

According to Dr. Jacques Vallée, this fictional scene offers a striking example of what is happening in UFO research today. An advocate of bringing critical thinking to a field dominated by crackpots and conspirators, Vallée has established himself as one of the most serious investigators of UFOs in the world today.

In his book, *Dimensions*, the first of his Alien Contact trilogy, Dr. Vallée presented a fascinating casebook of UFO activity. In its sequel, *Confrontations*, he reported his personal, worldwide investigation into reports of UFO sightings, contact, and, in some cases, abduction and human injury. Now in *Revelations* (Ballantine Books), Dr. Vallée examines the well constructed hoaxes and media manipulations that have misled UFO researchers, diverting them from the real issues at hand in the UFO phenomenon.

Focusing in-depth on cases reported in the United States and throughout the world in recent decades, Dr. Vallée reveals that some of the most remarkable sightings are actually complex hoaxes that have been carefully engineered—not by the witnesses who report them, but by an odd combination of UFO cults and government agencies. The result, according to Dr. Vallée, is that too many false reports of alien contact are accepted as real, while far too many actual cases have gone overlooked or have been misrepresented.

Dr. Jacques Vallée is a former principal investigator on Department of Defense computer networking projects. He was born in France where he was trained in astrophysics. He moved to the United States in 1962 and received his Ph.D. in computer science in 1967 from Northwestern University. He is the author of numerous articles and three books about high technology. His research into the phenomenon of UFOs has taken him to places around the globe including Scotland, Australia, France, and Brazil.

What is the state of UFO research today?

Jacques Vallée: There is an alarming level of insanity now in the field. The study of UFOs is increasingly polarized between two camps—the believers and the non-believers. All my colleagues in science and technology are telling me that it's just garbage, and many of my friends in ufology seem to be convinced that we're being visited by short gray aliens. Well, I believe that there is a real UFO phenomenon that is unexplained by science, but I'm not ready to jump to conclusions yet: That can derail the whole research process. It's not enough just to stand up to the skeptics who deny the existence of the phenomenon any more. You also must have the courage to question the believers themselves.

In your book Revelations, *you discuss the muddled thinking that has tainted much of the research. Could you give some examples?*

Jacques Vallée: There is an important pitfall I call the "transitivity of strangeness." This happens when somebody claims to explain one strange phenomenon with another. The classic example is someone who says he can prove he's in contact with an extraterrestrial civilization because they gave him the power to bend spoons. Well, even if he can bend spoons, that doesn't prove he's in contact with extraterrestrials. It just proves that he knows how to bend spoons.

Another pitfall that we seem to fall into consists in taking two slightly different mysteries and putting them together. The Roswell Incident is often cited as proof that UFOs have crashed on Earth. The Roswell Incident is certainly fascinating, but the published story is flawed because it jumps to certain assumptions without qualifying them.

Could you go into the Roswell Incident a little further?

Jacques Vallée: In July of 1947 something fell on a ranch near Roswell, New Mexico. Over 90 witnesses have reported on the curious debris that was scattered over the area. They found some very light material that couldn't be torn, bent, or burned. In addition, there were wooden boards, apparently of very light wood like balsa, with hieroglyphics on them. Excellent research was done by people like Bill Moore, Stan Friedman, Kevin Randle, Don Schmidt, and others. They don't always agree on the details, but there is no question that the field research was very thorough. The Air Force gave a stupid explanation at the time, a stupid cover, by saying it was a weather balloon. There was no way it could have been a weather balloon. The material did not even match what weather balloons were made of.

Five days later an egg-shaped object seems to have crashed some miles away, and some people reported bodies in connection with it. Now, obviously it's tempting to jump to the conclusion that these two incidents were related, and they may very well be, but the fact is that they were discovered by different sets of people, at different times, and under different conditions. Various authors have merged these two mysteries into a single one that they call "The Roswell Incident."

When people talk about Roswell, one of the first things they mention is the mysterious material, but a little research shows that it may not have been all that mysterious. It matches material that was under development at the time and was, in fact, made available in 1948 for general scientific use. Of course, in the absence of the material, we don't know what it was. All I'm saying is that from what we know today, we cannot jump to the conclusion that it was paranormal material.

Another thing I find interesting is that nobody has talked about any smell. It's very hot in July in New Mexico. If those two incidents were in fact the same, then those bodies were under the scorching New Mexico sun for five days before they were discovered. The first thing you hear when you talk to crisis intervention teams involved in airliner crashes, for example, is the awful memory of the stench of human bodies.

It's as if more and more information is coming out and it's just getting more and more confusing.

Jacques Vallée: Some of the confusion may be deliberate. In some cases false information about UFOs has been planted as a cover for military technological experiments. The expectations of extraterrestrials on the part of UFO believers can be easily manipulated. Then, once everyone is focused on the UFO cover, someone comes along and proves it was a hoax. The elegance of this kind of cover is that believers continue to believe and non-believers have the explanation they need. As a result, no one ever gets around to examining what really happened even when the hoax explanation doesn't make sense.

The crop circle phenomenon in England is a good example of the same process. The books that have been written to explain the circles were ridiculous explanations that no real scientist would consider for 10 minutes. It was as if the explanations themselves had been planted. Then, two old Englishmen came forward and claimed to have done all the crop circles with something like a two-by-four. As far as I can tell, most people are accepting that explanation. But I have a number of questions. For one, how did these two old geezers gain access to the world media? This was front page material in England, France, and the United States. Even when you have behind you an organization like a major publisher in New York, arranging access to the media is a difficult thing. It takes coordination. It takes logistics. You don't have access to the entire world media just because you show up and say, "I did it with a two-by-four." Somebody put those guys up front, distributed the story, and made sure the media picked it up.

Another interesting question to ask is how come those circles have been getting better and better every year? They started as plain circles. Then it was circles within other circles. Then it was circles with rings and satellite circles. And now it's very complex geometric graphs that obviously are not the process of nature. Another question: How come no known British scientist has bothered to get into his car from Oxford or Cambridge, both of which are within easy driving distance of those circles, to go there and study this? This should be a very fascinating botanical phenomenon, if nothing else. But nobody has bothered to do that.

Another curious question is, how come the farmers are not demanding to be compensated? There is a crop loss. Is somebody paying for that loss? And if so, how and how much?

And finally, how come those circles have been within space that is controlled by the military? A lot of people have pointed out that these fields are close to Stonehenge, but they're even closer to a number of British Air Force bases.

Do you have an explanation?

Jacques Vallée: No, I have not done any direct research, but I have friends in France who have gotten samples from both inside and outside the circles and they've looked at the samples under a microscope. What they find is very interesting. If you take any plant or stalk, especially cereal stalk and you bend it, it's going to break between the nodes. If an old geezer is going around England flattening crops with a two-by-four, he's going to break the stalks the same way. But that is not what's happening to the plants at all: When you look at the nodes under a microscope, the nodes are exploded. In fact, the fibers continue to grow. As it turns out, you can get this kind of effect if you couple energy into the nodes. Initially my friends thought it was infrared energy. Now it looks more like microwave energy.

Their speculation is that the most likely explanation is that somebody has been testing a microwave beam weapon, a Star Wars device, that's probably designed to zap electronics on board a satellite. Testing such a weapon with a target in space would be very expensive because you would have to launch targets every time you recalibrated the beam. So, they may simply be reflecting the beam down and using the corn fields as the target. If they really did do that, it's very clever because it means you can turn every stalk of corn into a microwave antenna and check the precision of the beam with exquisite resolution. That would explain why the circles are getting better and better—their technology or beam is getting finer and finer, and they are getting better and better at focusing it and reflecting it.

Such an experiment is bound to be classified. So, why not use the expectation of the paranormal to cover it up? Why not write symbolic messages in the corn fields? Then, when the paranormal explanation is close to being exposed, you can always release the hoax explanation. As far as I can tell, people are quite willing to believe the hoax. Most of the public at large really believe that 500 circles were done in one year by two old geezers pushing a two-by-four. It's absolutely amazing. I don't know if this will turn out to be the true explanation, but if that's the case, it is not only a brilliant physical experiment, but it's also a brilliant sociological experiment using New Age belief and the expectation of extraterrestrials as the channel to cover up a high tech experiment. What's scary is that it's obviously succeeding very well.

This is reminiscent of something that happens with UFO cases. I don't believe you can go into the field to investigate a UFO sighting today without being aware of the possibility of there being a hoax—not a hoax on the part of the witnesses, mind you, but a hoax on the part of somebody else, like the military. Some classified projects have not only one level of cover, but up to four levels of cover. There may be only five or six people who know what is really going on, and the UFO explanation may well be one of the levels of cover.

You're almost forced to say either you believe in nothing or you believe in everything.

Jacques Vallée: You have to consider everything and believe nothing, as Aimé Michel has said. What I try to do when I work in the field is to give highest priority to cases that have not come to the public's attention: confidential reports from people who want no publicity whatsoever. The cases that have not been reported to UFO organizations also have a higher chance of being legitimate.

When something has been given a lot of publicity like the Gulf Breeze episode, or when it happens close to an Air Force base, then there may be no way for you to find out what really happened.

In countries like the United States where information is controlled and where false information can easily be planted through the media, it can get very, very confusing. Suppose that some military experts have come to the conclusion that there really is a UFO phenomenon and that they want to keep the field to themselves. The best way to achieve that is to send everybody else on a wild goose chase for short gray aliens in New Mexico, since nobody could check it anyway, and discredit the people who are doing this kind of research on any independent basis.

I prefer to quietly study cases where I have access to the witnesses and to the site. I'm studying the phenomenon in countries that have a weak cover-up system. For example the Soviet Union now is in complete chaos, and there is genuine information coming out from witnesses, from military personnel, and from the press on the UFO phenomenon. I went there last year and I came back with new data, surprising data, that I'm going to publish later.

The Soviet Union is a big country, and there were many, many things happening in different parts of the country that were unconnected with each other. They were researched by different groups, but the patterns were the same. I think the cases in Voronezh that were ridiculed in the Western press are very solid. I met with a research group of Soviet engineers and physicists who had done research at the site. They convinced me that the different sightings were genuine. One of them involved 500 witnesses and an object flying at roof-top level near some of the apartment buildings in Voronezh. There were other cases of close encounters—actual landings with depressions left in the soil that could be tracked and analyzed. What impressed me most about the Soviet Union was the caliber of the people involved. We had a briefing in Moscow that involved a number of scientists. They had come to the conclusion that this is not a phenomenon that can be solved by using any single science. In other words, you don't just need physicists or aerospace engineers. They made it very clear that they wanted a multidisciplinary approach. In fact, that day in the room there were physicists; there were medical people; there were psychologists; there were anthropologists; there were students of mythology, all working together trying to make sense out of the data.

Could you talk some about abductions?

Jacques Vallée: Abduction reports are becoming more and more visible. I believe that those experiences have a legitimate basis. In other words, something really happened to those people. The problem I have with abduction research, the way it's done now, is that it relies so much on an amateurish use of hypnosis. I think this is irresponsible, unethical, and unscientific. If and when we get the attention of the scientific community, they will take one look at the methodology that has been used, and they will throw the whole thing out the window as complete garbage. No serious screening has taken place.

The first abduction that was widely publicized in this country was the Betty and Barney Hill abduction that took place in 1961. I spent two days with Betty and Barney Hill and with Dr. Simon who had done the hypnosis. I asked Dr. Simon if he could tell me if their experience was real. He said that there was no question that it was real "to them." I said, "Well, doctor, that's not what I'm asking. If you and I had been there sitting in that car, would we have seen Betty and Barney being carried off by little men or would we have seen something completely different?" And he said, "I have no way to answer that question." I think that is the true professional answer. It separates the reality as experienced by the participants—the two witnesses—from the external consensus reality—the physical reality as we could have tested it from the outside, assuming, of course, that we were unbiased observers, which is a big assumption in the vicinity of the phenomenon.

Most of the people hypnotizing contactees do not bother to find out what other kinds of crises may be going on in their lives. They ask very few questions about the backgrounds of these people. As a result, you have genuine UFO abduction cases mixed in with cases of people who have had trauma—for example, people who have been molested as children or people who have been victims of ritual crime. All those things are mixed in, and very few people have seriously taken a look at separating those different types of cases. In the cases that I have studied, I found that those different types of stories were in fact present. To simply hypnotize people and assume that you're going to get some sort of ultimate truth about UFOs is absurd.

A close encounter with a UFO is a very complex and traumatic event. It's as traumatic, for example, as a head-on crash on the freeway. People go into very complex stress patterns, complex altered states. And they may develop screen memories. The UFO itself is clearly something that distorts reality in its vicinity. Jenny Randles, who has done a lot of good research in England, calls this the "Oz factor." There is a point beyond which the witness is no longer in the normal consensus reality. The reality is being manipulated by other factors. In some cases, this kind of trauma may create a screen memory that may involve imagery from the collective unconscious or from the memory of the witness that may overlay what really happened. Fifteen years ago I reported on a case where two people were together; one of them remembered being abducted and the other one simply saw a bus that stopped and went by. And that person saw no UFO. So, you have two witnesses who were there at the same time but who experienced something completely different.

And both may be telling the truth?

Jacques Vallée: There may very well be hallucinations created in the presence of a real UFO. So, you might have genuine witnesses that report experiences in good faith that did not actually take place the way they experienced them.

You also have that in religious miracles. In Fatima, different people saw different things. There were people who saw the Virgin Mary. The children saw a vision of hell. They thought they were given a message. The rest of the crowd didn't see any of that. They simply saw a disc.

So far we've talked about hoaxes, military experiments and religious miracles. Are we being visited by extraterrestrials or aren't we?

Jacques Vallée: My speculation is that one of the many things we are dealing with here is a form of intelligence that is non-human. But I'm not ready to jump to the conclusion that we're being visited by extraterrestrials. In many cases, the witnesses of UFOs are not even describing spacecraft. Instead, they are describing something that appears out of nowhere, vanishes into nowhere, changes shape, merges with other physical objects, shrinks into a single point and disappears like the image on your television set when you turn the power off. To me, this suggests something that is more challenging than extraterrestrial visitors. After all, the possibility of other dimensions is no longer a marginal idea in physics. It is now a mainstream idea. Encounters with UFOs may provide a clue to other paranormal phenomena, and they give us an opportunity to test some advanced theories about reality. So, it is not only interesting from a scientific point of view, but it's also fascinating from a spiritual perspective.

In other words, these visitors may be subject to laws of nature that we haven't discovered yet?

Jacques Vallée: I believe the laws of nature are the same everywhere for everybody, but there are certainly many laws of nature that we haven't discovered. That's obvious from the contradictions in our science today. So, there must be laws of nature that we have not clearly articulated yet. Some of those laws of nature may have to do with other dimensions than the dimensions of space and time that we know. If there are other dimensions of space and time, that certainly opens the possibility that some forms of consciousness are doing exactly that. And they may be right here on Earth—an Earth that extends to other dimensions. That certainly is a direction we should look into since the aliens that have been described seem to be very close to us physiologically. Furthermore, they seem to be able to appear and disappear on the spot. And the phenomenon seems to be as old as mankind itself.

In the Middle Ages, people confronted with alien beings would have thought of them either as angels and demons or as elves and fairies and leprechauns. Today, it's natural for us, given our culture, to think of them as space visitors because that is an image we can relate to in our technological culture. We grew up with it.

In other words, we see what we expect to see?

Jacques Vallée: I'm simply saying that there are some interesting parallels between modern reports of encounters with UFOs and Medieval reports of supernatural beings. There seem to be two different types of events in which phenomena have been reported down through the ages. Some reports are intentional. They are similar to what happens in ceremonial magic when entities are invoked or evoked through ritual. There are similar claims of UFOs appearing as a result of some overt communication attempt on the part of human beings. Then you have other cases where the encounter seems to be accidental: A farmer back from his field encounters elves dancing in the moonlight. He dances with them for what seems like 10 minutes and 200 years have passed. Today, of course, the farmer is driving rather than walking back from his field. There is a bright light over the road, and all of a sudden he seems to be abducted in some kind of craft. Both instances involve a missing time phenomenon.

Do you think we'll ever get beyond the hype and hoax, the believers and the non-believers, and begin to sort all this out?

Jacques Vallée: The UFO phenomenon is challenging two very important things. First, our view of our history on this Earth and second our concept of reality—of what reality is. I think that eventually we will have no choice but to study it seriously. And when we do, it's going to change everything. It's going to be a revolution.

(Magical Blend issue #34)

Alternate Realities
UFO Phenomena

Whitley Strieber: Evolutionary Stimuli

with Richard Daab and Michael Peter Langevin

Following the phenomenal success of Whitley Strieber's firsthand encounters with non-human "visitors" in *Communion* and *Transformation*, he became something of a household name because of his insistence that the books were not fiction but fact. Taken together, *Communion* and *Transformation* related a hall-of-mirrors horror story of a life-long subjugation by alien (if not extraterrestrial) tormentors. His "They're here!" theme attracted intense media attention, not the least of which was focused on Strieber himself. As author of previous works of fiction, including *The Wolfen* and *The Hunger*, Strieber's nonfiction book of alien encounters was considered suspect by the rationally outraged press, who accused him of being that most villainous of creatures—a public relations genius.

Those who have talked to Strieber, or watched him on television, or heard him on radio, however, tend to have a different point of view. There is a sort of earnestness in the man himself that makes you willing to suspend disbelief, and with that obstacle out of the way what he says becomes imminently believable, even if for the most part you'd just as soon not believe it. Strieber himself would probably call this a case of indeterminate thinking, a willingness to accept the unacceptable in order to finally get around to understanding it.

In this interview Whitley Strieber discusses his book, *Majestic* (G.P. Putnam's Sons, New York). In *Majestic*, Strieber returns to the realm of fiction, but it is fiction with a difference. According to Strieber, *Majestic* is "informed fiction" that takes advantage of indeterminate thinking to approach the now-legendary Roswell Incident in which a UFO supposedly crashed and littered the New Mexico desert with aliens. The year was 1947; World War II was just over, and the Cold War was birthing the CIA. A military intelligence officer released a press statement which said that the army had possession of a crashed UFO. Later, the government denied its initial reports and said that the UFO was really just a wrecked weather balloon. There were, however, enough anomalies in the government's report to make it look like a cover-up to a lot of people, and intense speculation concerning what really happened in New Mexico in 1947 has continued to this day.

Whitley Strieber's informed fictional account of the Roswell Incident attempts to sew together the meager facts of the story using the thread of his own firsthand experiences and the needle of his subsequent understanding of the UFO phenomenon. The result is striking because of its profound ambivalence about the origin, nature and intentions of the "visitors." We are clearly looking at the fact of God here—God disguised as aliens—and God (as you might have guessed) is both more wonderful and more terrible than anything we can imagine. As such, *Majestic* is an object lesson in dualism.

In your newest book, Majestic, *you go into the controversy that there was a cover-up by the government of the crash of a UFO in New Mexico in July of 1947. Could you go into this cover-up in more detail?*

Whitley Strieber: I've never gotten directly into the controversy about whether or not the government is hiding things. What I do point out, however, are two statements that were made publicly by Admiral Roscoe Hillenkoetter who was director of the CIA in 1947. Later Admiral Hillenkoetter joined the National Investigation Committee on Aerial Phenomenon—NICAP—and was in it for a couple of years as a member of the board of directors. He then resigned, and on February 20, 1960, made an extraordinary statement. In his resignation he said, "The Air Force has revealed as much as it can about this matter, and it is up to the aliens to tell the rest of the story." To me that statement suggests that there was some kind of relationship between the government and these unknown entities whatever they may be, and that the government's policy was a policy of secrecy.

Do you know more than you're telling?

Whitley Strieber: Sadly, I've been placed in a position where I have to be very careful about what I say because there are certain secrets which must be kept. They are not terrible secrets; they are secrets that anyone with any moral sense would feel compelled to keep if they knew them. There are a lot of people in this world who would destroy something that is presently very fragile if they knew these secrets.

On a different tone, in Majestic *you speculate, in one of the scenes that you created, of a supposed aborted child being taken and raised and, perhaps mutated, by other beings. Is this something that you've run into widely in speculation from the UFO community?*

Whitley Strieber: I'm not really very interested in the speculations that go on in the UFO community. I think that the community is intellectually extremely weak. I would like to see some much more rigorous and deeper thinking than UFO investigators have displayed so far. My speculations in *Majestic* are based on my own personal observations. Admittedly my observations do, to a degree, coincide with certain things that are spoken about in the UFO community because other people have observed the same thing. However, I have had, in my own life, direct experience of someone who had one of these spontaneous abortions under extremely strange circumstances. I have also followed up, in investigation, a couple of cases where this was medically verified. Each time the miscarriage took place right at the end of the first trimester. The fetus suddenly disappeared with no trace under circumstances that were highly mysterious.

Bruce Lee of William Morrow and Company told me of a brief encounter with two beings who looked very much like the cover of *Communion* and who, upon talking with him, seemed to him to be very alien but still capable of functioning in a human environment in the sense that they were in a bookstore when he encountered them. This is mentioned in an appendix to *Transformation*, which you can look at if you want to get further facts about it. I, personally, encountered these same two people in the back seat of a car in Manhattan about a year ago during a time when I was trying to arrange to photograph them. The photography session failed but, nevertheless, the meeting was very real. I was able to observe them quite clearly and they looked very much to me like a mix between human beings and something radically different. They were extremely strange and very difficult to be with. My tendency was to want to jump out of the car. I therefore have been led by my own observation to feel that there may be something in the idea of genetic material being altered in some way. I played this out fictionally in *Majestic* because I have no proof of it, but it does seem to be one of the things that would make some sense of some of my own personal observations as well as the testimony of other people.

Can you speculate on what their goal might be if this, indeed, is something they might be doing?

Whitley Strieber: I think it's rather obvious that, whether it's been done by somebody or happened naturally, what we're dealing with is an exponential leap from one species to another. These beings that I have observed have properties and powers that I would suggest are far beyond what is present in normal human beings, and I would suspect that what we're looking at is the process of evolution in action.

Almost that they are to us as we are to Neanderthal man?

Whitley Strieber: No, I would say it's more like they are to us as we are to chimpanzees.

Do you think that they are here in our midst unseen?

Whitley Strieber: I know that for certain.

Does it take some shift in consciousness for us to perceive them in a physical being, or do they physically come from somewhere else, or are they on another plane here?

Whitley Strieber: My observations would lead me to conclude that all of the above is true. I have certainly seen beings that I would consider to be completely physical, and yet I've also seen them do things that would suggest that they can go beyond that level of being. Many other people have seen things like balls of light come into a house and then suddenly turn into a being or, in another situation, witness a being walk into a room and immediately be transformed into an entirely different looking being before one's eyes. This kind of phenomenon suggests that they have much more control over their relationship to the physical environment than we, that they are not necessarily stuck in the physical realm like we are, although I do think that they have reference to the physical, and that their fundamental origin may be physical. My impression is that the physical world is only a small instant in a much larger context and that reality is primarily unfolding in a non-physical way. I don't think that physical reality is the original source of being. I think that being, as consciousness, probably predates the physical.

What might you offer as hope for the future of the human race if, indeed, these godlike beings are as advanced above us as we are above chimpanzees?

Whitley Strieber: I suspect the human race is probably finished. In our attempt to capture consciousness by the use of reason we have ultimately deluded ourselves. Reason and consciousness are not the same, and in linking them inextricably one to the other, we've gone down a blind alley like the Neanderthals did, and we will not emerge from it intact. I think that over the next couple of thousand years environmental pressures and this inter-breeding process that is going on—if indeed that's happening—will materially alter the nature of the human species to the extent that it will be, in effect, a new species. What we now call humankind will have entered history. The soul of the species—of which we are all a part—will be separated from the physical.

Do you see these other beings as affecting or helping us in any way along these lines?

Whitley Strieber: What they are interested in is probably beyond the physical. I think that they are probably midwifing our birth into the nonphysical world—which is their origin. In fact, much of what we actually see may be completely different from what is there. I think that we have a tendency to anthropomorphize this "other" level of reality. What we may be seeing is the limits of our own ability to perceive rather than what is there. However, the physical beings that we are seeing—whether we are perceiving them correctly or not—are probably an evolutionary step beyond ours which has emerged into our world as a result of actions on the nonphysical plane. However we see it, and whatever we choose to call it, I believe that this other level represents the origin of all being, and it is the origin of the physical world as well. The really interesting question, to us, of what the physical world is, and what we are doing in it, is one that remains, to me, unanswered.

You say the aliens are indifferent, that they have no desire to....

Whitley Strieber: No, I didn't say aliens. I never said that. I don't use the word aliens because I don't know what they are. My impression is that the physical beings that are involved are from the Earth. They are an evolutionary leap of some kind, but that they are primarily Earth-oriented. That's my impression. We are not looking at aliens. We are looking at our replacements. They will fill the gap in consciousness that will occur when humanity departs from the physical realm. They are a new concept and a new soul...and also very old. They are alien and familiar at the same time. I know that this seems contradictory but it isn't. What it is, is indeterminate.

So, if these beings are not aliens from another planet, how do you explain the UFO wreckage, complete with bodies, that was supposedly found in the New Mexico desert?

Whitley Strieber: I believe it was a trick. It was an attempt to create the impression that they were aliens from another planet in order to make them seem more formidable than they really are. Let me give you an example that can, perhaps, answer a lot of the questions that have to do with why they want to play tricks and apparently plant things in people's heads that give them a subtle ability to influence those individuals' thoughts: Pretend that you and your family are shipwrecked on an island in some vast tropical sea. You don't know where you are, and nobody has any idea that you're even lost. You are going to be on that island, quite probably, for the rest of your life. You're going to have to raise your family and your children and your children's children on that island. Now let's say that it's quite a large island, and certainly it can sustain you. There's only one problem which is that living on that island with you are two million chimpanzees, and they are eating the fruits and vegetables at a furious rate with absolutely no idea of how to balance their intake and replant to keep the island's environment going. It becomes quite evident that they are, in fact, destroying it. But their numbers are so large that if they fully understood your vulnerability they would overwhelm you. So what do you do? You use your much greater insight and intelligence to subtly alter conditions on the island to enable the environment to continue longer than it would if the chimpanzees, alone, had control over it. You protect yourself from the chimpanzees by appearing much more formidable than you actually are—say by firing a few weapons or learning the chimpanzee's own language of display in such a way that you can frighten them away from you. Meanwhile you build up your own family and increase your control over the island in many, many ways—all of which are completely incomprehensible to the chimpanzees. Finally, at the end of 25 years or so, there are far fewer chimpanzees on the island because you have balanced their population. So now you are in absolute and complete control of the situation, and your family is thriving, and since there are fewer chimpanzees they are much healthier as well. Potentially that is what's happening with these other beings.

That's an interesting example. So, perhaps, the hope for our planet rests with these other beings?

Whitley Strieber: The hope for our planet rests on the return of the balance of nature. That's the only thing that will save the planet.

If some of these chimpanzees, or in our case individuals of the human race, wanted to help in the process by communicating our willingness to be of assistance, are there things that we might do?

Whitley Strieber: All I can say from my own experience is that getting involved is going to be an extremely challenging and difficult experience because it will take you directly to your own deepest truth about yourself and everyone around you. Other than that, I don't think that I'm in a position to give any specific advice about what needs to be done because I'm not sure that I understand the issues involved in this all that well myself. Everything that I've said today may very well be my own misapprehensions. I may be wrong. So, if I am wrong, then everything I've said should be taken with a grain of salt. I'm not in a strong enough position with this myself to give advice.

Is this why you wrote Majestic *as fiction?*

Whitley Strieber: That's right. *Majestic* is informed fiction. I think it's probably the best informed fiction about this subject that's ever been written, but it's fiction because there's no proof positive. I wouldn't have written it as anything but fiction for that reason. The number of facts are small, but they are very important. For example, I can certainly prove that at least one of the professionals who was involved in recovering the debris of the crash in 1947 in Roswell thought that it was an extremely strange thing that they had found, but the fact that the debris was strange doesn't prove anything more than that. So, just dealing with the facts doesn't take us any further into this matter than we already are. What *Majestic* represents is part of a process of leading people into the understanding that there is something very real happening that, at its core, remains a mystery. I think that I know what's going on, as I said a few minutes ago, but maybe I'm wrong. Maybe I'm dead wrong. I've tried to observe clearly and carefully, but maybe I've failed. Maybe I misunderstood. Maybe I drew the wrong conclusions. God knows I've criticized a lot of other people for drawing the incorrect conclusions, and maybe I've done the same thing. I can only say what I have observed and what those observations appear to me to mean.

Something strange happened out there in the desert. I used that fact as a springboard for my story, and I attached to it lots of my own speculations about what may have happened and about the origins and nature of the intelligence that caused these events to take place, but they remain speculations. This is why the book is fiction.

It's a very compelling book. What struck me is that you seem less ambivalent about the nature of these beings than you did in your two previous books. It appears as if you have come to the conclusion that these beings are benevolent where before you weren't so sure.

Whitley Strieber: They are benevolent insofar as they exist on behalf of the health of the Earth and consciousness. They are not, however, necessarily benevolent in the sense of perpetuating the human culture or the human species.

You spoke earlier of your criticism of the research and conclusions reached by the UFO community. What specifically is the problem?

Whitley Strieber: We haven't yet even begun to think clearly about the whole phenomenon. What we really need to do is to learn to think in a different way. We habitually think in a way that I believe Karl Popper described as linear thinking, that is to say we think from A to B. But it's not possible to think that way and to deal coherently with this experience. In regard to the presence of the visitors, it is necessary not only to think clearly but also indeterminately. Indeterminate thinking is absolutely essential to even the beginnings of understanding. One has got to be able to think about it, to theorize it, and to proceed on those theories as if they were true even though one continues to keep them in question because, in this particular case, truth is amorphous; it changes. As we change and grow, the nature of the truth changes and grows because our ability to perceive it changes. I believe that what we are dealing with now has probably been present for a very long time, but only recently have we begun to perceive it in a way that we, in modern terminology, would consider to be an orderly perception. I would submit that the practitioners of the faery faith in the past may have perceived the material in just as orderly a manner as we do, but in a different context. In fact, perhaps because their context was different than ours, their perceptions may actually have been a little bit more accurate in terms of the phenomenology of the experience, though perhaps a little bit less accurate in terms of its relation to the physical world. Now we have lost track of the phenomenology completely while, at the same time, we're getting a little bit more of an idea of what may actually be on a physical level, and the intelligence behind the phenomenon is responding by throwing illusions at us in the physical world, such as the illusion that it is a rather comprehensible intrusion from an extraterrestrial civilization. I would say that, if extraterrestrials are involved, then one thing they are not, at least in human terminology, is comprehensible. We need better minds involved in this very badly. I would like to see some of the great practitioners of the shamanic community really address this, to leave their belief systems behind and address this directly. I would also like to see some of the best minds of the scientific community address it with something other than ego.

Writers and artists have had a long tradition in history as functioning almost as unconscious shamans, channeling the unconscious and reflecting it through their art. Do you see this happening in, say, for example, science fiction?

Whitley Strieber: The fact that shamanic people, or creative people, function as unconscious shamans is representative of the fundamental breach in the relationship between humankind and Earth that is leading to our destruction. Shamanic thinking must not be an afterthought. Every single creative person is shamanic in the sense that they have access to another level of reality and can perceive it as phenomena. People should be consciously reaching into that world in an orderly manner, and bringing back their material for display in the culture. Creative minds are our means of communication, but in our particular culture they have had their eyes gouged out by reason, and their brains burned up by technology. The result is that our communicators, our shamans, those of us who reach into that other world to gather material essential to informing our lives are stumbling blind and crippled. The fact that they are doing it unconsciously, I think, is a great catastrophe. We should never communicate unconsciously.

How much can a human being really understand the unconscious? We have no idea what the real nature of our unconscious is.

Whitley Strieber: You say that, but it's not necessary to build the barrier inside of oneself that we do. It's not necessary to even have an unconscious. We didn't set that barrier up until the 19th and 20th centuries. What I mean when I say that it's not necessary to have an unconscious is that it's possible to be conscious of one's entire self. If that was the case then we wouldn't be in this pickle, but it is, and we are. We walled off part of ourselves, and the result is that we are a species in hiding; we are hiding from ourselves. The unconscious is the source of all hope and all salvation. It is what we are. When I speak, in the beginning of

Majestic, about returning to the forest, this is what I mean. Our own un-conscious is the forest which we must protect from burning. That doesn't mean that it has to be nice in that forest. It might not be a very pretty place at all. That's probably why we walled it off, and it's prob-ably why we yell and scream so much when we are confronted with the unconscious.

Are you aware of any esoteric groups that have more of the picture? I was recently reading some books about Sufism, and I got the impression that they have an idea of a fuller, more real picture, but they're not really saying...at least the writers that I'm reading are not really saying just what it is.

Whitley Strieber: Within their context they certainly do, but in terms of a modern Western grammar of experience, there aren't any. Certainly deep within the Sufi community there are traditions that would sug-gest a profound knowledge of reality. Among the Tibetan Buddhists there is also clearly a profound knowledge of reality. However, the dif-ficulty is that it becomes corrupted when it is translated to the grammar of modern Western thought, which is at once very rigid and extremely fantastic. I consider modern Western thinking far more fantasy prone than Tibetan Buddhist thought or Sufi thought. We, in the West, are liv-ing in a fantasy. Our fantasy is that we think we understand the physi-cal world. We do not understand the physical world. We don't understand its origin; we don't understand its destiny, and, therefore, we don't know what it is or where it is or where it's going, and we don't know our place in it. What we have done is that we have used our sci-ence to parcel out the physical world in infinite and meaningless detail like those Medieval academics who devoted their lives to trying to de-termine how many angels could stand on the head of a pin. Modern sci-ence is in exactly the same position as it probes more and more deeply into largely meaningless areas of discovery about the nature of the physical world without understanding either its origin or its destiny.

One of the themes that runs through many of the esoteric teachings con-cerns a secret body of teachers or directors who are in charge of the planet but who exist on another plane.

Whitley Strieber: I encountered such teachers, but they did not, to me, appear to be human. They seemed to be those sort of next-step beings that I mentioned earlier, and I don't think that their primary purpose was teaching; their primary purpose was clear; it was self preservation.

One of the most bizarre notions I've heard is that humans may serve as food for these higher beings?

Whitley Strieber: This is obviously and inevitably true, though not in the debased sense that it is talked about and written about in the UFO community. I can assure you from personal experience that there aren't any aliens sitting around black cauldrons eating bits of human flesh. However, what happens to the soul and the issue of the soul after life is a different question. I suspect that life is probably about the creation of souls and the fate of souls. This brings up the question of what a soul is. It is probably a concentration of awareness that is defined by the experiences it has as it moves through the physical world attached to sequential time. The final issue of every species is what its whole soul is like when it is completed, when every small soul within it has completed its journey. We will probably soon know the answer to that in the case of humankind because the human race is approaching completion. The human experiment wasn't a successful one, but then, again, there have been many other great species that have walked this Earth that have not been successful either. You could say that about every species that ever became extinct, and therefore about every species that will ever be. But that's not a tragedy, unless you find death a tragedy. I don't. I don't think that death is ever, necessarily, a tragedy. I think that death is simply another aspect of life, and so the extinction of a species is just another aspect of life.

The fact that humanity is coming to an end is not a tragedy at all. Humankind is an absolutely marvelous thing that has happened to the Earth. It has left the Earth exhausted, but it will be renewed. We are going to emerge into a new level of reality.

All my life I've been terrified of the dark. There's nothing I recall which accounts for this, but after reading your books I began to wonder if what lies behind this fear was similar in nature to the contact experience.

Whitley Strieber: Perhaps you were having a memory of the future. If you think that you were scared then, wait until the human race no longer has the shelter of the physical, then you will really be scared.

Well…OK. Not very comforting, but….

Whitley Strieber: I don't intend to be comforting. What I'm describing is not a pleasant thing, but it is incredibly beautiful. If it wasn't hard it wouldn't be appreciated.

I have a feeling that there's something there at almost the soul level that needs to be faced.

Whitley Strieber: This is what we have such a tremendous amount of difficulty doing, but what we have to do. We have no choice. We will do it, each of us together, as a species—all of us. There are no gurus; there are no gods; there are no leaders; there is no one to look up to. There is only one place to look, and that is inside yourself.

Is that what you have used to face your fears in this awesome and evolving information that you've been exposed to?

Whitley Strieber: You face the fears now, or you live the fears later. They become you. Your soul becomes the fears. You learn yourself now, or later you are pretty much whatever you refused to face or didn't understand about yourself. Those things you don't face in life dominate you after death. That's what hell is. That's what that ancient, pervasive idea of there being some terrible place that people go after they die if they don't behave correctly is all about. Hell is ignorance of self, and refusal to face the reality of one's soul and to face the consequences of one's actions. This is why I feel so strongly that some of the ideas in the New Age community are so devastatingly dangerous to the health of the soul. The idea that we create our own reality—having that extended into justification for anything terrible that's done by one person to another—is devastating because it forecloses the need to look at oneself. It obsoletes conscience, and, when conscience is obsoleted, people have ceased to have any chance at all to evolve.

We absolutely must listen to the wisdom of the self. We must do this, and it's hard. It's very difficult because every single one of us, for whatever reason, is full of fear. It is extremely difficult to say why we are this way, why we are turned in such strange directions that we are afraid to look into our hearts. Why are our hearts dark? I don't know, but it's true. My heart is as dark as yours. I'm afraid of the dark, too. I suspect that the reason that it is so difficult to look inside oneself is that what is in there is the sum of human experience. I've looked back at my own life and, frankly, it has not been the kind of life that I would think would give rise to extremely fearful, hidden imbalances and problems. It's not been a perfect life, but I've never committed a great sin. If I was Adolf Hitler then I would understand why I wouldn't want to look at myself. But I still have difficulty looking within myself. Everybody else I know does too, and I think that the reason for this is that when we look inside ourselves, we don't look simply at an isolated individual; what we are looking at when we look at those strange, symbolized communications, as it were, from the unconscious is the inner condition of the whole species—of all of us put together. So, when we look at ourselves we are looking not only at Krishna Murti and Jesus; we are also looking at Adolf Hitler, and that's a very hard thing to do. Everyone else is what is behind the curtain inside each one of us. This is what makes it so hard to look inside ourselves, and it's why, when you need comfort, there's no place to go except for the Earth itself. You can't find comfort inside a human being. This is why we go from one master, guru or religion to another endlessly searching through the debris of human experience for something beautiful and something that will sustain us, when, actually, the only thing that will sustain us is the purity of the planet. And since the rain is no longer pure, we're really in trouble.

Are there any closing statements that you would like to make, either about Majestic *or about things that you haven't touched on?*

Whitley Strieber: *Majestic* is an attempt to create or to explore reality through the medium of story, and it is fundamentally for this reason that it is indeterminate. It is not a statement of fact except in that one little kernel of what Col. Jesse Marcel had found near Roswell. All of the rest of it is a very serious, and very orderly attempt to explore something that I think will always remain extremely indeterminate, and I think it should be taken on that basis. I believe that if the human race is going to get on with the process of understanding what we are and where we're going—which presupposes that we have time to do that in a meaningful way, which I don't think we do—it is necessary for us on a smaller group basis to get on with it because there will come a time when the species has lost its contact with the physical realm and it is going to have to be something and go someplace and do something, and somebody is going to have to have some reference of experience that will give the rest of information that will be necessary in that situation. We don't want to have it said in the future that the human race had no point. We want a point. And if we have a point it's going to be because some of us, during our tenancy in the physical, gained some real understanding. We have to learn how to make order out of indeterminate thinking and how to use as a Western tool of thought the kind of indeterminate thinking that created shamanic reality. *Majestic* is an attempt to do that kind of thing—flawed I'm sure, but it is an attempt.

Technology

Technology

Technology has fundamentally altered both our external and internal landscapes, bringing the Magical Universe right down in the middle of consensus reality without so much as raising an eyebrow. We alternate between rejoicing in it and cursing it, but mostly we just take it for granted. The technologies that could elevate us to unprecedented heights of human achievement, that could end world hunger and ease human suffering, are used primarily as pacifiers to entertain us. Though we have harnessed the power of the Magical Universe, we remain either too mesmerized by it or too lazy to put it to good use.

One of Magical Blend's first articles on technology focused on Buckminster Fuller's "design science revolution." Fuller, who was affectionately known as the "planet's friendly genius," believed that all of the technology necessary for humanity to take a step up the evolutionary ladder was already in place, waiting only to be recognized and applied to the proper tasks. His lifelong devotion to "doing more with less" was aimed at breaking the spell of the illusion of scarcity and proving there were enough resources to provide for all of humanity. That was 15 years ago, and though technology has continued to do more and more with less and less, humanity still acts as if there is not enough to go around. It seems our most serious problems as a species is no longer a lack of resources, but a lack of imagination and a failure of will.

In recent years, technology's hottest new toy has been Virtual Reality (VR), and Magical Blend has followed its development with a watchful eye. Though still in its infancy and still limited largely to entertaining an increasingly bored population, several writers have seen in it the potential for a renaissance of perception. As Robert Anton Wilson has noted, "We cannot grow if we have a conditioned attachment to conditioned perceptions. Once the fiction of one 'reality' dies as a concept, and the operational fact of 'realities' (plural) becomes generally recognized, we might all discover that human beings can actually live together without constantly making war over who has the 'real' reality." I believe the late Buckminster Fuller would have agreed wholeheartedly with Wilson's assessment.

But how do we get there from here? Fortunately it may not be as difficult as it first appears. VR is an interactive medium. It does not feed images to us the way television does, but allows us to choose perspective, to create, in the words of psychology, both set and circumstance. We do not observe VR, we inhabit it, and since anything is possible in a virtual world, it is, first and foremost, a fun place to be. Jaron Lanier, known as the "Father of VR," captures the adventure of VR when he talks about experiments in "trading eyes" with *another person, so that one person's head controls the other's point of view. It is, he says, an exercise in intimacy and trust.*

Over the years, Magical Blend has talked to numerous visionaries of various persuasions, and a recurring complaint has been the inability of the species to alter perception. While technology has handed us a brave new world, we continue to inhabit the old one, primarily because our perception is conditioned by centuries of habit. Terence McKenna speaks of the "VR of Culture," by which he means that the reality we experience is largely a matter of consensus. Lanier adds to the discussion by observing that the world we see "out there" is to a great degree an act of imagination, noting that "our direct perception of this world is actually highly flawed. For starters, the blind spot is a great example. Near the center of each of your eyes is this big, black hole where you don't see anything, but you're never aware of it. Your mind fills it in perfectly for itself, which it can do because it holds all the cards. Even aside from that, what your eyes actually see is not what you perceive them seeing. Your eyes see edges and boundaries and patterns. They don't really see the picture that you see—that's constructed on a running basis in your brain. Physiologically, they just do not pick up the picture you're seeing now."

If our perceptions of reality are flawed, this flaw is only accentuated by our dependence on language to pass on information. Language is a second-hand way of presenting reality. A word is not a thing but a symbol pointing toward a thing. When, for example, we say the word "red," our brains must interpret the symbol for what it stands for. The fact that we forget that our brains are doing this for us only further confuses the issue. Lanier sees the greatest potential of VR in the development of a "post-symbolic communication," which he says will have a clarifying effect on the boundaries of imagination. According to Lanier, post-symbolic communication "amounts to a spontaneous way of creating a sensual world between people without requiring interpretive symbols. It's sort of like cutting out the middleman, and you actually make stuff instead of just referencing it.... In language we have a notion of a quality, such as redness or pudginess or something. In post-symbolic communication...you can bring a jar containing everything you consider pudgy. Then the concept of pudgy becomes unnecessary, because you can look at them all at once and experientially get what's alike about them." Terence McKenna makes the same point in a slightly more whimsical way, noting that "Each age takes its self-image from the animal world.... I believe the totemic image for the future is the octopus." The octopus, he points out, uses its ability to change the color of its skin as a visual form of communication. "The octopus," he says, "becomes its own linguistic intent." He compares it to a "naked nervous system" in which "the inner stats, the thoughts, if you will, of the oc-

topus are directly reflected in its outward appearance. It is as though the octo-pus were wearing its mind on its exterior.... In the world of the octopus, to behold is to understand.... Like the octopus, our destiny is to become what we think, to have our thoughts become our bodies and our bodies become our thoughts."

The potential of VR to effortlessly alter our perceptual patterns and to provide a new avenue of communication is one of technology's boldest and most exciting developments. It promises not only to dissolve the artificial bar-riers we have constructed around ourselves, but to increase our awareness of the natural world, for as Jaron Lanier observes, "When people emerge from VR sessions, they have increased sensitivity to the world around them." This in-creased sensitivity may be evolution's ultimate goal for all of technology. Buck-minster Fuller summed up the design-science revolution by saying, "We are being taught to assume as closely as possible the viewpoint, the patience and the competence of God." Should our species ever ascend even halfway to Full-er's expectations, the doors of the Magical Universe will at last be flung wide open, and its wonders will be available for all to see.

Technology
High Tech's Highest Goal

Timothy Leary: Mind-Altering Software

with Christopher Miles

In the foothills over Hollywood, Dr. Timothy Leary, psychologist, iconoclast, prophet, outlaw, historian and visionary, resided with his family and looks at the future and the world of "thought technologies." Forty years of transition as a doctor, drop-out and prison inmate had brought him to the "brave new world" of computers. Mind Mirror, Leary's software innovation; is an intelligence appliance which will sharpen our minds and prepare us for the future. His company, Futique, ("opposite of antique") has completed this headware appliance, published by Electronic Arts of San Mateo, California.

"If we can lift the thinking of the American people just 1%, we can change the whole culture," he told us. "We must be facile communicators with every form of thought processing—muscular, hand-made, mechanical, electronic."

Leary revealed his 40 years of a world in change, moving from the industrial age through the electronic revolution, helping to teach people how to, "Think for Yourselves, Question Authority. TFYQA. "In this interview, he gave his historical insights, from Gutenberg to how the microcomputer will affect the individual, and the world of work, religion and art.

Leary was a no-nonsense person who got straight to the heart of the issues he faced. His comical description of "Top Management," and his lucid attention to the variety of historical details, separate him from the prophets of doom who would have us give up on our future.

"We shall evolve," he stated simply.

Come with us into the fascinating mind of Timothy Leary.

Many of our readers may have heard of you by reputation, but don't really have an accurate picture of your background. Could you give us an idea of where your training and education have taken you and briefly bring us up to date on where you are now?

Timothy Leary: Well, I am by profession a psychologist. I consider myself a nuts and bolts technician for change— a sales agent for change, a mechanic, or engineer of change. For the last 40 years I have seen more changes happen, in our culture, and in my own personal life, than perhaps could ever have happened in history before.

At the present time I am the president of Futique, Inc., a start-up company which designs and produces interactive software for personal computers. It is centered around the concept of Mind Mirror, an intelligence appliance which helps someone qualify their thoughts, modify their thoughts, study their thoughts, plot their thoughts on diagrams, change their mind and communicate their thoughts more clearly to others.

Let's cut back. Forty years ago this year (1986) I had just finished five years of service in the military and was starting a career as a graduate student. I was doing my first research on interactive psycho-metrics, that is, designing tests that would get rid of the doctor/patient, expert/victim relationship, and give the power of diagnosis and change to the so-called "patient." I was a crew-cut graduate student with coat and tie.

At what University?

Timothy Leary: The University of California at Berkeley. I was convinced then that the only way to solve my own personal career plans and problems and to help solve the problems of our country and our species, was to improve our thinking, get control of our brains and learn how to use our heads.

What flaws did you see in the culture at that time that were very important to you?

Timothy Leary: I was instinctively reacting (as I think our entire culture was in 1946) to the changes that WWII brought about. It was the beginning of Dr. Spock's theory that parents should treat their children as individuals. It was the beginning of the electronic age. The electronic technology that was developed in WWII—sonar, radar and mass computers which were used for bomber tracking—were now going to be available for civilian use. The television culture and the information age had begun in 1946. The baby boom had begun (1946-1964). This was a watershed year in which all of us felt that, coming off WW II, a new and better world was available, and it was our duty to bring it about. I believed that psychology—understanding your own mind—learning how to use your own head—was the key.

Thirty years ago, in 1956, I was a successful young psychologist. I had two kids who were raised on Dr. Spock's manual. I was living in Berkeley, California. I was a hot-shot research director publishing tests which allowed people to study themselves without the necessity of having an expert. I was developing the idea that a doctor or a therapist or a counselor or a psychiatrist should be a coach helping someone to improve their performance, rather than as a medical authority helping them cure a disease. I was "hanging out" at that time with professional people, although I was somewhat active in the beginnings of the "beat" culture in San Francisco North Beach. I met Alan Ginsberg at the time he was writing "Howl."

How were these tests you were developing being received by your fellow professionals in psychology and psychiatry?

Timothy Leary: They were enthusiastically accepted. Over a thousand clinics and hospitals used my tests. Even the CIA used my tests in their never-ending quest to control the human mind. I was a respected and admired successful young psychologist. (quite middle class...lots of martini drinking....

Ten years later in 1966—and this is a chronology of change not only of myself but of the culture—I had lost everything! I had been fired from Harvard, was living in Millbrook, NY, being arrested regularly by G. Gordon Liddy. I was an outcast. I had lost my credit cards. I was a disgrace to professional psychology. I was hanging out with such people as Richard Alpert, Alan Watts, Aldous Huxley—heroes of consciousness, and with the poets, heralds and popular conveyors of this new movement of individuality which involved the rejection of the industrial factory society, the urge for self-discovery, self-reliance, self-fulfillment and self-enhancement. In 1966 I was wearing long hair, a pony tail and a headband. My button-down uniform had changed.

Ten years ago, in 1976, I was in a maximum-security federal prison. I belonged to the prison class of 1976, including people like G. Gordon Liddy, Eldridge Cleaver, and John Dean. I was wearing the uniform of a prison inmate. Some of my friends were Mafia capos and other dangerous people.

So, you see, in the last 40 years I have been through some changes. Now I am a suit-and-tie computer executive. This is one chronology of change. I am sure that everyone who has lived through that period could sit down and list what has happened to him/her: the changes in role, dress, and style over the last 40 years. I am sure many would come out with a similar chronology.

From the period since your incarceration until now, where would you say you have led your mind in relationship to consciousness?

Timothy Leary: Consciousness! That is one of the "Macro-thoughts," one of those huge boulder thoughts that we must qualify! Here is my scientific definition of consciousness. Consciousness emerged in the human species when we developed technologies for thinking—cave drawings, icons, chipping thoughts on marble tablets, illuminated manuscripts. You can always judge the level of consciousness, I think, by the level of technology that is used by the individual or the culture.

These symbols...these communicating tools you are talking about...

Timothy Leary: They are technologies for processing, storing, and communicating thought with increasing precision. I must tell you and your readers that I am a nuts-and-bolts person. I don't like concepts like consciousness, illumination and revelation. I am a skeptical, tough-minded, soft-touch, hard-boiled, romantic, nitty-gritty person. I define consciousness as the level of the information technology that you use.

Twenty-five thousand years ago the tribal, oral society used vocal chords and gestures. Knowledge was stored in the human brain, therefore the wise old sages were the repositories of wisdom. The units of knowledge, the units of thought, were vocal. This is wonderful! Even today we still use the vocal method. In fact, I am using my vocal chords right now to communicate, so I am not denigrating the need and form and wonder of the oral tradition.

When people began writing thoughts down in letters—the Phoenician alphabet—a new level of consciousness developed. This is called a feudal-consciousness. Once you had letters to convey thoughts, the voice of the authority—the shaman or the tribal leader—was no longer necessary. Once you could put thoughts down with letters, illuminated manuscripts, or even Babylonian tile chips, you harnessed a means of telecommunication. This means that the king, or the Pope, or the sultan—in his headquarters—could control thought through this telemedium. Also, the hand-made culture of feudalism allowed knowledge to be stored in the "Sacred Mainframe"—the illuminated manuscript kept in the palace of the duke or the cardinal. These thought tools (illuminated manuscripts) were their "computers" (because that is what a computer is —*putare* is Latin for "to think"...*com* means "with." A computer is an appliance to think with).

The mainframe illuminated manuscripts were guarded by security-cleared, socially alienated "hackers" called monks who knew the machine language (Latin). And the use of the illuminated manuscripts was kept from the serfs and the slaves in the feudal society by Top Management.

The first level of consciousness was voice. The second was writing. The third level of consciousness developed in 1456 when Gutenberg invented the printing press and made possible the "micro-book," a cheap portable home computer that encouraged everybody to read and write and think more accurately. Now it never occurred to Top Management (the Vatican, the bishops, the kings and dukes) that the printing press would be used by individuals as a tool for personal growth. Recall that everything that I have done—going back to '46 when I was a psychologist, to '56 when I was a psychometrician, to '66 when I was an alternate reality scholar, to '76 when I was writing by books in prison, right down to today—can be summed up in five wonderful, red-white-and-blue American words: "Think For Yourself, Question Authority"—TFYQA.

The think-for-yourself movement took a tremendous jump—a quantum leap—when Gutenberg invented the printing press. That meant everybody could have a personal, cheap, home wood-pulp computer and could read, write and therefore think. Within a hundred years that led to the Protestant Reformation. Hundreds of new sects surfaced composed of small groups of people who were learning how to think for themselves with this new medium.

There was an unfortunate side-effect to this: Anytime you give power to the individuals you have chaos. That was when several hundred different religions started. That's wonderful, but many of them were of the Calvinist persuasion—a kind of psychopathic, paranoid tool—to generate weird new mind-control. Many problems we face today are caused by fundamentalist religion—Middle East crises, terrorism, the current warlike atmosphere based on fanaticism—people who totally believe in their own cause, who sincerely believe that anyone who doesn't agree with their position in not just an antagonist or another human being with a different point of view but literally the "devil" or the representative of evil. This is Calvinism, which developed during the Reformation and is based on pre-destination—the pernicious doctrine that there is a certain "elect" that God has nominated for salvation, and it doesn't make any difference if you do good works or not. If you don't belong to the "elect" then you're going to hell.

This is the familiar position taken by the Fundamentalist Jew, the Fundamentalist Moslem (as represented by Ayatollah Khomeini), the right-wing Christian, *etc*. If you are not one of us, you are Satan—or the emissary of the Devil—and it is our "duty" to eliminate you. This is the prime cause of the current malaise in America today. And this is partly due to the use of the printing press. Because when you look at it, the printing press did not change the "units" of thought. It is still this insane notion that you could use 26 letters, A to Z, to represent thought or to represent the complexities of the universe, and of course to pass on the "word of God." So, in a sense, the printing press was simply a technique of mass producing the feudal thought technology.

At the present time it is my duty to call attention to the fact that books—words which have been printed by clawlike presses on wood pulp paper—are the leading block to the evolution of thought. The fiber-based computer, which is Gutenberg's legacy, did free us from the hand-made illuminated manuscript and did democratize knowledge. But, then, Top Management took it over. And the theology of the industrial age, which was made possible by the Gutenberg book, is the theology of the engineer factory god. This Newtonian god has constructed a clockwork-engineered universe which is wearing out, step-by-step, due to the second law of thermodynamics—entropy.

Consider the morality of the society which Gutenberg helped produce—the industrial age. The ethics of this society is as follows: The "good" man is the one who is prompt, practical, industrious, reliable, dependable, replaceable, but, above all, productive. In other words, the "good" man is the "good" cog in the overall machinery of society and of God himself.

The fourth level of thought technology, or consciousness, emerged with the invention of the personal computer. Now, instead of thinking in terms of clumps of letters gathered together by grammatical rules and used to produce unchangeable thoughts, the personal computer allows us to qualify, modify, and quantify our thoughts; put them into digital language; put them on screens so that we can see clearly what we are thinking. We can communicate clearly by reflecting each other's thoughts through screens.

I have just given you a very quick history of the four stages of human thought technology. By definition human beings are thought-making species. We are called *homo sapiens*. We are distinguished form the other species, because we develop technologies for externalizing our ideas so that we can reflect our thoughts or communicate our thoughts at a distance. So, if you are going to live up to your label of *homo sapiens*, you have to define yourself as a thought-making person. *Think for Yourself, Question Authority*—TFYQA. We come back to that motto as the bumper sticker, or tee-shirt guide. Specifically, the intelligent member of our species has got to feel familiar with every form of thought storage, and thought-making, and thought communication— the oral, the hand-made, the mass assembled book, and the electronic mirrors which are provided by computers.

So, what type of ethics do you envision in the computer age?

Timothy Leary: Well, this question has been answered fairly well by authors like Toffler, Nesbitt and others who are involved in the futurist movement. We will witness a tremendous emphasis on the individual as opposed to the bureaucracy, and we will see decentralization. The person's home will become the center of his/her productivity. The notion of work will be replaced. It is an insult and a humiliation for any human being—and certainly for any American— to be forced by economics to do work which can be performed better, more effectively, more cheaply by a machine.

Within ten years, we could eliminate all work and turn it over to robots and computers. But, if you do *that*, what's a human being going to do? Remember, in an oral society a human being was part of the herd, tribe, or hive. In the feudal society an individual was a serf in bondage to the liege Lord, who was in turn in bondage to God. In the industrial society, the human being was a worker. You defined yourself by your occupation. "What are you?" "Well, I am a plumber," or "I am a carpenter. I am a Lawyer. I am a psychologist. I am a doctor. I belong to one of the knowledge monopoly professions. I am a librarian. I am a journalist, or an editor." People defined themselves by their work. Now, if we have eliminated work, then what is the function of a human being?

Obviously, the function of a human being is to grow, to evolve...to become more intelligent. In the future, we will be moving away from a work society where you are forced to do something you don't want to do, to contribute to the bureaucratic machinery. This notion will be replaced by free agentry. Everyone will be a free agent. Futurists say that the "service professions" will be the work of the future. I think this is a silly and somewhat ominous, though understandable and forgivable, application of the industrial language to the future.

If you are not producing something in hardware, like a book or an automobile, you are in "service." I prefer to say that we are going to be personal enhancers. We are here to help each other grow. Our function is to be human interactors in the new network society of the future. But, we are not going to work. We are going to nurture each other, activate each other, help each other to grow. So, in the post-industrial society, everyone is considered an expert in some particular field and can share that expertise. Everyone is here basically to fulfill the duties of a member of our species— to get smarter, to enhance our intelligence. It is our duty to increase our intelligence because everyone's got some certain perspective or aspect of knowledge that can be useful to others.

Obviously the political and religious structures that are in place during this transitionary period are not tuned in to this idea. Do you see this as a natural progression as the computer proliferates?

Timothy Leary: Yes. It is going to happen naturally. The idea that people could write in illuminated manuscripts was considered heretical. You copy. To write your own manuscript was considered sinful, and the Inquisition would kill you. Every new advance in human thought technology has been very carefully controlled by Top Management. To this very day, printing presses—even Xerox machines and typewriters are controlled in Iron Curtain countries like Russia, Bulgaria, and Hungary. The idea that you could write your own book is considered treason and cause for imprisonment. So, Top Management is always going to throw barriers against the evolution of thought. The ideas of individuals getting smarter is anathema to most bureaucracies. There is nothing right or wrong about this. It's the function of intelligent individuals to dissolve that bureaucracy when we are smart enough to do so.

At the present time there is tremendous anguish, nervousness and paranoia—a paroxysm of fear and anger which you can sense throughout the world today, because of this agonizing transition from a factory society to an information society.

People's definitions of themselves and of authority, and even the purpose of life, are being shattered. The rugs of security are being pulled away from everyone who is committed to the old industrial society. So, people get frightened. That is why you have this paranoia expressed in the Rambo-Reagan foreign policy which toes back to the Crusades and the religious wars that followed the invention of the printing press.

All of this calls for tremendous compassion and tolerance on the part of those of us who know what is going on. We should try to explain, coherently and clearly to everyone, and particularly to young people, the nature of the game and how it is changing. At least if you know what is happening, then you will be able to protect yourself, and you will be able to survive and grow in spite of the vexing and depressing things that are happening around you.

For many of us stuck in between these two periods...

Timothy Leary: We are all stuck.

What can we do to smooth this transition, both personally and globally?

Timothy Leary: My role is always the same, and my answer is always the same: *Think For Yourself, Question Authority.* My role is to encourage you and empower you to TFYQA. I encourage you to do this through my anecdotal versions of history, my satirical humor and my attempts to make fun of Top Management. I try to give a very gentle nudge to people. The way I empower people to think for themselves is through the technologies. I was using interactive, interpersonal psychological tests in the '50s. In the '60s, I felt drugs should be used by the individual, not just by the CIA, and not just by the psychiatric clinics or the government in approved projects. I urged that drugs should be used by individuals who were well informed and well motivated to improve themselves and to grow. The advice is always the same. Think more clearly. Understand your thoughts and change your mind in a more precise direction. Develop your own psychological excellence. The most revolutionary thing any of us can do is to improve our own performance, to become a better person in terms of intelligence and thought. You can't do that unless you are thinking clearly.

How will your program, Mind Mirror, help people to do that?

Timothy Leary: When you come to think of it, any computer is a "Mind Mirror." The terminal is the screen, and the screen is reflecting back thoughts. At the present time the thoughts reflecting back from computer screens are pretty prosaic—spreadsheets, tax accounts, checkbook balancing and word processing—but, that is inevitable. Top Management, or the unthinking individual, will use a new technology in service to the old philosophy. Recently you see more and more people using computers as expressions of art—the new computers like the Macintosh, Amiga, and the new Jack-in-Tosh by Atari, the ST; are doing away with the keyboard, which is wonderful! They are doing away with the literal Phoenician feudal mentality of the alphabet. They are doing away with the snobbish literacy of the industrial age. They are replacing the keyboard with the "mouse" and the "joystick," and now by the "electronic glove." Just point to the screen and made changes. And there are programs like the one you are working with, in which you use the human voice rather than the words printed in the Phoenician alphabet.

All computers are "Mind Mirrors." The real function of the computer is to help you clarify your own thinking, and to help you think more clearly and communicate more clearly. Everything that is now printed on a wood pulp book could probably be expressed better and more effectively on a screen because you can interact with it. You have broken down the Newtonian dichotomy of writer/reader—the all-wise, empowered, clever, scholarly writer, and the passive, dumb, receptive reader who just sits there and takes in all this stuff. The "interactive book," the "electronic book" engages the dumb reader who becomes co-author. At the end of each paragraph the "book" requests, invites, demands, a response from the so-called "reader," before going on to the next step in the "book," no matter what it is.

For example, at the end of every paragraph in a chemistry textbook the book might ask the student to demonstrate his/her understanding of the text. If the student's answer shows that the student hasn't mastered the preceding paragraph the author says, "Where did I go wrong? Let's go back and try it again.'" The formerly passive reader becomes an equal interactive partner in the new version of the book.

In, for example, *Huckleberry Finn*—the reader might decide to alter the personality of Huckleberry and the contrasting personality of Becky Thatcher. Is Becky a wimp? Is she bossy? Is she spacey, or moralistic? It is a continual invitation to clarify your thinking about the book, and to interact with the author. So the author of an "electronic book" is using a new art form, an interactive exchange that is initiated by the author. The book is not designed for passive readers who just sit there and react; it has to anticipate the enormous range of response by readers who participate in an ongoing dialogue. This is going to raise the intelligence of the human race, because it is going to demand, instead of passive learning, *active* learning.

The bureaucracies are going to oppose this. The knowledge monopolies are not going to feel too happy about ordinary people being able to interact with a "sacred text." As a matter of fact, many currently famous authors who pride themselves on making their living by being a "masters of literature," are going to be really pissed off at the idea of people being able to go in and change their prose. I've had people get upset at the notion that a mere reader can change Huckleberry's character in Tom Sawyer or, perhaps, decide that Napoleon was a little dwarfy, compensating wimp instead of being a glorious emperor. The "sacred authors" are going to fight the notion that anyone can change their thoughts. They don't want their words changed. Just as the original Jehovah said, "Thou shalt not bear false witness," or "Have no other graven images," the sacred author commands, "You shan't compete with me." That's the way the typical literary man from the industrial age feels about his writing. So there is going to be a lot of controversy as we move into the age of the active reader/writer.

And once again, the old monopolies are going to be broken. Just as the handicraftsman was pushed aside to a certain extent by the tool-making machine, thought monopolists are going to be very upset as they get pushed aside by the "thought-making appliances" that are going to be made available to anybody. Any dummy without a Ph.D. can start putting his thoughts down on the screen.

The new technologies are going to increase the power of individual intelligence entrancement. The use of laser-disks, new machines like the Amiga, modems, and voice-activated systems like yours are all signs that we are at the beginning of a glorious revolution in thought-processing that is going to lift the evolutionary level of our species.

Currently, we are looking at a small percentage of the population who are using computers In one study approximately 15% of the population were using them. Quantitatively, it is impossible to tell how much more intelligent we will become. How do you look at that?

Timothy Leary: You refer to the disturbing fact that we are becoming a two-tiered society, one that has access to computers and one that doesn't. There is a monopoly here. At the present time it costs several thousand dollars to get a personal computer system.

Our company, Futique, has a goal. We hope that within two years we will have on the market a Mind Mirror hand-held computer, that will be no larger than a hand-held audio tape player or calculator and will cost less than 20 dollars You could actually give it away. There is no excuse for any poor kid or Third World kid—or any person—not to have several hand-held Mind Mirrors that will allow them to process their thoughts minute-to-minute. This is going to eliminate the tremendous problem of illiteracy. At the present time, illiteracy is growing. I would flatly say that roughly 50% of young people today are functionally illiterate. They can barely read the letters on labels. The solution is not to draw all these kids into school and make little Shakespeares out of them. Johnny and Joanna can't write...and they don't have to write. Writing is just as outmoded as oil painting or illuminated manuscripts.

But, even the kid from the most impoverished background its going to take immediately to a screen because that doesn't require the left brain mentality of the industrial age literary society. So, this disastrous and ominous division between the literate and the illiterate which is increasing in our country and our planet...this problem can be eliminated by the distribution of these hand-held computers. You would no more think about stealing someone's personal computer than you would think about stealing someone's Nikes, because it will be that personalized. Each computer will be immediately processed with your data base. Each of these hand-helds will be tied to the records of your performances with your mental abilities coded in along with the knowledge that you have and the language that you speak. Your personal diary and your goal plan will be included as well, so that no one would be that interested in stealing someone else's, unless they really wanted to know. In that case you could put it in code with your MOS— "Mind Operating System." Oh, it's granted that Big Brother or Big Sister could "crack" your code and get into it, and the solution there is not to put anything that secret into your hand-held computer. The intimacies and privacies and wonderfully rich personal exchanges and secrets of life will not be put into these personal machines, which can be tapped and "busted" by others. They will be passed on in whispers and murmurs and double-meaning jokes and tones of voices as they always have been.

It seems, from what we have talked about, that you feel that even though we have just begun this type of evolutionary pattern, it's still happening very rapidly, I mean, we are right in the middle of it, even though we just started yesterday.

Timothy Leary: Many of us who are "crusading" (if I may use that terrible word) enthusiastically for the computer or electronic mirror to be used for TFYQA and individual growth are disturbed because it is going so slow. But let's be patient! It was just ten short years ago, in 1976, that Jobs and Wozniak popularized the personal computer.

Now, to help understand the present transition it is useful to look back at other transitions that our species has gone through. I see my role as being that of Henry Ford. When automobiles were first invented the "hackers"—mechanics—took over, just as it is with computers today. And, if you were a "car person" in those days, you had wrenches, you could get under the hood, your car would break down, and you would be covered with grease. A whole jargon of automotive mechanics sprung up that the average person couldn't grasp. The same thing is happening with computers. This "hacker"—electronic engineer, graduate of computer sciences—is like the early automobile mechanic talking their new jargon of bytes and K's and so forth. They are deliberately trying to make the thing look grease-stained and tough to operate.

Listen, I don't even know what model car l have! I don't know how many cylinders it has. I don't know any details of its mechanics, but I know it is exactly the car I want. I have been using cars for 45 years, so I know what I want in a car, but I don't know anything about automobile engineering.... I don't even know how to change a tire. The same thing is true for computers. I don't know anything about computers. I couldn't change the tire on my IBM and I couldn't get under the hood of my Apple. I am totally ignorant about that. But why not? There are plenty of people out there, like garage mechanics, who can repair it. I want to get into the driver's seat of my computer and drive around my mind and zoom and soar around my brain. I know exactly what I want and I can upgrade. My first car was a Model T, my second was a Model A. I just keep upgrading. I am not committed to Apple or IBM, but don't be intimidated. I speak here to the people in the New Age or the humanist futurist soft-touch field. Don't be intimidated by all this high tech stuff and the pomposity of the engineers. If you can drive a car, you can drive a computer, and it's much easier on the environment.

So how does Mind Mirror help people?

Timothy Leary: Mind Mirror doesn't really need a computer to operate. The computer simply makes the information available faster and with more precision. Mind Mirror is a system of linguistic thought processing that allows you to take large thoughts and choose attributes or qualities, modifiers or quantifiers, to describe that massive thought. Take a massive thought like Christianity.... What does that mean?

Well, you have to take a bunch of attributes. To one person Christianity means brotherliness and divinity, to another it means intolerance and warfare. The program will ask you questions, and you define it. Then your pal will come along and define Christianity, and you can see the two views on the screen and how they differ.

What Mind Mirror does to thinking is what Mendeleev and the chemical periodical table of elements did. We help you reduce your massive molecules of thought into elements so you can see clearly what your thoughts are made of and then re-combine the elements into new thoughts. It is a psycho-metric, linguistic methodology which can be learned in ten minutes and allow you to clarify your thoughts and communicate more clearly. Now, a lot of people—we have to face this fact—don't want to think for themselves. They would rather have Jesus —or the boss or Swami Rajneesh or the Pentagon—do it. Most people find it too hard. Their morale has been broken. Their self-confidence has been eroded.

Society discourages people from thinking for themselves. "Who are you, some kind of nut? You are no expert. Who are you to be thinking for yourself? Who are you to argue with the experts? You must be a kook. Put on a propeller and spin it on your beanie." If you think for yourself, the full weight of a totalitarian society will come down on you. If you think for yourself, they will ridicule you and ostracize you. Don't be discouraged by that.

According to a recent study, 22% of our society is "inner directed." Do you think this appliance, Mind Mirror, can impact that figure, and help people change from "outer directed" to an inner type of experience?

Timothy Leary: I would have to take a mega-thought like "inner directed" and put it on the X-ray screen. What do you mean by "inner directed?" What are the attributes? Does it mean they think for themselves? Does it mean they are yuppies? Does it mean they are ambitious? Does it mean they are sensual? I would put qualifiers on "inner directed." Does it mean that they are vegetarians? Does it mean they believe in politics? We would have to define what we mean by "inner directed." The advertisers want to know if that means someone is likely to buy Perrier or Budweiser, or likely to drive a BMW or a Detroit model car.

So, can you do this with people in your life?

Timothy Leary: Listen, the most important subject to study and clarify your thoughts about is *yourself!* Many people don't want to change, don't want to find out about themselves. I have demonstrated Mind Mirror to over 1,000 people now, and it is amazing. People come up, and I say, "Put any thought you want up there." The truly courageous person will want to put themselves on the screen, but many people will not.

They will pick, say, Christianity or Judaism, or good or evil. The subject one selects is very diagnostic about what part of you mind you want to know about.

If I ask you, "What are the important subjects you want to clarify your thinking about?" What do you pick? You might pick a different subject if you were alone than if you were with me. The subject you select only reflects what is on your mind. My programs don't tell you anything but what you put in.

Do they store the data you put in? Let's say I do a scorecard on ten people, will it store all this information?

Timothy Leary: Yes, every time you do a "micro-scope" (pun) or "thought-scan" you can store the results so that you can go back a year later and see how you were doing. It is a diary of your mind.

Part of the paradox in human history is that nobody knows what anybody is thinking, not even themselves. And there is no way of knowing what you thought in the past. Mind Mirror allows you to record your daily thoughts in a very precise form, and a year later you can go back and reflect upon what you looked like in the Mirror before.

Some people might want to enter themselves and their girl or boyfriend. What are their attributes' For example' someone may say, "For me the most important thing is that they are Armenian." Now I wouldn't say that and you might not, but for many...Who knows? Whether it's being rich, or skinny, or Irish, or thin. the attributes you choose to modify and qualify are showing you where you are at.

So, this product will help me do that? Clarify and modify my thinking to help me be more clear?

Timothy Leary: That is correct.

Do you have any final comments?

Timothy Leary: I would like to say this. These are very confusing, perplexing and disturbing times. These changes have provoked a savage reaction that goes back to feudal attitudes. Ancient blood—genetic and religious strife—is sweeping the world. Assassinations, hostages, terrorism—this is nothing new. It has been played over in centuries past. This is the old game which, in our idealism, we thought would never occur again, but it is recurring. During this period of confusing transition from the old society, the smoke-stack industrial society to the information society many are losing heart. And it is my obligation to encourage and empower people to become active and *not* to be confused and *not* to be discouraged by what is going on today.

If 1% of America can catch on and start moving together, we can change the rest of America. I am not talking about written IQ or some vague philosophical concept. I am talking about tolerance, humor, and good feeling. If we can lift by 1% the thinking of the American people, we can change the whole culture. The model, or metaphor, here is the human body. Normal temperature is 98.6°. If you raise this a little over 1% to 100°, you are sick. Raise it 2%, and you are really kind of "out-of-it." On the good side...*lower it*, and you are healthy again, lower it 1%, lower it 2%, and you are healthy again.

The point I am making is that society and the human species is an incredibly complex, interactive network of forces that can be easily directed. We can change this fevered, sick return to feudal barbarism just as quickly as it popped up in the last five years, just as any feverish disease can be healed.

Be of good heart my friends. Anyone who wants to bring about change has got to clarify his/her own thinking, and become very active in the new modes of thought processing. You are not going to change society using the old forms of meditation and prayer and the printed word. You have to become a facile skilled communicator. Because our cause is freedom and our cause is growth and our cause is humanistic, we shall *win*! We shall grow and advance together.

Everything I have said in this interview has been dedicated to my lifelong career motto—TFYQA!

Technology
Virtual Wonderlands

Jaron Lanier: Creating Virtual Reality

with David Jay Brown and Rebecca McClen Novick

When virtual reality (VR) first took the national spotlight, Jaron Lanier stood center stage. The possibility of full sensory immersion into computer-generated worlds caught the collective imagination, and Jaron became the hero of cyberspace.

Jaron began his journey into VR after quitting high school, when he engineered his own education in computer science by spending time with mentors such as Marvin Minsky at MIT. After a stint performing as a street musician in Santa Cruz, CA, Jaron began programming electronic sound effects into video games. He quickly became a pioneer in computer programming, and soon he started the first VR company out of his home. That company, VPL Research, produced most of the world's VR equipment for many years. He is the co-inventor of such fundamental VR components as interface gloves and VR networking.

Jaron coined the phrase "VR" and founded the VR industry. He appears regularly on national TV shows, such as *Nightline* and *60 Minutes*. His work with computer languages and VR was twice chosen for the cover of *Scientific American*, and has appeared on the cover of the *Wall Street Journal* in a piece entitled "Electronic LSD."

But music is Jaron's first love. Since the late seventies, he has been an active composer and performer in the world of new classical music. He writes chamber and orchestral music, and is a pianist and a specialist in unusual musical instruments. Jaron has a large collection of exotic instruments from around the world and can play them all. He has performed with artists as diverse as Philip Glass, Ornette Colernan, Terry Riley, Barbara Higble, and Stanley Jordan.

Jaron has a powerful presence. His large eyes, which alternate between dreamy reflectiveness and focused intensity, peer out from behind long, brown dreadlocks. He appears gentle and relaxed, although he gets very animated when he starts talking about something that excites him. His nervous system is unusually balanced with a blend of artistic sensitivity, sharp scientific mindfulness and great imagination.

What is your definition of reality and how do you think it's created? And in that context, what is Virtual Reality?

Jaron Lanier: You'll be shocked to know that I don't have definitive answers to all deep philosophical questions. I do have some thoughts, though. I'll start with one definition, which is a biological one. *Reality* is the global expectation of the nervous system for the next moment. In other words, the most flexible parts of the psyche and your body mold themselves to a rolling guess of what will probably come next.

The continuous, cinematic-style experience of reality we have is an illusion created by our nervous systems. Our direct perception of this world is actually highly flawed. For starters, the blind spot is a great example. Near the center of each of your eyes is this big, black hole where you don't see anything, but you're never aware of it. Your mind fills it in perfectly for itself, which it can do because it holds all the cards. Even aside from that, what your eyes actually see is not what you perceive them seeing. Your eyes see edges and boundaries and patterns. They don't really see the picture that you see—that's constructed on a running basis in your brain. Physiologically, they just do not pick up the picture you're seeing now.

Philip K. Dick once said, "Reality is that which doesn't go away when you stop believing in it."

Jaron Lanier: That's absolutely excellent. There are only a few things that fall in that category—I think there are three. There's this everyday, mundane, physical world, which seems awfully persistent, and the fact that Marin hasn't made it disappear is good evidence that nobody can (laughter). And then there's the world of moods and essences and artistic feelings and styles, and those things are intensely real to me on a deep level. The other stubborn item is that mysterious thing called mathematics—it's just really stubbornly there.

And just a brief definition of mathematics in that context?

Jaron Lanier: *Mathematics* is the inevitable path you go down when you start thinking about things in some way other than as an undifferentiated whole—which is any kind of thinking, really.

So what is VR?

Jaron Lanier: VR is the use of technology to generate the sensory experiences of people, under human control. The neurophysiological strategies used to perceive, manipulate and learn about VR are the same that your body has evolved to use. So your experience of it is with the natural language of your own body, as opposed to your intelligence or cultural perception.

What happens when VR changes the physical laws, and you are able to do things you're not accustomed to doing?

Jaron Lanier: If you deviate too far, VR becomes imperceptible, because it is too weird for the brain to recognize. But there is a wide gray zone in which you can experience a radically unnatural world. You can slow everything down. You can make your arm two miles long relative to the rest of your body. But if you want to really create a surreal experience in VR, you don't play with physics, you play with your sensory motor loop. One of my favorites is trading eyes with another person, so that one person's head controls the other's point of view, and vice versa. What you discover is a very intimate and trusting approach to the other person. It's a remarkable experience of a shared body.

One really radical experience is controlling a virtual body with more limbs than a physical body. Ann Lasko, who was at VPL for a long time, made a lobster body. Initially, the extra limbs just kind of sat there, but eventually she was able to control them.

How?

Jaron Lanier: There are different approaches for controlling extra limbs. One takes all the movement data from all over your body and puts it through some tricky algorithms so you have a function that relies a bit on all that global data to control just one local joint on an extra limb. There's a field of study of tactile illusions that is vital to the development of tactile feedback in VR. One of the illusions has to do with putting buzzers or vibrators against the skin and creating phantom third buzzers between them. It turns out that, apparently, the way the brain understands that type of sensation is very nicely linear or metrical, so you can put a buzzer on one hand, and another on another hand, and create a sensation that's from an out-of-body point.

Now, if you match up the position of such a sensation with one of these phantom, visually existing limbs that you're controlling, all of a sudden you have a new limb to your body you can control *and* feel. I just cite this and the example of trading eyes as two of the types of things you can do with playing at a deep level with the way you perceive your own body and the world, and how you interact. That, to me, is the most fascinating area for aesthetic exploration of VR. I think all of the great art coming out of VR is going to be playing with the very intimate sensory motor loop in that way, as opposed to the current, early trend of making weird external virtual environments.

You have said you feel VR's greatest potential is for communication and empathy?

Jaron Lanier: Absolutely. But I'm thinking in the very long term. I'm not thinking about tomorrow, but about generations hence. This really hinges on the idea of post-symbolic communication. Some generations from now, if we've survived as a species—which is not clear—there will be many wonderful, cheap VR setups around, and there will be access points everywhere. A generation of kids will grow up using tools with great user interfaces for inventing stuff in virtual worlds.

So they're going to grow up differently from previous kids, because, aside from using symbols to refer to the things they can't directly create and do, they'll have this other way of making up for each other any imagined stuff as objective sensory objects. They'll develop a facility for "reality conversations," or "intentional waking-state shared dreaming," or co-dreaming, what I call post-symbolic communication.

Post-symbolic communication amounts to a spontaneous way of creating a sensual world between people without requiring interpretive symbols. It's sort of like cutting out the middleman, and you actually *make* stuff instead of just referring to it.

If we were conducting this interview right now in some kind of post-symbolic world, how would we be doing it?

Jaron Lanier: The first thing is that the types of things you'd communicate would start to shift in a very wonderful way. Don't get me wrong, language isn't going to disappear. There's actually a part of our cortex that's specialized to it. That's how committed we've become to it. This is going to become a new, wonderful adventure that grows up *alongside* the adventure of language, increasing our sensitivity to language.

A lot of linguists believe that abstraction has to exist for communication to occur.

Jaron Lanier: I disagree. In VR, if you need to refer to a quality, you don't need categories to communicate because you can have every single thing that's perceived alike in some way in some giant planet that you can carry around. I mean, why not? Instead of saying something's red, just put everything that's red in a planet and let others look at it and perceive for themselves what these things have in common. So that's an example of how the whole idea of communication changes.

In language we have a notion of a quality, such as redness or pudginess or something. In post-symbolic communication, why bother with those things when you can bring a jar containing everything you consider pudgy. Then the concept of pudgy becomes unnecessary, because you can look at them all at once and experientially get what's alike about them.

VR will probably have a clarifying effect on the boundaries of imagination. In our everyday physical lives, there's a very confusing division between the internal and external worlds. In VR, however, there is a much sharper division between what is objectively created and what is subjectively perceived, because the external world is exactly defined by computer software.

Now, there are some things about VR that are not perfect. VR will always be of a lower quality than the physical world. After the next few early decades of development, the veracity of VR will not depend on how good the technology becomes, but rather on how good we become at perceiving the difference between it and nature. A good precedent for this is the way stereophiles can compare a $50,000 pair of speakers to a $70,000 pair of speakers and hear a difference. But they also can hear a difference between that and natural sound. So here you have a whole aesthetic of creating ever-better speakers, but it never ends, because we're also increasing our own sensitivity to sound. Sensitivity is a global or systemic property of perception; it's not a simple, measurable parameter that can be maxed out. I think it goes on forever, and you can achieve entirely new, unforeseen strategies of sensitivity that cannot be predicted. Good media technologies make us more sensitive to nature by providing a basis for comparison. That should be treated as one of their best gifts.

Doesn't technology desensitize and desanctify the world? If you can create virtual environments with virtual trees and bring back extinct animals, why would you care about the environment and other people? You can just plug them in?

Jaron Lanier: One thing about VR I have found to be true for almost everyone who uses it is that when you leave it, you get this thrill of seeing the physical world again. Actually, one of the patterns of use I've noticed with people is they tend to want to build up some time in VR so that they can experience that thrill of the transition back to the physical world. You have such an increased sensitivity to detail when you come out—it's like your sense organs have been widened. The first time I came out of VR, I noticed the rainbows in the individual threads in the weave of the carpet for the first time. So it actually increases sensitivity, rather than decreases it.

Except for a few fortunate individuals, corporations are going to pretty much monopolize this technology. How much freedom will there be for autonomy in VR programming? Will people have to be content to buy another person's dream?

Jaron Lanier: That's the single most important question about the future of VR. Obviously I want everybody to be able to make their own world all the time. I'd like that to be so standard that it's spontaneously happening at conversational and improvisatory speeds all the time. That's the future I want to see, but it won't be there right away.

Do we have the technology now for this to be possible?

Jaron Lanier: That's more of a cultural question than a technological one. On the one hand, there's the evolution of wonderful user-interfaces for creating content of worlds quickly, and on the other, there's the social phenomenon of a generation of kids growing up using that with fluidity and expertise. Both have to happen, and it'll take a while. The shortest time I can imagine is maybe 3 or 4 generations hence.

We touched briefly on the applications of VR. What other possibilities excite you?

Jaron Lanier: Well, education is one of them. You could create a virtual world for the express purpose of making a memorable place where you learn something new, like dinosaurs. You can simulate the old forest and have these big dinosaurs tramping around, and even better, the kids can become dinosaurs themselves. They can become the thing they're studying and achieve identity with it. They can become molecules such as DNA, or mathematical shapes—it goes on and on. It's a very effective way of learning something.

Unfortunately, I don't think this society has a commitment to spend any money on education. I've talked to schools a lot about this, and there are very few that can afford this. Many in the country today can't even afford a new basketball hoop. It'll happen eventually, but it might not happen right away.

Tell us something about VR's potential for physically challenged people.

Jaron Lanier: I did a juggling teaching demo a long time ago. If you juggle virtual balls, you can sort of simulate the experience of juggling. You don't feel the balls hit your hand as much with the current types of gloves, but you can still approximate the experience. Let's suppose you decide to make the balls move slowly, but keep your hands moving at the natural speed. So now you have lots of time to get your hand under the balls. That by itself is just a cheat, but what's really interesting is you can slowly speed up the balls and have a gradual approach to learning a physical skill that previously required a leap. For people recovering from strokes, this could give them some learning feedback earlier than they would get otherwise. So there's a whole range of learning uses.

Do you see VR as being a turning point in humanity's relationship with the machine?

Jaron Lanier: It is in a number of ways. First of all, it defines our agenda with machines as being primarily cultural and sensual, as opposed to power oriented. We've reached a remarkable moment now that, with the exception of diseases and natural disasters, all of our other problems are created by our own behavior.

We can't stop making technology, because we're in love with it. So what we have to do is shift to a cultural way of choosing our technologies and justifying them. VR is an interesting technology; it's something that's being taken very seriously. But everybody recognizes its justification is fundamentally cultural. To me, that's a marvelous shift in which life can be explored as if it were a work of art.

(Magical Blend issue #48)

David Jay Brown and Rebecca McClen Novick are the authors of two collections of interviews with renowned thinkers: Mavericks of the Mind *and* Voices from the Edge *(both by Crossing Press, 1-800-777-1048.)*

Technology
Virtual Wonderlands

Terence McKenna: Virtual Realities & E-Highs

Looking like a cross between a T'ai Chi master, a Navy frogman and the Terminator, a man harnessed to electronic leads and fitted with a piece of headgear slowly turns and gestures. The pointing hand and the ballet of sign language, combined with an air of intense concentration, give the unmistakable impression that the person is far away from the brightly lit Bay Area laboratory in which he stands. You might also say that he seems as if he was in another world.

You would be right. Before you stands a true astronaut of inner space, a researcher who is in the process of going where few have gone before. But look quickly; what is today the visionary dream of the techie few will soon be reality for all of us. Virtual Reality (VR), that is.

Is it mechanistic multi-media masturbation or a doorway swinging open on the flower-strewn fields of the romantic imagination? A tool for discovery and navigation in new esthetic domains, or the final trivializing of the drive to be mindlessly entertained? These are questions that I asked myself one morning recently as I drove toward a rendezvous with one of the mavens of VR, the redoubtable Eric Gullichsen, then of Autodesk, currently a free agent. For, as I was to learn later that day, not even VR is immune to corporate change and upheaval. Gullichsen and his associate Patrice Gelband are now virtual guns for hire; the status of Autodesk's future commitment to R & D of VR remains undecided.

Corporate intrigues aside, worlds are being created by such pioneers in the VR field as Jaron Lanier and the Autodesk special design team Gullichsen headed. It was logical that Autodesk should be a leader in the VR field; their Auto/Cad software has based much of its appeal on the idea that the user can actually "walk around" in a high-resolution, 3-D simulation of 2-D blueprints. Pursuit of this idea grew naturally into the idea of computer-generated worlds. And Lanier and VTL, his corporation, have been the persistent leaders in the field of body and hand imagining in VR. The magical gloves and body stockings that are the keys to entry into VR remain Lanier's specialty.

What is VR? It is a technology currently under development by NASA and private companies in the Bay Area and on the East Coast. It began with the modest intent of simulating the experience of flying high-performance fighter aircraft under combat conditions. Think of it this way: You are the Defense Department. Would you turn over a fighter plane costing upwards of one hundred million dollars to some apple-cheeked hayseed so he can learn to fly it? If you spend the cost of one plane on simulation, and thereby prevent even one crash, you are saving a lot of money and possibly even human lives. And one hundred million dollars buys a lot of simulation.

What I saw at Autodesk was considerably more modest than the classified government efforts. Gullichsen estimated that the whole VR apparatus could be recreated for around $50,000—chicken feed in the world of high-tech R&D. The 5th-floor lab was a sparsely furnished office approximately 15 by 20 feet with a humongous high-res color monitor, and a quite ordinary computer work station. Introduced around, I was asked if I had any questions. Figuring I had done my homework, I suggested we cut to the chase.

The glove, wonderfully redolent with all the associations that are carried by black silk gloves everywhere, was slipped onto my hand. I had found it difficult to visualize the motion sensors that I knew were stitched onto the back of the gloves on top of each flex point. They appeared to be small blue beads. The whole thing fitted smoothly. I was asked to close and open my hand while the software sensed and entered the flex values of my particular hand. Next came the helmet, looking like a fancy, overweight scuba mask. Once on, it put a Sony Watchman color mini-screen about an inch from the eye; a slight discontinuity between the screens created the impression of 3-D space.

Once everything was in place, I could see the fuzzy, but colored and recognizable outlines of a cartoon version of an office. Hovering in space in front of me was what appeared to be a foreshortened spaghetti fork. This, I was told, was the virtual image of the glove I was wearing. Sure enough, wiggle thumb, left-most tong of spaghetti fork wiggles. No Roger Rabbit appeared, but as I pondered the mechanics of the glove, I burst noiselessly and effortlessly through a wall and into a burnt sienna space that seemed to, and probably did, extend to infinity.

Eric explained about pointing. I had been pointing without realizing it. Pointing is how you get around in VR, or cyberspace, as the true believers call it. When you point at something you move toward it. When you open your hand the motion ceases. It is that simple. The eye goes where the finger points, and the image of your gloved hand comes along and can be used to "pick up," by intersecting, objects in the VR. After a few moments, the lag time in the refreshing of the images, the weightlessness, the newly insubstantial nature of the objects and the newfound nature of my right index finger were all familiar enough to me that I could slowly make my way around the office without moving through walls and objects or taking off through the ceiling or the floor.

In short, I got it. Talking with Eric and his associate mathematician Patrice Gelband, I had the eerie feeling that this might be what it would have been like to stop by the Wright brothers' bicycle shop to shoot the breeze with Wilber and Orville about the latest ideas concerning lift ratios of air foils. These folks are onto something. They know it, and I will wager that soon the whole world will know it. We are on the brink of another leap in evolution, folks.

From fighter simulations to simulations of architectural models that you can literally "fly the client into," it is only a short step, and from a 3-D blueprint of an imaginary office to the simulation of the Taj Mahal on a moonlight-flooded summer night is only a slightly longer step—in VR.

If all this sounds too far-out to be true, or like a rehash of Philip Dick's novel *A God Named Jones*, then that is just the universe's way of telling you that you haven't been keeping up. Remember the feelies in Aldous Huxley's science fiction distopia *Brave New World*? Everyone went to them and held onto a knob on each side of the velvet-cushioned seat and was conveyed away to the latest risqué and ribald fantasy that the schlock meisters of future pop culture had prepared for public consumption. Of course we have had the operational equivalent of the feelies since at least the intro of television. And the effect of vast narcotized masses of people hooked on a drug whose content is culturally sanctioned and institutionally controlled is certainly debatable. Some have blamed TV for the creeping crap-for-brains disease that seems to have become endemic in America. However, on one level, TV, and now VR, are nothing more than the latest instances of neotany, the carrying over into adulthood of infantile physical or behavioral characteristics. The world is a complicated place; if millions of people choose to retreat into an electronically reinforced state of semi-infantilism, it may end up making the total system ultimately easier to pilot into a safe harbor.

VR is easy to denounce in the same breath with MTV and perhaps HDTV—upon which it will in some degree depend. But the fact is that VR is more than simply further movement down a primrose path strewn with *The Price of His Toys* catalogs. It is a technology that will not only allow us to make more and better art, but potentially will dissolve the boundaries between us and allow us to see the contents of each other's minds. There is also the possibility that improved forms of communication—states of near-telepathy among participating human beings—can be coaxed out of imaginative use of the technology. Because of what VR is intrinsically, there are several ways in which it could be the basis of an entirely new kind of communication between people.

Each age takes its self-image from the animal world. The 19th century, with its obsession with the power to reshape the earth and abolish distances through the new technology of the steam engine, took as its guiding image that of the thoroughbred race horse. The early 20th century focused on speed, conquest of the air, and the integration of human beings and machines into an even more lethal symbiosis. This process found its realization in high-performance fighter aircraft; the animal image was that of the raptor, the relentless bird of prey.

Jaron Lanier is fond of saying that in VR one can choose to be anything; a piano, for example. Fine. Having surveyed the smorgasboard of morphogenetic options offered by Mother Nature, I would choose to be a virtual octopus. Many people, once informed, would make the same choice. I believe that the totemic image for the future is the octopus. This is because the cephalopods, the squids and octopi, have perfected a form of communication that is both psychedelic and telepathic, a model for the communications of the future. In the not-too distant future, men and women may shed the monkey body to become virtual octopi swimming in a silicon sea.

Consider: Nature offers the example of the octopus, a creature in which well developed eyes and an ability to change the color, banding, and general appearance of the skin surface have favored a visual, and hence telepathic form of communication. An octopus does not communicate with small mouth noises as we do, even though water is a good medium for acoustic signaling; rather the octopus becomes its own linguistic intent. The octopus is like a naked nervous system, say rather a naked mind: The inner states— the thoughts, if you will—of the octopus are directly reflected in its outward appearance. It is as if the octopus were wearing its mind on it exterior. This is, in fact, the case. The octopus literally dances its thoughts through expression of a series of color changes and position changes that require no linguistic conventions for understanding as do our words and sentences. In the world of the octopus, to behold is to understand. Octopi have a large repertoire of color changes, dots, blushes and traveling bars that move across their surfaces, this ability in combination with the soft bodied physique of the creature allows it to be obscure and reveal its linguistic intent simply by rapidly folding and unfolding different parts of the body. The octopus does not transmit its linguistic intent; it *becomes* its linguistic intent. The mind and the body of the octopus are the same and are equally visible. This means that the octopus wears its language like a kind of second skin; it appears to be and becomes what it seeks to mean. There is very little loss of definition or signal strength among communicating octopi. Indeed, their well known use of "ink" clouds to conceal themselves may indicate that this is the only way that they can have anything like a private thought. The ink cloud may be a kind of correction fluid for voluble octopi who have mis-spoken themselves.

Like the octopus, our destiny is to become what we think, to have our thoughts become our bodies and our bodies become our thoughts. This is the essence of a more perfect Logos, a Logos not heard, but beheld. VR can help here; electronics can change vocal utterance into visually beheld color output in the VR. This output can then be manipulated, by tools still uncreated, tools to be found in the tool kit of the VR hacker/mechanic soon to be. This means that a three-dimensional syntax, one that is seen, not heard, becomes possible as an experience of VR. What is the point of being able to see one's voice, even in VR, you may ask. The point is that others will be able to see it as well. The ambiguity of invisible meanings which attend audio speech is replaced by the unambiguous topology of meanings beheld. At last we will truly *see* what we mean. And we will see what others mean too, for cyberspace will be a dimension where anything that can be imagined can be made to seem real.

When we are in the act of seeing what is meant, the communicator and the one communicated with become as one. In other words, the visible languages possible in VR will overcome the subject-object dualism as well as the self-other dualism.

In trying to imagine the futures onto which these doors open, let us not forget that culture and language were the first virtual realities. A child is born into a world of unspeakable wonder. Each part of the world is seen to glow with animate mystery and the beckoning light of the unknown. But quickly our parents and our siblings provide us with words. At first these are nouns; that shimmering pattern of sound and iridescence is a "bird," that cool, silky, undulating surface is "water." As young children we respond to our cultural programming and quickly replace mysterious things and feelings with culturally validated and familiar words. We literally tile over reality with a mosaic of interconnected words. Later, as we grow in ability and understanding, the culture in which we find ourselves provides conventionalized relationships for us to model. Lover, father, investor, property owner. Each role has its own rules and its own conventions. These roles too tile over and replace the amorphous wonder of simply being alive. As we learn our lines and the blocking that goes with them, we move out of the inchoate realm of the pre-verbal child and into the realm of the first VR, the VR of culture. Many of us never realize that this domain is virtual, and instead we assume that we are discovering the true nature of the real world.

Musing on this in a recent interview, Jaron Lanier observed: "I think VR will have an effect of enhancing and, in a sense, completing the culture. My view is that our culture has been abnormally distorted by being incredibly molded by technology.... VR, by creating a technology that's general enough to be rather like reality was before there was technology, sort of completes a cycle."

Lanier's remarks concerning the field that he helped to create have an eerie aura of unfocused prescience. He speaks in terms of a non-symbolic language, and in terms of bifocal glasses with real reality on top, yesterday's VR on the bottom. He oscillates between the profound and the quirky, but the idea that VR completes a cycle of neurotic behavior that is as old as our use of tools is interesting. VR asks us to imagine a future in which there will be virtual realities within virtual realities. A man slept, and while asleep dreamed he was a butterfly. Upon awakening, the man asked himself, "Am I a man who slept and dreamed he was a butterfly, or am I a butterfly who sleeps and is now dreaming he is a man?"

The promise of VR is that in the near future we will walk the beaches and byways of twice ten thousand planets, a virtual new galaxy to explore, whose name will be Imagination. The rest of our lifetimes, our busy mind's eye is culturally destined to peer out at thousands of shimmering realities: Ankor Wat and the volcanoes of Io, many of our own memories, and the memories of others who have shared this or that engineered vista or thrill.

My take on this is all different. I wish all these folks luck. I think that we can look forward to terrific pornography based on this technology, to simulations of fixing broken machinery in outer space and tidying up inside radioactive zones. Surgeons can already operate on virtual cadavers in one advanced medical teaching facility. But somehow I am haunted by a deeper hope for VR. After all, technology has already proven that it is the drug most palatable to the Western mind. Could not VR allow us to blaze a high trail into the wilderness of the human imagination? Then where each went, all would be free to follow through the miracle of instant VR replay? Can the riches of the imagination be made a commodity that can be sold back to the consumer who is also their producer? Selling the self should be the easiest of tasks in a society as narcissistic as our own.

And speaking of drugs, just where on the spectrum of the cultural pharmaphobia can public and governmental attitudes towards VR be expected to fall? Is VR to be seen as a "safe and harmless substitute for drugs" or is it "electronic illusions from hell?" It is a dreary comment on the current infantile state of public dialogue that there is little doubt that we will be subject to both claims in the debate ahead.

Certainly VR represents a technology of escapism that dwarfs the modest intent of the opium smoker or the video game addict. But on the other hand, so does modern film. Through color photography, most people on earth have vicariously experienced sufficient data to allow them to create VR fantasies based on imagination and media-fanned expectation. It seems highly unlikely that the development of VR will be treated as the spread of a new drug; rather it is seen as a new frontier for marketing and product development. Indeed, the non-destructive nature of VR means that the talent of many artists, designers, and engineers can be absorbed in VR projects with no impact whatsoever on ordinary reality. Finally, VR, with its capacity for virtual replay of constructions of the imagination, may hold the key to accessing the mapping of the imagination. The dream of artists, to be able to show the fabric of their dreams and visions, may be fast approaching VR.

The more extreme, inventive, and *avant garde* of the VR constructions are likely to resemble experiences with psychedelic plants and drugs rather than the more conventionalized forms of art. The doorway to the realms of dream and the unconscious will be opened, and what had been merely symbolic representations of eccentric individual experience will become that experience itself.

Does Lanier's "non-symbolic communication" have anything to do with the visible languages of the DMT Ecstasy? It was this un-obvious question that had gotten me interested in VR in the first place. My experiences with shamanic hallucinogens, especially *ayahuasca* use in the Upper Amazon Basin, had shown me the reality of vocal performances that are experienced as visual. The magical songs of the *ayahuas-ceros,* the folk *medicos* of the Indians, and Mestizos of the jungle-back rivers, are not songs as we understand the term. Rather they are intended to be seen, and to be judged primarily as visual works of art. To those intoxicated and adrift upon the visionary reveries unleashed by the brew, the singing of the shaman becomes a magical airbrush of color and organized imagery that is breathtaking in its alien and comic grandeur. My hope is that VR at its best may be the perfect mind space in which to experimentally explore and entrain the higher forms of visual linguistic processing that accompany tryptamine intoxication. In other words, the VR technology can be used to create a tool kit for the construction of objects made of visual language. These objects would be experienced in the VR mode as three-dimensional manifolds devoid of ordinary verbal ambiguity. This phase shift is a move toward a kind of telepathy. The shared beholding of the same linguistic intention in an objectified manifold is a true union. We become as one mind with this style of communication. Language beheld could perhaps serve as the basis for a deeper web of interlocking understandings between human beings that would represent a kind of technically aided evolutionary forward leap of the species. The near future may hold a public utility that will provide access to a hyper-dimensional ocean of visibly expressed public thoughts via cable. This service will be delivered over cable simply because the very large computers necessary to create moving, real time, high-resolution Virtual Realities will be state of the art mainframes for the next few years at least. A kind of informational network that one can actually enter into and control through the use of visual icons. Is this not true cyberspace? I believe that it is, that it is what cyberpunk hyper-prophet William Gibson was thinking of in his novel *Neuromancer* when he introduced the notion of cyberspace as a....

   "... consensual hallucination experienced daily by billions of legitimate operators, in every nation.... A graphic representation of data abstracted from

the banks of every computer in the human system. Unthinkable complexity. Lines of light ranged in the nonspace of the mind, clusters and constellations of data. Like city lights, receding...."

My hope for VR would be that exploration of such new frontiers of language and communication could be built into research strategies from the start. Then the loop from the trivial to the archetypal might be appreciably shortened as the VR option becomes well known.

A major career option of the near-term future is that of professional cyberspace architect/engineer. Such folks will design and direct the construction of virtual realities and scenarios. Gullichsen, in an article for *Nexus* wrote:

"The talents of a cyberspace architect will be akin to those of traditional architects, film directors, novelists, generals, coaches, playwrights, and video game designers. The job of the cyberspace engineer will be to make the experience seem real. This job is as artistic as it is technical, for experience is something manufactured spontaneously in the mind and senses, not something that can be built, packaged and sold like a car or refrigerator."

Consciousness is no better than the quality of the codes that convey it. Virtual Reality may hold the possibility of an icon based-visual language that could be universally understood while being much more wide spectrum in its portrayal of emotions and spatial relationships than is even theoretically possible for spoken language. But we will not find the fountain of pure visual poetry if we do not look for it.

Terence McKenna is the author of numerous books, including True Hallucinations, *his first-hand account of Amazonian tribal people and their shamanic traditions.*

Spirituality

Spirituality

Spirituality today is a moveable feast. With a smorgasbord of world religions and spiritual traditions (both ancient and modern) to choose from, food for the soul is no longer a one-course proposition, but can be mixed and matched like Chinese takeout, one belief from column A, another from column B. Not surprisingly, the result is more often than not metaphysical heartburn. Digesting the meat of one religion can be a challenge, gorging on a stew of world beliefs can stop you up for decades. And while one might expect some spiritual indigestion from a reliance on New Age junk food, even a traditional diet of spoon-fed dogma can create painful bloating and excess gas when it is only half-baked. And so our stomachs (which, by the way, several traditions consider the seat of the soul) continue to growl. The fact is, we need some form of spiritual nourishment, and we are hungry for it. We can't simply starve ourselves. The Soviet regime proved this when it tried, with disastrous results, to remove religion from the state menu. Neither can we gorge on empty calories or swallow ideologies whole. For spirit to nourish, it must have substance, something lacking in too many frothy New Age meringues. And just as food needs to be broken down and digested for its nutrients to be absorbed, so does religion, something all but impossible to do with refried fundamentalism.

All of this is not to deny the existence of some very holy souls on our planet. Every religion has them still. But they are far too rare. If this were not the case, intolerance and prejudice would not be as pervasive as they still are. The problem with today's spiritual smorgasbord is that much of it is passion unleavened by love. Together, these two forces still have the power to change the world, but until we stop trying to substitute sentimentality for love, our religious recipes will continue to leave a bitter aftertaste.

In its 17 years of publishing, **Magical Blend** *has sampled many spiritual approaches. Variety and diversity have been its hallmark. As editors, we have tried not to let this focus on breadth come at the expense of depth, but considering that scholars spend lifetimes examining a single tradition, we readily admit the limitations inherent in our approach. True spirituality requires depth, which comes not from religion but from the person practicing it. We also realize the written word is an avenue for information, not enlightenment. While we have looked for both heart and soul in the spiritual approaches we have presented, we cannot pass those qualities on to the reader. What we can pass on are ideas, and the ideas contained in the articles and interviews in this section are powerful ones, changing the way we view spirituality today.*

Take, for example, the rediscovery of the Goddess tradition of pre-Christian Europe, which does not, as many would like to believe, simply replace a

male deity with a female one. The Goddess is not Jehovah in drag, but repre-
sents a fundamentally different approach to spirituality. While God inhabits
the heavens, sitting atop a detailed hierarchy, the Goddess energy permeates
the body of the Earth and stresses partnership and equality, not just between
male and female but between all living creatures. Nature is considered not a
fallen state but an exalted one. These ideas are potent ones in a time when the
concept of "man's dominion" has resulted in separating man from woman, hu-
manity from nature and justified exploitation at every level. The biggest mis-
understanding about the reemergence of the Goddess tradition is that it
represents an assault on God. But the Goddess is not a personage in the same
sense as our traditional image of God. Instead, She is more a personification of
natural energies. Followers of the modern Goddess tradition are not at odds so
much with God as with certain ideas about God, ideas which have elevated
domination and subjugation to a spiritual level. Indeed, there is a growing
cadre of Christian theologians who feel that the modern Goddess tradition con-
tains ideas that are central to Jesus's teachings but which have been misplaced
by centuries of dogmatic interpretation and political agendas. This approach
recognizes that the human tendency to try to capture spirit in form sometimes
elevates form over spirit and seeks to turn the emphasis around.

This approach recognizes that the human tendency to try to capture spirit
in form sometimes elevates form over spirit and seeks to turn the emphasis
around.

If spirituality does not ennoble us—all of us—it has failed to connect with
the Magical Universe. The articles and interviews in this section represent a
groundswell of interest in alternative routes to the Magical Universe, any one
of which is worthy of a lifetime of devotion. And in the long run, they are per-
haps not as diverse as they first appear. Rather than dismissing a culture's or
tradition's beliefs out of hand, we can at least consider them as ideas. We do
not have to surrender our own faith in order to attempt to see the Light in an-
other. The remarkable thing about ideas is that they generally benefit from
cross-pollination. An idea grows stronger when informed by other ideas. Per-
haps the same is true of spirituality. If so, these differing approaches may point
to a metareligion of the future, where diversity is considered a blessing rather
than a threat. When this happens, the human spirit will at last be free to soar
to the heights it has so long aspired.

Spirituality
Modern Mysticism: A Practical Approach

James Redfield: Beyond the Celestine Prophecy

with Sirona Knight and Michael Starwyn

With the phenomenal success of *The Celestine Prophecy*, James Redfield has re-awakened New Age interest in mainstream America. Not since Shirley MacLaine danced into the light have we heard such a commotion over ideas that many of our readers no doubt find quite familiar. They are not, however, that familiar to everyone yet.

What Redfield has done in *The Celestine Prophecy* is to take the cannons of New Age thought, sift out key "insights," find a logical order for them and unfold them in the course of a futuristic adventure story.

First rejected by a string of publishers, Redfield self-published the book, turned it into an underground success, sold it to Warner Books for $800,000 and watched it stay on the *New York Times* bestseller list for twenty-five straight weeks. A companion reader is out, a movie is in the works and a sequel is already planned. It's a nice job, but is it that good?

Showing a remarkable resilience to sudden fame, Redfield humbly credits much of *The Celestine Prophecy*'s success not to his own talent, but to the recognition of readers that the awakening phenomenon he writes about is happening in their lives, too. So, while reading an adventure story, they are at the same time coming to grips with their own unexplained synchronicities and brushes with the ineffable. In other words, they awaken with the protagonist to the dawning of a new age.

Perhaps the most hopeful new age concept is the idea of the "hundredth monkey" or "quantum leap" or magic threshold or number of people it takes to "grok" the experience and suddenly trip reality's wire, transcending to a higher plane. That's what Redfield's book is about and, if all the hub bub over it is indicative, that's what his book is doing—opening readers' eyes to the possibility.

Wouldn't it be interesting if one of Redfield's readers becomes the hundredth monkey who will take us over the top?

How do you explain the incredible influence your work has had on large groups of people? Your books are being devoured by the mainstream.

James Redfield: We're all pretty much at the same place and these insights seem real to readers of the book because they are coming to all of us at the same time. The insights and the books put into words what so many people are already experiencing. It's archetypal in the sense that cultures as they mature and civilizations as they mature, naturally and archetypically go through these insights. The more materialistically secure we get, the more we want to know why we're here in the first place. The more we ask those questions, the more we begin to pull the information together. Human culture is reaching a point where it's beginning to understand the purposes behind its existence.

What are the deepest truths are in your work for yourself and others?

James Redfield: The most important idea is it's not as easy to open up to spiritual experience as we would like. There are some psychological breakthroughs that need to happen. Learning how not to control others and how not to control our lives so intensely, are two of those breakthroughs. We have to let go. That has been a spiritual truism for a long time. What we're putting together now is the psychological process involved in letting go, to understand the steps we have to go through inside to open up to our fullest spiritual potential.

The "Celestine View" encompasses a time when class, power, status, and property will no longer be motivating factors or definitions of success. When do you think this is going to take place?

James Redfield: It's a gradual evolution. In other words, right now our old paradigm or old world view is about creating material security to feel abundant, to feel taken care of, to have enough money, so we can take care of our children. In my view, this was a necessary step that human culture has had to go through and we're still going through it. But the fact is, we already technologically have the means to take care of everybody on the planet. The thing that stands in our way is the fear of scarcity. We have to evolve to a place where we no longer gain our self-image or status from controlling the means to material security. But we can only get there when we have another preoccupation, another reason for living beyond the need for material security. First, we've got to develop a spiritual culture on the planet and then we'll be too busy to fool with whose going to be in charge. There won't be any greed about it because life will be about something else. Again, it can't be centralized. It has to be something that comes from individual decisions made by individual persons.

How far are we from establishing a global unification of human awareness? Is that what excites you most about the future, this whole concept of global unification, of our awareness of becoming one?

James Redfield: I think that's the purpose of history. The purpose of our existence on the planet is to come to an agreement about what life is about from a spiritual perspective. We're still in a consensus making process—from which the new world view will fully emerge.

It seems to me that all religions have been about humankind finding relationship to oneness, to the higher self, to the inner seat of truth. If this is so, what do you think causes conflict and is still causing conflict between different religious groups? Does it go back to control?

James Redfield: Of course. What happens is all institutionalized forms of religion become dogmatic. They fall short because they don't continue to evolve an understanding. The people that gain personal power by being at the head of these institutions don't want them to change because if they change, they lose their personal power.

What do you feel are the reasons for this current shift in perception and awareness? Why do people really seem to be making a big leap now?

James Redfield: For the first time, we've entered a mass shift. We're not motivated by what other people tell us and what the authority figures in the culture want us to believe. We're motivated more by what we've come to understand based on our own experience. It's part of the maturing of human consciousness and it's happening very rapidly.

One example of how it's happening is synchronicity, or those so-called "coincidences" that are charged with meaning. A characteristic of synchronicity is that it excites us. It gives us a sense of our lives as an adventure unfolding. The whole idea of coming to spiritual awareness on the planet lies in realizing our lives are these very mysterious experiences. We're in an adventure here. There's no way we can feel bored if we stay in touch with these guiding coincidences.

We're fighting through a kind of materialistic cynicism where we think there are no miracles. And even those of us that believe there are sometimes have a problem intending for there to be more miracles in our lives—really holding that image and being open to the vision.

The important thing for us in our time period is developing an alternative to intellectuality as a way of relating to each other and the world. We're not content with doing that anymore.

You mention in The Celestine Prophecy *and also in the companion* Experiential Guide *that the competition for energy is the source of all conflict. How can we move away from competition towards cooperation? How can we move out of conflict?*

James Redfield: The first thing you do is get centered—developing a connection with the divine which keeps you in a state of love. We have two measures for our connection to the divine. One is love and one is a sense of buoyancy and lightness. These are two measures which are becoming very experientially understood. Staying in a positive relationship with others has to begin by staying in a state of love. Then if someone tries to steal our energy, it's theirs to have. We don't run out of energy, and we don't run out of status, because our status is inwardly defined rather than by those around us. It's the centeredness that gives us the energy to interact with people in a different way.

What are the primary steps for moving towards creativity rather than control?

James Redfield: It comes from realizing what our best creativity is, and once we maintain this interconnection and work through our control dramas, what happens is we discover a set of talents we have. We discover a kind of preparation our own life experience has given us—preparation to do something.

Is this like a calling, the old-fashioned concept of a calling?

James Redfield: That's right. It always comes, and it's our calling that energizes our existence and really amplifies the sense of adventure we have. We have to find a place to perform this calling and it comes synchronistically, just like everything else. If we can't actualize our calling in our jobs, then we move to some other place to perform it or we create our own work. It all happens synchronistically as long as we're not trying to control it with preconceived images of what it is. As we let go and let our highest self draw the conclusions, then we're going to move into a space where we're going to complete this calling.

As we become more aware and in touch with our calling, what we will find is that, at every level, every problem that exists, whether it's crime, hunger or our threatened environment, people are perfectly in place to change the way we do things, to bring a new truth. Everybody is in place synchronistically to make a difference. That's what is happening now and will continue to happen as more people get in touch with their true calling or mission in life.

You see a world where our bodies will ultimately transform into spiritual form, uniting this dimension of existence with the afterlife dimension, ending the cycle of birth and death. What do you sense this existence would be like?

James Redfield: It's going to be gradual. Just because we remove the veil between the two dimensions doesn't mean we aren't going to continue growing and learning and striving, and having missions and so on. What we're evolving to is ending this cycle of dying and being re-incarnated into a dense bodily form. What will happen is we will find ourselves in a very active culture like the one we're in now.

Then whole groups of people will become invisible to those vibrating at a lower level. In a recent interview with Whitley Strieber, he stated a similar concept, saying this multidimensional view of reality or awareness is something that is happening all of the time. It's here in front of us, yet it's something we're just now becoming aware of.

James Redfield: That's right. The most important element is staying in a state of love, so we have a world community using this interconnection of love from which springs all knowledge and from which springs our most creative path of helping the world. In community with each other, we can help each other redefine and expand our calling—exactly what it is we should be doing with our time here. It's a highly interpersonal world where we help each other as we make our dreams come true. The main factor determining whether we can reach that world or not is whether we can hold the vision in a very conscious and clear way, and project it outward with a creative prayer.

Sirona Knight, M.S., C.H.T. is a contributing editor for Magical Blend. *She is the author of* Greenfire: Making Love with the Goddess *and* Moonflower: Erotic Dreaming with the Goddess *(Llewellyn Worldwide). Michael Starwyn is a composer and author who lives in the Sierra Nevada Foothills. He has produced a series of self-help guided imagery tapes.*

Spirituality
Modern Mysticism: A Practical Approach

Dan Millman: Being a Peaceful Warrior

with Michael Peter Langevin and Mike Ferris

The night he met his mentor, Socrates, at a Berkeley gas station was an important one for Dan Millman and the many readers of his *Way of the Peaceful Warrior*. In his new book, *No Ordinary Moments* (HJ Kramer Inc., Tiburon, CA), Millman provides advice for turning intentions into action and learning to live in the present moment. Different from his two metaphysical novels, the new book is primarily, as Millman writes in the preface, a "guide to the way I teach and live."

Born in Los Angeles in 1946, Millman won the US Gymnastics Federal National Championship and the World Championship for trampoline before entering college. He was an international gymnastics competitor at the University of California at Berkeley, where he earned his BA in Psychology.

Besides *Way of the Peaceful Warrior*, Millman's other books include *The Warrior Athlete*, *Secret of the Peaceful Warrior*, and two children's books. In this interview, Millman explains the transformative process through which each individual must go in order to become a "peaceful warrior."

What do you mean by the title of your new book, No Ordinary Moments?

Dan Millman: In *Way of the Peaceful Warrior*, I wrote about a man being chased by two tigers. He leapt off a cliff to escape from the tigers and managed to hold onto a single vine that was hanging there. He saw two other tigers waiting below. Just then, two rats ran down the vine and started gnawing it above his hands. The man looked up and saw a strawberry growing on the face of the cliff. He plucked the strawberry and ate it, and how sweet it tasted!

That's really my approach to life. It tastes sweet when you recognize that this moment counts. That recognition keeps us from sleepwalking through life. It keeps us from letting life pass us by while we wait for our next sexual encounter, the next movie or whatever. It keeps us from always waiting for happiness.

In *No Ordinary Moments*, I wrote about a friend named Michael who was parking his car in Philadelphia when someone in a car parked right behind the space he was pulling into flashed their lights and honked their horn. Michael figured it must have been a mistake because there was a clear space, so he continued to pull in. Then, the fellow honked his horn again, and my friend got out of the car and went to the driver's side and said "Is there a problem?" At that point, the man in the car raised a shotgun right to Michael's face, who didn't know whether he'd be alive or dead the next instant. It was certainly no longer an ordinary day. The man said, "Get out of here," and Michael complied. As he drove away, he saw someone coming out of a liquor store with a gun in one hand and a satchel in the other. It became apparent that the fellow who had pulled the gun on him was a get-away driver whose escape would have been blocked if Michael had parked where he had intended. Whatever the reason for the incident, the fact that it happened reminded Michael that every moment is the moment of truth—that there are no ordinary moments.

In No Ordinary Moments, *you make the point that happiness is something projected from within rather than found outside one self.*

Dan Millman: Happiness is one of our most fundamental drives. Yet most of us only find symbols for happiness, not the state itself. We may think we want a love partner, a house, more money or a career, but behind all those things, we just want to feel happy.

Happiness—especially personal happiness—is a controversial topic, because it seems somehow offensive to be happy in a world filled with injustice and poverty. Well, there are always going to be good reasons to be unhappy in this world. There will always be inequities. Socrates once said, "You can choose to be reasonably unhappy, or you can choose to be unreasonably happy."

Happiness is not simply the *me generation's* search for personal fulfillment. It's the recognition that no miserable person is much good to anybody. I doubt Mother Theresa ever went off to work muttering, "Damn! I've got to go help those lepers today." She saw the face of Jesus in everyone. The Dalai Lama, whose country suffers from torture and atrocities of every kind, is always smiling, radiating, and tirelessly working for his people, for people everywhere.

I define happiness as the ability to radiate positive energy. Joseph Campbell spoke of "going with joy among the sorrows of the world." If you're happy, if you're radiating positive energy, you're more effective in what you do. Happiness is not waiting to feel good "one day when I've learned these techniques, when I've struck it rich, or when I've found my soul mate." Happiness is now or never.

How does one deal with a great loss? The loss of a loved one, for example?

Dan Millman: I haven't lost a loved one recently, so to be honest, I can only hypothesize about that. My sense is that I'll cry when I lose a loved one. I'll feel sad. I'll feel grief. All those feelings are like the waves in the ocean. They come and they go, and they're totally natural. I believe in accepting one's emotions. But at the same time that I experience these feelings, I will also do my best to radiate as much energy as I can to be a support for other people involved, rather than just collapsing and becoming an energy drain.

Talking about happiness tends to suggest repression, suppression or playing pretend—like wearing a happy face. What I'm talking about is deeper than that. It takes courage to radiate energy despite what's going on.

Your books emphasize the issues of living. What are your feelings about the other side, on dying and the mysteries of the unknown?

Dan Millman: These issues, as you stated in your question, are "unknown." Ultimately, there's not much we can say about death, though we can philosophize about it. We have near-death experiences and reports from mystics who speak with some authority from their deep meditations, such as the Tibetans who talk about the Bardo: the space between lives.

In one sense I'm looking forward to my death, not out of any negative view, but because I will finally have the opportunity to see this facet of mystery. Death is an opportunity to find out if what all the spiritual masters have been telling us is correct. I understand that if they're incorrect we get our money back.

On the other hand, I believe we're here to live out the longest, healthiest life we can because every day is another day to learn, another day to teach, another day to serve and discover. In God's script, you never know what's going to be around the corner when the page turns.

My own speculation is that the state of consciousness we've developed during life will be the one that we experience at our moment of death. Whether, as some scientists say, we finally just flash out and experience a final hallucination or if we indeed are going through a space between lives, people who are unconscious and fearful in their lives will experience a degree of unconsciousness and fear when they die. Even if they see a tunnel to the light they won't know what to do with it.

Some of your critics have labeled you a "commercialized Castaneda." How do you respond to that'?

Dan Millman: I appreciate critics, but I don't believe there's anything wrong with earning a living from my books and teaching. As Joan Baez once said, "I am not for voluntary poverty; I'm against involuntary poverty." It costs money to live in the world. For example, giving my children the best education I can is important to me. I don't see money as inconsistent with living a full, spiritual life.

What about the comparison between you and Castaneda?

Dan Millman: Castaneda probably had some level of influence, but I wouldn't say he was terribly influential. I don't know Carlos personally. I met him once, briefly, a long time ago. I did read his first three books when they came out, and I enjoyed them. I didn't read his subsequent books. The comparison probably comes from the title of my book, *Way of the Peaceful Warrior*. I've been a martial artist for years, so the term "warrior" is not new to me. I know one spiritual teacher who is also an expert martial artist, and he was offended by Castaneda's use of the term "warrior" because the natives of the part of Sonora, Mexico that Castaneda writes about don't have an indigenous martial art. In other words, the term "warrior" is not indigenous to that culture. He feels Castaneda implanted it. All I can say is that I believe Castaneda inspired many people, and his books certainly reflect some deep wisdom. But Castaneda's experiences took place in the desert. I found Socrates in a gas station in Berkeley. Our teachers are everywhere; daily life is the arena. You don't have to go elsewhere.

You say although we're not responsible for what happens in the world around us, we are responsible for how we deal with it. How do you contrast this theory with those who say that we create our reality?

Dan Millman: To say you create your reality may be absolutely true on the transcendental level. The question is, who is the operational "you" that creates the reality? If you are your divine, expanded self, then sure, you create it. But the little piddling ego, thinking that it goes around creating all these things—no, I don't think so. Rather than create realities, what I think we do is create meaning. What happens just happens until we view it subjectively and give it meaning. As infants, we are ignorant; we have no meanings. Then, as we grow, we create meaning out of associations, interpretations, and beliefs. We create a subjective sense of what otherwise just is.

Once, about a year ago, a gigantic tree fell on four cars outside a training hall where I was teaching. Having a tree fall on their cars was an inconvenience for all four people, but each reacted differently. The most interesting reaction was from a woman who paced back and forth asking herself, "What's the lesson in this?" Then she saw a big raven fly by the window. She may have been reading too much Carlos Castaneda because she said, "Oh, that's an omen! It must mean I shouldn't have been here today!" That was her "lesson." If I was going to find a lesson in the experience it would be: Can you be happy anyway? Again, that doesn't mean putting on a happy face and pretending to be happy. It means finding a way to stay positive while honoring one's emotions.

Take two people who get hit by a car and are in the hospital. To one it's a complete catastrophe, to the other it's a challenge. In that sense, their realities are different. They create their realities in terms of their minds' filters. But they both got hit by a car that they didn't necessarily create. If somebody has a cold and they've been staying up late, eating a bunch of food that toxifies them and not taking care of themselves, then there certainly is an element of responsibility for "creating" the cold.

In No Ordinary Moments, *you write about the effect of diet on people's lives. What are your theories on diet?*

Dan Millman: A fellow told me, "I once had three theories about child rearing. Now I have three children and no theories." I used to have a lot of theories about diet. Now I don't. What I have, instead, are principles, or foundation elements, that I've come to live by. Diet and exercise are both foundation elements in our spiritual disciplines. For example, each day, over time, I've simplified my diet to the point where I recognize food as a kind of medicine. A dessert can be medicine too—for the soul. But I don't have any hard and fast rules. I believe it's better not to impose one's philosophy on the way one eats, or exercises, or on one's sexual life, or anything else. We have to trust our own instincts and respect our own individual directions.

There are several theories making the rounds that human beings are undergoing a fundamental change. Michael Murphy, for example, speaks of the psychic evolution of human beings. Do you feel that the species is undergoing that dramatic an evolution?

Dan Millman: Some of us are fascinated with physical powers out of boredom with life as it is, but I'm not personally that fascinated with physical powers or changes. If we were suddenly able to fly, we'd be ecstatic, but I suspect we would get as bored with that as we do with any other miracle. Pretty soon we'd be saying "Damn! I'm late. I wish I could fly faster!" I prefer to concentrate on everyday things.

The ability to see is a miracle. Imagine a race of blind people speculating about what it would be like to actually see the things around them. The gift of sight would be incredible for them, and yet we take it for granted.

I think our most significant evolution will happen in the arena of consciousness, in our expanded understanding of who we are. Though this view may differ from Michael Murphy's area of interest, I honor his work.

Another popular theory that's been around for a while concerns dramatic changes in the earth that will require humanity to alter its behavior. Do you have feelings about what you expect to take place on the planet or with society?

Dan Millman: Yes, I do. Many people talk about polar shifts and their concern about where safe ground is going to be. While they're worrying about that, they may cross the street and get hit by a truck. I'm not going to look for safe ground; I want to be where the action is. That's where the excitement is, where I can make a difference.

My own sense of earth changes is that they're already happening right in front of our noses. Edgar Cayce wrote about Atlantis rising. I think it is—in the form of EST, Silva Mind Control, Scientology, and Neuro-Linguistic Programming. These are all technologies straight out of Atlantis. Psychic healing, crystals—it's happening right now, but never quite the way we expect. Cayce also talked about countries changing. If you look at an old globe, there is a huge block called the "Union of Soviet Socialist Republics" and an other called "East and West Germany." They no longer exist. They have "vanished."

There may certainly be earth changes because the earth does reflect human consciousness to a large degree. We influence it through nuclear testing and so on. So, it's back to the question, "Do we create our own reality?" I do think we are creating the earth's reality to a large extent, but I don't think it's going to be in polar shifts. I think it's going to be a shift in consciousness that may be more radical than anybody anticipated.

We occupy a territory that we basically stole from the native peoples. Now we're becoming Native Americans. It breaks my heart to think about what our ancestors did and to see how the Native American people have been scattered to the four winds, and yet their spirit is going to live on. It has to if we are going to survive on this Earth.

Feminine consciousness and the balance between men and women are also parts of our polar shift in consciousness, but again, I think we're misinterpreting what's going on. Feminism has nothing to do with putting female bodies in the White House. What it has to do with is putting female consciousness in the males and more male consciousness in the females, to balance the anima and animus, in Jung's terms, and become whole.

What are your feelings about religion's role in this polar shift in consciousness? Traditional religions are certainly going through all sorts of changes.

Dan Millman: Everything has its place. All religion, I believe, is about the loving quest for the presence of spirit. The approach to life that I describe as the way of the peaceful warrior embraces the heart of all religions. I don't mean that as a platitude. I think it literally does. Christian Mysticism, Sufism, Buddhism, and Shintoism all touch upon the same thing even though they approach it differently. Different fingers pointing at the moon, as Bruce Lee used to say.

The problem is one of beliefs. There are two kinds of beliefs: conscious and unconscious. Unconscious beliefs get mistaken as the "absolute truth," which means that anybody who doesn't agree with them is wrong. People kill and fight and die over unconscious beliefs that they mistake for "truth." That's the root of fundamentalism. We usually think of fundamentalism as connected to religions, but it also happens in martial arts schools, acting schools, or wherever we view our way as the only or best way for everyone. Unconscious beliefs tend to isolate and divide.

Conscious beliefs allow a certain respect for other people's processes. Bringing our beliefs into consciousness allows us to say, "This is my belief. This is true for me. It doesn't have to be true for you." I think we are ready to move beyond belief and go with our own experience. It's not enough to believe in God. We need to develop within ourselves an unconditional feeling that we are okay. To do that, we need to re-think who the "I" is. When you say "I am going to my house," you know what that means. Semantically, that seems pretty clear to all parties. The "I" is separate from the house. If you were not separate from the house you couldn't say you were going to it. But if you say, "I feel good about my body," then I'd have to ask who the "I" is that's making the statement. Our language does reflect our meanings and in some sense our reality. Maybe we're not the body. Maybe we're the mind. But you can also say, "My mind feels sharp today." Who is the "me" talking about "my mind?" We also can say that maybe we're the soul talking about the mind. Maybe we're not the body or mind. But you can also say "My soul is uplifted." Well, if we're not the soul, what are we? That is an important question worth considering—could it be that we are awareness itself?

Is there anything else you'd like to add?

Dan Millman: What it ultimately comes down to is to stop second-guessing ourselves. If we make a mistake, okay, learn from it and go on. That requires trusting the process of our own lives. In spite of the world's difficulties we read about in the newspaper, in spite of the difficulties in our own lives, everything is going as it needs to, step-by-step. Recognizing that requires a larger awareness, an ability to see the bigger picture. When we step into space and look at the earth, we regain our senses—our sense of humor, our sense of compassion, our sense of understanding. It can be useful to step outside our usual limits and view life from the eyes of the heart. As we begin to think less and feel more, we may even get a glimpse of life from the eyes of God. And then we will know for certain what I suggest in my newest book—that there are no ordinary moments.

Spirituality
Modern Mysticism: A Practical Approach

Larry Dossey, M.D.: Prayer Most Powerful

with Jerry Snider

A lifelong student of religion, philosophy, meditation, parapsychology and quantum physics, Larry Dossey, MD is one of an increasing number of medical professionals who do not believe that science and spirituality are irreconcilably separated. Though as a writer and international lecturer Dossey often focuses on the fascinating fringe of medical science, the doctor himself is far from the fringe. His professional credentials are impeccable, ranging from former Chief of Staff of Humana Medical City Dallas to current co-chairman of the newly established Panel on Mind/Body Interventions, Office of Alternative Medicine for the National Institutes of Health.

Dr. Dossey is the author of *Space, Time and Medicine; Beyond Illness; Recovering the Soul;* and *Meaning and Medicine.* In 1988 he was invited to deliver the annual Mahatma Gandhi Memorial Lecture in New Delhi, the only physician ever invited to do so.

Dr. Dossey discusses his most recent book, *Healing Words, The Power of Prayer and the Practice of Medicine* (HarperSanFrancisco) in which he brings to light one of science's buried treasures—over a hundred carefully performed studies that provide clear evidence that prayer produces a significant effect in laboratory experiments.

What led you to write a book on prayer?

Larry Dossey: I must say that I was dragged into it kicking and screaming. I was a typical physician educated to believe in things that have some apparent physical basis like medication, surgery, and radiation.

I had my come-uppance back around 1987 or 1988, when I discovered a study that really looked like good science. It showed that prayer made a major difference for heart attack patients at a coronary care unit. This study came out of San Francisco General Hospital. It was what is called a randomized, prospective double-blind study in which a prayed-for group did terrifically better on several accounts than an unprayed-for group. I was disturbed by the results. Did this mean there was something I should be doing that I wasn't? So I began to poke around the literature, looking for other studies that might corroborate or invalidate this. I was stunned at what I found:

There are easily 130 studies that show that if you take prayer into the laboratory under controlled situations, it does something remarkable, not just to human beings but to bacteria, fungi, germinating seeds, rats, mice, and baby gerbils. One of the things that intrigued me about the studies was how this material has been marginalized. You certainly don't hear anything about these studies in medical school. But after considering the evidence, I decided to incorporate prayer rituals into my medical practice. It seemed to me that not to do so was the equivalent of withholding a potent medication or a needed operation.

So these studies are all out there, but they're not well known?

Larry Dossey: They've been gathering dust on the sidelines of medical research for a couple of decades at least.

Why do you think that is?

Larry Dossey: Most physicians in medical science won't even look at prayer because it doesn't fit their theories. Well, if a pet theory doesn't work maybe it's time to get rid of it. The whole point of the scientific method is to guard against self-delusion. Refusing to give the evidence a fair hearing is not the way you play science. It's true we don't have a clue about how prayer works, but when penicillin was first introduced, we didn't have a clue about how it worked either. All I'm saying is that it's time we looked at the data. I was fascinated by the clarity of a lot of these experiments. Some of them were extremely clean, well designed, and very precise. And well over half of these 130 studies show statistical significance that something major is going on with prayer. A lot of physicians would like to write it off as placebo effect, but that's difficult to do considering that bacteria, fungi and germinating seeds aren't generally considered to be susceptible to suggestion.

What has been the reaction to your book from the medical world?

Larry Dossey: Well, it's interesting. I talk to a lot of doctors in the course of my work, in hospitals and medical schools. There are two reactions.

One is a public reaction and one is a private reaction. The public reaction is to look at this data and just be silent about it. It's odd presenting this material to a medical school; all the physicians just sit there silently. The interesting thing is that, by and large, they don't object to the data. But neither do they stand up and cheer.

That's the public response. The private response is entirely different. Doctors approach me on the side and imply that they sort of hope that this turns out to be true. They write letters that read like carbon copies of each other: "I attended your talk when you were here, and I don't have any trouble with your proposals, but if I stood up for what you talked about, I would never get another promotion, I'd never get another research grant..." One even said, "This situation is killing me."

The good news, according to your book, is that because prayer works at a distance and because a sacred attitude seems just as important as a "Our Father who art..." you can use prayer without making a big deal of it.

Larry Dossey: The fact that prayer is nonlocal—that it functions at a distance and that spatial separation doesn't diminish the affect—means that it doesn't have to be intrusive. You don't have to visit your own religious or spiritual views on the patient. In fact, you don't even have to be in the presence of the patient.

You take a wide view of what prayer is. A lot of what you're calling prayer, I think of as visualization or meditation. How do you describe prayer?

Larry Dossey: Let me tell you what prayer is not. I object to the way that we have defined prayer in this Western, Christianized culture as somehow talking out loud to a male cosmic parent figure, who basically prefers being addressed in English. That definition is extremely limiting. If you go to the Orient and look at what goes on in Buddhist cultures, you find that Buddhists pray like nuts. They go through their lives twirling prayer wheels. Buddhism, however, is not a theistic religion; they don't even believe in God, but they believe that their prayers are answered.

So right away I think there's cross-cultural evidence that you need to rethink the presence of a personal God in the prayer loop. I think what is important are qualities of consciousness like caring, compassion, empathy and love. That's what seem to make the studies work. When you take them away, the studies don't work. In fact, if you flip these empathic, warm feelings in the prayer experiments to the negative, and the person doing the praying generates hatred or negativity, frequently the subject is affected. In experiments bacteria died and plants withered.

And outside of that, you say that there's no wrong or right way to pray, because it's an individual connection with the absolute.

Larry Dossey: Yes. One of the things that causes me immense concern about this so-called New Age we're supposed to be living in is the formula approach. You find a lot of books by well meaning people who get very specific about strategies and imagery. But I think that if you try to get prayer technique from a book, you're asking for big trouble. A person's prayer strategies should be in sync with their innate temperament. Extroverts are much more at home with the graphic go-get-em, in-your-face, aggressive prayer imagery. Introverts are more comfortable with a let-it-be, Thy-will-be-done, may-the-best-thing-happen approach. If you try to get an introvert to pray according to an extroverted standard, they will very likely become discouraged. Where this really gets to be a problem is when they start to feel guilty and think there's something wrong with them because they don't fit the authority's formula. To me this is metaphysical malpractice in action.

What you just addressed is, to me, the most liberating aspect of Healing Words. *The truth is, whenever I pray I get caught in a labyrinth of irreconcilable images between an anthropomorphic "it," and an ineffable "something." Although I find it easy to pray for specific results for other people, I always feel guilty praying for my own health. Your book said, "Stop worrying." It made me accept what I already knew—being still in a sacred attitude is enough.*

Larry Dossey: What your comment raises for me is the question, "What do we need to expect of prayer?" There's a quote by Manly P. Hall who says, "There is a type of person in whose mind God is always getting mixed up with vitamins." His point is that vitamins and God are not identical; they're two different hierarchical dimensions. When people forget this they treat prayer like a vitamin. You want to be healthier? Take a vitamin.

My personal feeling is that it's okay to use imagery, visualization, and prayer for a specific goal. That's what petitionary prayer is all about—praying for something for yourself. If the cancer goes away, if the AIDS is cured, that's a blessing. We should be thankful for that. But the potential payoff for prayer is far more glorious. It allows us to reach out, independent of spatial separation. Studies have shown that prayer can range back and forth into the past and the future. This says that there's something about who we are that's nonlocal in space and time, which means that something about us must be omnipresent, infinite, immortal, and eternal. In other words, prayer is the big cure for the big disease; it cuts through the superiority of death. The lesson of prayer is that there's something more. The benefit of this recognition dwarfs whether or not your particular physical problem gets better or not. I hope it does, but if that doesn't happen, you just may have to settle for immortality.

Tell us about how prayer can affect events in the past.

Larry Dossey: If I get locked up in the looney bin for anything in this book, it's going to be that. There are actually laboratory experiments that show if an event happens at the quantum level, and if that event is not observed by a living being, then it's not fixed, even though we presume that it's already happened. What they indicate is that if an event is not fixed, then an observer may later be able to use his consciousness to influence the outcome of the event *when* it is observed. This sounds like witchcraft—the ability of the mind to reach back into the past and influence events that are already supposed to have happened.

The experiments involve random event generators and they've been done by physicist Helmut Schmidt and Robert Jahn's group at Princeton, among others. I don't want to get too esoteric here but let me give you an example: The random event generator is spitting out events, half of them are above a certain line and half are below. This is random distribution of whatever you're trying to measure, let's say radioactive decay. So you've got the random event generator going and its events are being recorded on a magnetic tape of some sort. If not otherwise influenced, half of the events are in the positive direction and half are in the negative direction. The way the experiment is set up is that *after* the REG has already done its thing, a so-called operator tries to influence the distribution of the events by pushing them either in the positive or negative direction. The experiments show that, statistically speaking, the operator can will a change in direction. Remember, this is done after the fact but before the record is examined. The experiments also show that if somebody looks at the tape before the operator tries to skew the information, there is no statistical affect.

Now, what does this have to do with health? Well, science is heading toward the view that disease originates at the quantum level. Since these laboratory experiments show that a person can reach back into the past and affect events at the quantum level even though they're supposed to have already happened, this seems to open the possibility that we might use our consciousness to reach back into our pasts and skew our quantum events in a positive direction toward health rather than illness. How do we do that? By thinking positive thoughts, by simply saying, "Thy will be done, may the best thing happen." We don't need to know the ins and outs of the origins of the disease. The studies in nonspecific imagery show that you don't have to know the biochemical pathway business in order to influence the outcome in a positive direction.

In our culture, God tends to be regarded as this big, nice power. But "nice" isn't really sufficient for God. You point out in Healing Words *that in other times and in other cultures, there was a recognition that there is a great paradox, a great power that we can't understand.*

Larry Dossey: Right. So let's emphasize the mystery. There is something about this that we can't seem to wrap our minds around with total understanding. People have arisen in this culture who do acknowledge the paradox. Probably the most famous is Carl Jung, who talked about the importance of the light and the shadow going together. You also see this in the Bible, but people don't seem to notice it. There's a chapter in the forty-fifth Book of Isaiah that says, "I am the Lord and there is none else. I create light and make darkness. I create good and evil." I mean, there it is. But when people want to claim their inner divinity, the God within, and so on, they seem to think these days that that's just the equivalent of having the nice stuff. It isn't. You get the whole enchilada if you want to claim your inner divinity. If you want to say that something about you is absolute, you get it all. There's nothing left outside the absolute. If there were, it would not be the absolute.

I think you see this in the lives of some of the God-realized saints and mystics. Frequently, their health histories are just atrocious. They die of some of the most dreadful diseases. So being God-realized is no guarantee of having perfect health. You get a lot more in the bargain than just the nice things. If we want to talk spirituality, then we're going to have to enlarge what we mean in terms of the impact of spirituality on our existence because it certainly involves the shadow as well as the light.

Your book has some interesting historical oddities. Would you tell us about the "Snap Diagnosticians?"

Larry Dossey: Yes. The faculty members of the great medical schools of Europe in the late 1700s and early 1800s would play this game of just trying to come up with a diagnosis with practically no information on the patient. Sometimes they would just look at a picture of the patient and make a diagnosis based on that. Napoleon's favorite doctor used this method. I think these fabulous diagnosticians were using nonlocal mental capabilities. Doctors today don't even want to talk about this possibility even though many of these diagnoses were quite successful.

You also tell a story about the explorer De Vaca that would certainly liven up the history books.

Larry Dossey: That story is very illuminating. It portrays what can happen if we are willing to go through the shadow. De Vaca was shipwrecked. He and two shipmates dug a pit to escape the cannibals, covered themselves up and stayed there three days, dug themselves out, and all three of these guys emerged from the pit with the power to heal. And these were big time healings. It saved their skin. The only reason they were able to walk halfway across the United States and finally arrive in Mexico, where they were rescued, was because the word of their fabulous healing ability went ahead of them. The Indians brought their sick by the tens of thousands and these guys healed them. So there is a powerful possibility for incredible transformation if we're willing to endure the darkness.

Probably the only thing more incredible than the fact that there actually is an Office of Alternative Medicine within the National Institutes of Health is how it came into being. Could you fill us in?

Larry Dossey: Yes. In 1992, Congress established the Office of Alternative Medicine within the National Institutes of Health, which really is the most powerful medical research body in the world. One of the senators, Tom Harkin of Iowa, was one of these guys who could go through two boxes of Kleenex in a day from a runny nose and allergy. Then one of his friends told him to try bee pollen. Imagine this prestigious senator eating handfuls of bee pollen. He said it was like somebody had turned a switch on in his body. The drainage stopped and he got well. This really got his attention.

A friend of Harkin, Representative Berkley Bedell, developed prostate cancer, had conventional treatment in this country, the cancer came back, and he tapped into the underground network and went off to Canada and did something alternative and strange, came back, and claimed he was cured. He then went to Harkin and said, "Hey, listen. It's a tragedy that the American people don't have access to these very effective, very cheap therapies "

From these two experiences, Harkin decided that the NIH, whether they liked it or not, should be investigating something other than drugs and surgery. He's in a powerful position; he is chairman of the Senate Appropriations Committee, which controls the funding for—guess what?—The National Institutes of Health. So he has the purse strings in his hand. And he said, "You *will* do this, otherwise we're going to cut off funding." That was basically the power play involved.

So the Office of Alternative Medicine was set up by law. I happen to be the co-chairman, along with Dr. Jeanne Achterberg and Dr. James Gordon of the Panel of Mind/Body Intervention and have been centrally involved in this office. Our mandate is to first of all assess the scientific status, such as it may be, for probably most of the alternative therapies that your readers have ever heard of. Practically everything's on the table for one of these seven panels. And also we're charged with making recommendations for funding specific research studies in various areas. Approximately twenty studies have been funded, looking at various alternative measures. This is critically important. This has never happened in this culture before.

This is a fabulous window of opportunity to look at therapies that have not been honored—everything from herbal medicine to homeopathy to meditation to therapy with touch. If you can believe this, my panel was charged with looking at the evidence for prayer and spiritual healing. So there are really no boundaries about what we can and can't look at. The criteria is: Does it work? What's the proof? Are there any side effects? And what's the cost effectiveness? Some therapies will rise to the top and some won't. If readers want to help this project along, which I would highly urge, they can write their congressmen and congresswomen and tell them that this new Office of Alternative Medicine exists, because it's so new that a lot of congress people don't even know it's out there. And, also, readers could advise sufficient funding for this office, because if it doesn't get funded liberally, it's not going to be able to do its job as well. And if anyone believes in the power of prayer, they might pray for the continuation of this endeavor.

I understand you met with Hillary Clinton. What did you tell her?

Larry Dossey: Actually, I testified to Hillary Rodham Clinton's committee that we need to stop being so shy in the alternative health care business. There is a tremendous body of evidence that some of these therapies are very, very effective and, if we're going to play science, we need to honor all the data. I just made a plea for playing science honestly.

I also had an interesting exchange with Hillary. I was struck by the speeches that she gave earlier this year, after her father's death, in which she used the phrase "the politics of meaning." She was asking people to get involved in the political process to make this stuff mean something to people. She was crucified in Washington for this, but the speech prompted me to send her a copy of my last book, *Meaning and Medicine*. I sent it with a brief letter saying that it looks like you're trying to do in politics what I'm trying to do with my profession, that we're both talking about the paramount importance of meaning in people's lives. This was a presumptuous thing to do—as if all she has to do is sit around and read her own mail and read books. But she wrote back saying, "Yes, we're on the same wavelength and we're going to make a difference. We're going to see change here." I was deeply moved by this. I think Hillary Clinton is the most precious thing I've seen emerge in Washington in a very long time. I don't line up completely with everything she's proposed, but this woman brings an openness and an integrity to the process that I really find refreshing.

I know we're almost out of time, so I would like to try to summarize everything we've been talking about. Most people, in one way or another, are looking for Utopia. They're looking for fabulous outcomes and the nice stuff. I'm no different than anyone else in that regard. But if you look at the origin of the word "Utopia" comes from Greek words meaning "not in a place." Utopia is nonlocal. And if people are able to follow the reasoning behind this concept of non locality, they'll realize that if something's nonlocal, it's omnipresent, which means that it's everywhere. So that means that Utopia is right here already. And if something is nonlocal with regard to space, it's also nonlocal with respect to time, which is why Utopia is not only right here, but it's right now. So at some dimension of the psyche, we're living in perfection. Utopia is here and it's now. The recognition of this has been called, in various spiritual traditions, enlightenment, which means waking up to what is, to what is already present. Although I'm much in favor of using prayer practically to achieve some nice outcome, I think the best lesson is that it can help us get in touch with what is already present. That's the starting and ending point of *Healing Words*.

Spirituality
Modern Mysticism: A Practical Approach

Van Ault: The Joy of Spiritual Service

One of life's unavoidable assignments is learning how to take care of yourself. Understanding your own needs and how to respond appropriately to them is an essential step in living as an empowered individual. You've taken that step if you're in the process of discovering how to release stress, nurture and respect yourself, communicate clearly, and most importantly, to awaken and express the love and compassion within you. As that love and compassion naturally unfolds, so does the desire to share it through service to others. Spiritual service is one of the most joyful and educational aspects of personal growth you can experience.

Wherever you are in your own inner voyage, there is some way that you can serve to bring a steadying support to someone else who is ready for it. There is a need for all of us to contribute in this way, because there are so many illusions to confront on the route to enlightenment. The path may be bumpy, and stumbling is all too common, particularly during critical moments. Spiritual service enters the scenario through the time-honored tradition of one person extending the hand of kindness to the person coming down the path behind him. Information is exchanged, directions are given, insights are shared, and strength is imparted. You become the signpost, through your own presence, to that person's next step in the journey towards wholeness.

Anyone can serve. You never have to pass any test of spiritual "correctness." You need no special intelligence; you don't need to have resolved all your personal problems, nor do you have to be fully healed or enlightened. If you had to be perfect, the world would be in far worse shape than it is, and no sharing of support would ever occur. The "attitudinal healing" school of thought is a good case in point. In attitudinal healing, people who are seriously ill reach out to assist others in the same situation. Those who give such support have reported that it helps them work through their own issues, and gives them strength for the road ahead. Many addiction recovery programs (e.g. Alcoholics Anonymous) encourage each participant to have a sponsor who assists him in walking the "twelve steps" to healing. The addicts help other addicts, illustrating just how egalitarian the power of spiritual service really is.

While you may find yourself drawn to special outlets for your energy, service doesn't have to be situated in a special, separate compartment from the rest of your affairs. You can integrate your spiritual service into things you already do. Right where you are—in the neighborhood where you live, in the school you attend, the company where you work, or the spiritual community you join is the place to put your love into action. An awakened heart has a way of pulling you towards the place of your most appropriate expression anyway. There is a perfect place of service for everyone, and when you find it you'll notice that it fits you as well as your most comfortable clothing, and that it brings you an inner satisfaction you may have experienced in no other way.

You can render spiritual service without even trying to do anything. You can just be yourself, making your way along the path, when someone brushes up against your little light, receives it, and is transformed. For example, a close friend of mine passed an acquaintance on the street one day, and though they didn't speak audibly, she silently blessed him. Weeks later, she received a letter from him saying, "I don't know what you did to me on the street that day, but I think you're a very powerful person." He explained that moments after that non-verbal encounter, he realized that his drug addiction had "nothing further to offer me," and he immediately went into recovery.

My friend never knew he was an addict, and had no ideas about intervening in that process. She was just silently, actively generating the love that always glowed within her, and it was effortless. The moment that she shared that energy was obviously a time of great receptivity for that man, and he allowed it to catalyze him in the most appropriate direction. Incidents like this, I believe, occur all the time although we don't recognize them or discuss them.

It's important to realize that spiritual service is not a new, improved way to give all your power away to the external world, or to lose yourself in pleasing everyone else. Service and codependence are not the same. It's not appropriate to use service as an escape from your own challenges, for neglecting your individual growth process is a dis-service to yourself and all who come into contact with you. A woman I know, for example, regularly volunteered to do massage work with dying cancer patients, and she experienced a considerable charge from the intoxicatingly powerful role of caregiver. Unfortunately, the way she played that role distracted her from working on her own personal issues, which eventually erupted and brought conflict and grief directly to those she thought she was "helping." The highest service is generated through those who take care of themselves, and remain in integrity with their own journey.

Service doesn't involve sacrificing your strength, only sharing it. True spiritual service will not bring harm to you. You won't be contributing anything by acting out the destructive ego-dramas of the saint, the martyr, the rescuer, the doormat, or anything else that undermines your own well-being. Conversely, you set a dynamic example for others by respecting your own needs and attending to them lovingly. Then, whatever you give can unfold from genuine self-esteem and self-authority, and perhaps stimulate the same qualities in those around you.

Service can be exalting and humbling at the same time. You may find that as you serve, you're doing work that doesn't match the world's spiritual pictures, or doesn't jibe with your own image of yourself. A friend of mine—a very highly paid, successful professional—was a student at an ashram and was invited to give some service in, of all places, the kitchen, on cleanup duty. He scheduled some time off from his lucrative work to participate in this task, and reported afterwards, to his surprise, the most gentle feeling of joy and bliss. Yes, from washing dishes! It probably wouldn't have mattered what he did at the ashram, because he approached it with an open heart, and it awakened his natural generosity, which, of course, uplifted him.

As always, anything you give out comes back to you, multiplied. Every bit of service you contribute is energy invested in your own well-being; it always returns to support you, one way or another, upholding, at the very least, your highest sense of identity. It encourages the best in you to emerge, increasing your sense of wellness and joy, and diminishes the pull of the denser aspects of your existence. By your spiritual service, you are the one who benefits.

The Need for Non-Attachment

Non-attachment is essential when you go about serving. Sometimes when you extend the hand of compassion, it is refused. Not everyone can accept love, and many people would rather maintain the status quo of limitation than be nurtured toward transformation. Or, they can't recognize the value in something, and so they sidestep it. For example, I remember once offering to a student the gift of some special, private training that I felt would have assisted her through a personal crisis. She declined the gift, saying, "I don't have time" (which was not true) and soon thereafter, her life plunged into a dramatic, downward spiral. It wasn't my place to demand that she accept something she obviously didn't want. It would have helped no one for me to insist that she take it, or to view her refusal as a personal insult. I had the feeling that my service had been rendered just through standing in that gateway, and inviting her to enter. That is really all that anyone can do in such a situation. To do more is to venture into control, which is frustrating and energy draining at best.

Non-attachment is your best protection against burnout. Non-attachment frees you from the compulsion to change the world, and allows you to just plant your seed and keep moving along the path of your own journey. As you eventually spiral back around to that place of planting, you may find the seed has sprouted, and you can celebrate its growth. If the seed has withered, you can relax in the knowledge that you gave what you could, and you need not be devastated by the outcome. Besides, there are more seeds to plant.

You'll know you're moving away from genuine service into martyrdom when you start feeling burned out. The planet really doesn't need any more exhausted, resentful people depleting themselves for the "greater good." If you find this happening in your area of contribution, re-evaluate the motives for your efforts, and see if you can find a way to realign the situation so that it works for you. There are always times to withdraw from active service, for your own rest, renewal, and reflection.

A sure clue that your ego has usurped the intended spiritual service is when you are attached to receiving loud, public recognition. Non-attachment allows you to release your gift, and that empowers it to come back to you in its own way and time. You don't have to demand that your reward—which is simply the energy returning via the law of "what you give comes back multiplied"—take a specific form.

Give it some room, and see what surprises drop into your lap. Let the power of love expand in your reality in its own way and time, and then watch how much you enjoy it!

Service on the Inner Planes

Spiritual service can take place on the outer or inner planes of consciousness. The outer planes include the physical-material world, and the mental and emotional realms. The inner planes are where the higher selves of all humanity are connected, a realm of transcendence where there is no material form, only energy. You can do your work strictly on the inner planes, have as profound an experience, and give as much (or more) service as you can on the outer planes. No one ever has to know you're active in this area, and there is a real point of departure from the ego's clamor for recognition.

A man I know works exclusively on the inner planes, through prayer and meditation, serving the souls of all who have died. He clips the obituary columns and sends light to each individual who has made that transition. When asked why he does this, and what he gets out of it, he replies, simply: "I'd want someone to do that for me if I died. Besides, it decreases my fear of death, and I feel more love every time I do it. I enjoy it." The fact that he finds it rewarding without any applause or recompense is a good sign he's doing his perfect form of service.

Other people I know pick out a certain animal species and send energy to its collective consciousness for its survival and well-being. I know some who focus on specific eco-regions, or particular trees, plants, or flowers. Still others will make outer-plane challenges, such as diseases or social conditions or even the earth in general, the recipients of their continuous, inner-plane service. They get no ovations for their work; they just keep stepping along, in the spirit of love and compassion, doing what is the appropriate thing for them to do.

Yes, spiritual service is simply the appropriate thing to do. That attitude seems to uphold all forms of genuine spiritual service, whether it's on the inner- or outer-planes, no matter what the circumstance being addressed. It is, after all, the radiant power of love within us which impels us to serve. And it is the nature of love to expand its influence through contribution. If we can open an avenue through our activities for love to escape into the world, it can accomplish things that we, in our personal, fragmented egos, never dreamed of, and, in the process, bring more meaning and joy to our lives than we could have hoped for.

Questions For Contemplation

1. What particular activities do you engage in that make a difference in the lives of others, or the well-being of the planet? What is your individual method of outreach?

2. Are you able to see the impact of your service, and how important is it to you to see it? What reward-mental, emotional, spiritual or physical-have you experienced through service? Is it commensurate with the energy you've put into it?

3. Is it possible to serve through refraining from participation in certain activities, attitudes, or beliefs, or by withdrawing support for same? How do you do that?

4. How have you been served by the spiritual support of others: (a) on a one-to-one basis, (b) in group contexts, and (c) in a larger, collective and social level? Did you recognize the service at the time it was rendered, or did it take you some time to perceive it? Did you acknowledge receiving it, and its value to you, and if so, how? Does acknowledging the service of others contribute anything to you?

(Magical Blend issue #35)

Spirituality
The Spirit of Diversity

Marlo Morgan: The Aboriginal Spirit

A Westerner's Walkabout

I originally went to Australia to get involved with a health care group. Then one day I happened to witness a group of people sniffing leaded gasoline out of containers. They were getting drunk from the fumes, falling over and so forth, but I didn't do anything. I just sat there and watched. A couple of days later, our clinic was notified about a young aborigine who had died from respiratory failure due to lead toxicity. At the morgue I recognized the face of one of the young men I had seen just a few days before.

The experience shook me. I felt guilty and decided to do something. So I started looking for the aborigines in Australia and discovered they're very difficult to find. They're really only in two places: they're at the tourist centers talking about dreamtime and performing, and they're in the inner city slums, unemployed and alcoholic. I got some of the ones together who live in the slums and helped them form their own company. It was a funny little company that made window screens, but it made a difference. All 22 people who started with us changed their lives around and were no longer sniffing things.

I was on a high. I was doing everything right, and the world was just wonderful. So it did not surprise me when one day I received a telephone call from a group of aborigines who wanted to arrange a meeting with me. After all, back home when you do good deeds, somebody ultimately comes and gives you a little pin or something. What intrigued me was that this group was across the continent from where I was staying. That's the distance between Los Angeles and New York. I thought it was interesting that they would even know what I was doing that far away. So I agreed to the meeting, we set a meeting place, and, because the man on the phone told me he would pick me up at noon, I assumed that they were planning a luncheon.

I flew across Australia to attend my awards banquet, and at noon on the appointed day, a Black man dressed in short pants, a grungy tee-shirt, and some tennis shoes that didn't have laces in them, pulled up in an open-air jeep. He motioned for me, so I climbed into the jeep. We drove, and we drove, and we drove. We went past the city, and pretty soon we were on this dirt road, and then, before long, there was no road at all. The jeep was literally jumping across the ruts.

About two hours into this I thought to myself: "You know, you don't even know for sure you're in the right vehicle." The driver seemed to know who I was, but he hadn't said a word since we started. Finally, after another couple of hours, we came to this corrugated tin shed in the middle of nowhere. One side of it was totally open. There was a fire, and two Black ladies stood outside. The driver stopped the jeep, turned to me and said, "Oh, by the way, I'm the only one who speaks English. I'll be the interpreter."

One of the ladies handed him something, and he handed it to me. "Put this on," he said. "Before you can go into the meeting, you must be cleansed." I looked around for cleansing facilities but saw nothing. So I opened up this thing they gave me, and it was literally a rag with a couple of ties on it. Observing that the two ladies standing there were wearing matching outfits to this thing, I took off my clothes, stacked them in a pile, and put on the rag. When my driver came back to me, he, too, had changed into a tiny little rag. He also wore a really disgusted look on his face.

"I told you to take off everything," he said. I still had my underwear on, so I took it off and modestly put it in the middle of the stack of my other clothes.

"I said you have to take off every thing," the man repeated. "You have to take off your jewelry. You have to take the pins out of your hair. Everything." So I took the pins out of my hair, the rings off my fingers, and removed this wonderful watch that had diamonds around it. These things I stuck in the toe of my shoe, which I put on the top of the pile.

One of the women motioned me to the fire, where they fanned me with smoke until I was covered with soot. Then they did my back. When I was filthy with smoke, I was told, "Now you're cleansed. You can go into the meeting." So we walked around to the open side of the shed where 62 people sat or stood around another fire. There was one teenage boy and a few people in their 30s and 40s, but most of the people were 60, 70, 80, and 90 years old.

They had designs painted on their faces and along their arms and legs. They had used yellow, red, white and black to make dots, stripes and elaborate patterns. Drawings of lizards adorned their arms, while snakes, kangaroos, and birds appeared upon their legs and back. They had feathers tied around them, and there was a guy in the center with a special kind of plumage, whom I took to be the head honcho. Around the periphery there was a group of men who, although they were smiling as if welcoming me, held gleaming spears that looked razor sharp. This was clearly not the awards banquet I had envisioned.

It was then that a lady on the outside picked up my stack of belongings, walked over to the fire, and, with a grin, dumped everything into the flames. As I watched my belongings go up in smoke, I was nearly numb.

At the meeting we went through a number of rituals that didn't make sense to me. I realized later that what they were doing was testing me. They wanted to know what they were dealing with—not who I said I was, and not what I acted like. They wanted to know, down at the very marrow of my being, who it was that they were dealing with. My concept of the "Creator" seemed very important to them. They wanted to know if I believed that God was a sometimes-mean-tempered, white-bearded old man who sat in a chair up in the sky in judgment, as they had heard from countless missionaries. To them, that is not God. God is an essence. God is unconditional love. God is everything. So that's what the test was about, but at the time I had no idea I was being tested, and they didn't give me a clue that I was passing the test.

After they finished questioning me, they put out the fire, dismantled the drums, packed up their few belongings, and started walking out into the sand, leaving me standing there dumbfounded. The interpreter, whose name was Uta (meaning "messenger between two cultures"), turned to me and said, "Come now. We're leaving. We're going on a walkabout across Australia."

"How long will you be gone?" I asked, and was told three changes of the moon. "No," I told them flatly. "I can't just go off for three months. If I disappear, my government will come looking for me."

"Everyone who is to know, will know," said Uta. "This tribe heard your cry for help, and if any one of us had voted against you, you would not take this journey, which is the most important thing you will do in your life. It is what you were born to do. Come and follow." With that he turned and walked away.

I looked at the jeep sitting there with the keys in it and realized I didn't even know how I got here. The journey had taken four hours across barren Australian outback, the last leg of which hadn't even been on any roads. It was now 110°, and I didn't have any water. I had already decided these people were nuttier than fruitcakes, but at least they knew their way around. I honestly didn't believe that they would be gone for much more than a night, since they weren't carrying food. The idea of actually walking across Australia seemed totally ludicrous. In the end, I decided, "What's a night in the desert?" Then I looked up at the sky and said, "OK, God, I know you have a really funny sense of humor." That was my attitude when we started. It soon changed.

The group walked in total silence through thorny ground cover. We hadn't traveled far before both my feet were covered with thorns and bleeding profusely. "There's no way I can do this," I thought to myself, whereupon Uta turned around and said, "Forget about your feet. There's nothing you can do about them anyway. We will help you with your feet when we camp tonight. Just focus your attention elsewhere." (As I would later learn, this tribe considers telepathy the most natural way to communicate.)

When we finally reached the end of the ground cover, burning sand took its place. My feet literally sizzled as I walked. Just when they hurt so bad I didn't think I could go on, they stopped hurting. They turned black and became numb.

When we finally stopped to camp, one old lady came up to me, took my feet, and began pulling the thorns out. After applying some ointment, she gently rocked my feet in her lap and sang a lullaby. After a meal of grub worms—they were very gracious hosts and hostesses in that they cooked things for me that they didn't ordinarily cook—we retired.

That was my introduction to the tribe who call themselves the Real People.

Over the following months I would get to know them well. I was their messenger, but to deliver the message, I first had to live it.

These people do not believe that they are human beings, and they don't think we're human beings either. They believe that we are all spiritual beings inhabiting human bodies. In their opinion, Westerners have forgotten this, and, in turning away from our spiritual nature, have mutated.

Because we "mutants" no longer recognize our place in the natural order, we have interrupted patterns that have existed for millennia.

Now, due to rising temperatures and a changing water pattern in the Outback, the Real People know that, within fifty years, a baby born to them today would have to choose between starving to death or going into the city and living with us mutants. To them, that's too high a price to pay.

And so they have decided to leave. The tribe will die out, and, according to their beliefs, return to the spiritual dimension from which they came. That, I discovered, was why there were so few young faces; they had stopped having children some time ago. (Birth has always been a matter of choice for them. Both men and women regularly eat a natural contraceptive, and only stop eating it when they choose to take on the responsibility of guiding another spirit through its journey.)

During my time with the Real People my perceptions of life have changed completely, but at first I felt mainly disorientation and discomfort. For one thing, there was no differentiation in days of the week. Nor was there any way of knowing in which month we were living. One of the things that bugs the Aussies more than anything is the aborigines' lack of respect for watch and calendar. The Real People think in terms of eternity, and they simply cannot be rushed. Whenever I would get frustrated about this, they would tell me the same thing. I must have heard it a hundred times: "Do you understand eternity? It is forever. That's a long, long time. Time is of no concern."

They are very wise people even though they don't read. They have symbols that they use, but they don't have an alphabet and they don't actually write anything down. They said to me, "You know, reading is real handy in your society but you have to understand that it's not a part of everybody's journey. You needn't try and make everybody conform to your ways. You should understand that there is no reading test in the next dimension. Besides, you've paid a terrible price for your reading and you don't even know it." They were referring to the fact that they are so mentally alert. They have no senility whatsoever in their society. There were only a few times that they cried when I talked about mutants, and one of them was when I talked about how we lose our mental faculties as we get old. They're convinced that reading is partly responsible, because when you write things down, you don't have to remember them. "At least when you had it written down in books, your knowledge was safe," they said. "But now you're storing it in computers. You folks haven't seemed to figure out that your machines don't work real good. Now, if you have a power failure, your whole brain is wiped out. We find remembering things is much better."

Their 50,000 years of history is remembered through song, and they have to remember every stanza of every song to preserve it.

They believe that we're all multitalented, that each one of us can be a healer, an artist, or whatever we want to be. Their names reflect this. Although parents name a child, they realize that the child will outgrow his or her name. If a child got interested in cooking and kind of grooved on grubs or something, he or she might pick a name like Worm Watcher. As you progress through life, you can change your name whenever it seems appropriate.

One evening we had a concert, and there was a man whose name meant Composer. After the concert, he stuck his thumbs underneath his armpits and said, "Hey! Pretty great concert, huh?" And everybody said, "Fantastic concert." And he said, "Yeah, couple more concerts like that, and I'll have to rename myself Great Composer." Of course, he might go from Great Composer to Worm Watcher, and that's okay. The important thing is that he felt good about what he was doing, that he was on track with his own purpose.

The same respect they show for each other, they show for the earth. That was also apparent at the concert. They make their musical instruments out of whatever is available. For this concert, they punched holes in some reeds, tied them together, then cut and fine-tuned them until they had some thing like a piccolo or harmonica. By tying flat pieces of rock to my hair, they turned me into a kind of walking wind chimes. Then we had this wonderful concert, and afterwards they dismantled their instruments and carefully returned each piece back where they found it.

They take water from the earth the same way. Water is very scarce but they can find it anywhere. They use their bodies to dowse, and they'll crouch down and listen to the ground and hear the water running twenty feet down in the sand. Then they take these little hollow reeds and put a reed inside of a reed inside of a reed and push it down into the sand until it reaches water. They ask the water permission to bring it to the surface, and tell it that it will now have an experience that it hasn't had before—running through the sand—and that it can come up and experience the upper world and become a part of their bodies and their lives. Only then do they suck on the reed and siphon the water. Once they have filled their containers, they remove the reed and close off the hole. As they walk away, they put their feet in the same tracks that they made in their approach and then brush their footsteps away.

They don't plant and they don't hunt. They pray to the universe to provide their needs, and it does. They never take anything for granted. Each day when the food showed up, it was like, "Oh! Wow! It happened again today! We're going to eat again today!" And it is not a joke. It is totally sincere. Every single day is a celebration and at the end of the day it was like, "What a really great day! We did great things today." In the morning they wake up, and it's, "Wow! What are we going to do today?" When I first started with these people, and they'd jump up with all this enthusiasm, I'd be looking out at the sand and wondering what all the excitement was about. But it rubs off on you, and it's a fun way to live.

They are wise and complex people, and yet there is a childlike simplicity at the core of their being. Once, during our walkabout, we went to the ocean. The Real People built a raft, and we sat on it and waited for the tide to take us out to the dolphins. We played with these creatures, who the Real People have a great affinity for, and then we sat on the raft and waited for the tide to take us back to shore. When I suggested a paddle might be handy, they responded, "Why would we need that?"

I said, "So you can paddle to where you want to be."

They said, "But how do you know where you're supposed to be? It seems to us that while you are paddling, you might miss everything and end up in the wrong place. We've been doing it our way for fifty-thousand years, and it's worked really good. We always go to the right place, and we are always brought back."

One of their abilities, which I've already mentioned, is telepathy. They say it's the most natural way to communicate. The reason mutants are unable to master telepathy is that they have walled off their hearts and heads with secrets and lies, and can no longer allow just anyone inside. The Real People also have the ability to travel out of their bodies. Sometimes we would be walking along and one of them would send their consciousness out twenty miles ahead to scout, and they would inevitably know what we were going to come to before we reached it.

These people are incredibly healthy. They live about 110 years and they don't have any of the diseases that we have. Once I was trying to explain arthritis, about how, when you get older, a knee or a joint may get bad and so forth. Their response was, "Interesting. But why would one knee be older than the other?"

I said, "You got me, but that's the way that it works. Sometimes parts wear out and we have to have them removed."

"When we're put together," they responded, "we don't get used stuff that wears out. All of our pieces fit together clear to the end."

They don't believe that disease or accidents are a natural way to die. The natural way to die is the same way you got here, and that is by choice. After you have spent your life trying to be a better person, you finally come to the point where you're really anxious to get back home. So then you tell everybody that you have meditated and prayed and have decided it is time to go. They have a big party for you, and then they pick up their things and walk on. Finally, you sit, shut down your body's systems, and die.

The Real People are, in my opinion, the most enlightened group of beings on the planet. Their whole lives are devoted to the consciousness of unconditional love. When a child is born, it is greeted with a statement: "I love you, and I support your journey." And whenever one of them dies they are told the same thing.

The interesting thing about their remarks and observations was that I never felt that I or my people were being criticized or judged. It was more like a loving adult observing a child struggling to learn an important lesson. As they explained it to me, "It just appears to us as though we have retained the instructions for life, and you have lost the manual. You've lost what it is to be real."

They once told me that, as spiritual beings, we were given freedom of choice. The reason we were given this is for the sole purpose of choosing not to use it. So we have the choice of holding on to fear and judgment, or else tapping into perfection and learning to bless everything that is happening. There is no wrong. The mutants' problem is that they look around and see everything as dead; the Real People know that everything is alive. We are all spiritual beings on this planet, and every thing is doing the best that it can.

I would like to close with the prayer that they said for me when they said farewell:

"Hello divine oneness. We stand here with the mutant, and we have walked with her and we have touched her and we have changed her much. But transforming a mutant is a very difficult task. You will see that her strange color hair is growing out from her head. At the base of it is beautiful black—aborigine roots. We have been unable to change the pale color of her eyes. But we've learned from the mutants. We've learned that they have something in their life called frosting. And it seems to be symbolic of how they live their lives in superficial, artificial, decorative, sweet-tasting, temporary pursuits, with very few seconds of their lives spent trying to understand their own beingness. We have selected this mutant as our messenger, and we release her today as a bird would be released from the edge of a nest to fly away far and wide and high and to squeak as loud as a cuckabera and to tell the world that the Real People are leaving. We do not judge the mutants. We love them and we pray for them and we release them as we pray for ourselves and love ourselves and release ourselves. And we only hope that they will understand what they are doing to each other and what they are doing to the earth, and will save it."

(Magical Blend issue #41)

Marlo Morgan's four-month walkabout with a nomad tribe of aborigines is recounted in her book Mutant Message Down Under, *(HarperSanFrancisco). This article was compiled from a talk given at Unity Church in Seattle, WA.*

Spirituality
Presence of the Past

Natalie Goldberg: The Marathon Monks of Mt. Hiei

There is an order of Buddhist monks in Japan whose practice is running. They are called the marathon monks of Mount Hiei. They begin running at one thirty A.M. and run from eighteen to twenty-five miles per night, covering several of Mount Hiei's most treacherous slopes. Because of the high altitude, Mount Hiei has long, cold winters, and part of the mountain is called the Slope of Instant Sobriety; because it is so cold, it penetrates any kind of illusion or intoxication. The monks run all year round. They do not adjust their running schedule to the snow, wind, or ice. They wear white robes when they run, rather than the traditional Buddhist black. White is the color of death: There is always the chance of dying on the way. In fact, when they run they carry with them a sheathed knife and a rope to remind them to take their life by disembowelment or hanging if they fail to complete their route.

After monks complete a thousand-day mountain marathon within seven years, they go on a nine-day fast without food, water or sleep. At the end of the nine days, they are at the edge of death. Completely emptied, they become extremely sensitive. "They can hear ashes fall from the incense sticks... and they can smell food prepared miles away." Their sight is vivid and clear, and after the fast they come back into life radiant with a vision of ultimate existence.

I read about these monks in a book entitled *The Marathon Monks of Mount Hiei*, by John Stevens (Shambhala, 1988). It was just before I went to teach the first of four Sunday afternoon writing seminars at The Loft in Minneapolis. I was excited by what I read and naturally I wanted to share it. I stood behind the podium and carried on to fifty Midwestern writers and would-be writers about how the monks became one with the mountain they ran on, how they knew the exact time each species of bird and insect began to sing, and when the moon rose, the sun set, the wind changed direction.

I was twenty minutes into the seminar's two hours, telling about the monks, when I looked up and paused. "I guess you want to know what the marathon monks have to do with writing? Well, they have everything to do with it. The way I see it, you either break through in your writing—say what you really need to say—or head for Mount Hiei. As a matter of fact, take a gun with you next time you go to a cafe to write. If you don't connect in your writing that day, just shoot yourself. Vague writing on Monday—off with the little toe. Tuesday, no better—the big toe. Get the idea?"

Why do the marathon monks go to such extremes? They want to wake up. That's how thick we human beings are. We are lazy, content in our discontent, sloppy, and asleep. To wake up takes the total effort that a marathon monk can exert. I told my class on the last day of the four-week seminar, "Well, you have two choices: Mount Hiei or writing. Which one will you choose? Believe me, if you take on writing, it is as hard as being a marathon monk."

There is a story about Hui-k'o, the Second Ancestor of Zen, who found Bodhidharma in a cave where he was meditating for nine years. Bodhidharma was the first patriarch, or ancestor, of Zen in China and, in fact, he brought Zen there from India. Day and night, Hui-k'o begged Bodhidharma for the teachings. "Please, master, I beseech you. Make my mind peaceful." Bodhidharma ignored him and continued to sit in meditation. This went on for a long time: the beseeching and the ignoring. Then one evening in December, there was a huge blizzard. It snowed all night and all the next day. Hui-k'o just stood outside the cave without moving, until the snow was waist high. He was waiting to be recognized by Bodhidharma. Finally, he took out a knife and cut off his left arm. He threw it in front of Bodhidharma. You can imagine the red blood on the white snow. With this, Bodhidharma looked up and asked what he wanted.

There is another Zen story about a beautiful woman who came to a monastery and wanted to practice. The head monk said, "If you want to join a monastery, first you must get married and raise three children. Then you can come back." She did this and returned years later. She was still refused entry into the monastery. The head monk said she was too beautiful. She would cause trouble for the other monks. She wanted to practice so badly that she went home and scarred her face. This time when she went to the monastery, they let her in.

Are these stories metaphorical or are they true? I believe they are true. There are people burning to realize the truth of existence and these are the extremes they will go to. Why so violent? Is Zen a violent practice? No. No more so than Jesus Christ being pinned to the cross or Abraham taking his son to be sacrificed.

There is a proliferation of writing books in America. They are very popular. People would rather read about how to become a writer than read the actual products of writing: poems, novels, short stories. Americans see writing as a way to break through their own inertia and become awake, to connect with their deepest selves.

Yes, writing can do this for us, but becoming awake is not easy. One must be persistent under all circumstances and it is not always exciting. It is hard. It is a long, quiet highway.

Recently, I drove alone from Minneapolis to New Mexico in late December, the darkest time of the year. I had to cross the southern border of Minnesota, drive straight through Iowa, across Kansas, into Oklahoma and Texas. I had to drive through an hour of sleet near Des Moines, past empty fields and funky cafes that said Elvis ate here. I had a great moment listening to Jessye Norman blast out spirituals in her operatic voice on my car stereo, just as I turned a corner on a thin highway in Kansas. The half moon and one evening star were directly in front of me. A train roared by on my right. The moment was over and I was tired, pulling into a Best Western at ten PM in the town of Liberty on the Oklahoma border. What I wanted was to love all of this: my weariness, the wind lifting as I got out of the car at the Texaco station.

To love is to wake up. How do we wake up without becoming a marathon monk on Mount Hiei? Well, some of us will have to go to Mount Hiei. There is no other way. The rest of us must work as tellers in banks, drive our children to school, wash the kitchen floor, buy groceries. The marathon monks go all the way to the edge of death, so they may come back and be alive, so they can know gratitude for this moment. We need to wake up when we buy groceries, push the cart down the aisle, see labels, count out change, feel our step on the floor tile. Every moment is enormous, and it is all we have.

About twelve years ago, Chris Pirsig, the son of Robert Pirsig, who wrote *Zen and the Art of Motorcycle Maintenance,* was senselessly murdered near the San Francisco Zen Center. The killers knifed Chris and ran. They did not take a wallet (I don't even know if Chris had one on him). I was sitting at a seven-day meditation retreat in Minnesota. It was December. We all knew Chris. Rumors spread quickly during breaks, even though we were supposed to remain silent. We all awaited our teacher's talk that morning. Katagiri Roshi was close to Chris. He would make it all better.

Roshi walked into the meditation hall, bowed, lit incense, sat down. We chanted. Then he spoke: "Human beings have an idea they are very fond of: that we die in old age. This is just an idea. We don't know when our death will come. Chris Pirsig's death has come now. It is a great teaching in impermanence."

The bell was rung. It was the end of the lecture. I was furious. What kind of thing was that to say? How could Roshi be so cruel? I knew he cared about Chris.

Years later, distraught by learning that Katagiri Roshi had cancer, I cried for many weeks. In May, as I drove to the airport in Albuquerque to fly to see him, I suddenly remembered his talk about Chris. His talk had not been cruel. It was brave. He was willing to cut through all sentiment and touch the fundamental truth of impermanence. I appreciated it. What he said then helped my life now.

This is how we learn. Human life is very big. There is no short cut from Minneapolis to New Mexico. My car had to cover every mile. We learn with every cell and with time, care, pain and love. I'm sure that many times when the marathon monks woke at midnight to prepare to run, they had an urge to go back to sleep, but the path was ahead of them. We, who are not marathon monks, wake up and have the toothbrush before us—brushing our teeth! The great ritual that gets us out of bed—and then we have the blank page in front of us, or the school bus, or the phone ringing. We all must go on down that highway. Our life is the path of learning, to wake up before we die.

(Magical Blend issue #45)

From Long Quiet Highway *by Natalie Goldberg. Copyright © 1993 by Natalie Goldberg. Used by permission of Bantam Books, a division of Bantam Doubleday Dell Publishing Group, Inc.*

Spirituality
The Spirit of Diversity

Zsuzsanna Budapest: The Goddess Rising

with Jerry Snider and Michael Peter Langevin

Affectionately known as the "Good Witch of the West," Zsuzsanna Budapest has been dodging falling houses for years. The first came crashing down in 1956 when she fled the Russian occupation of her Hungarian homeland. Deeply tied to the ancestral roots of her native Transylvania, Budapest still feels the "righteous pain" of the political manipulation and military force that tried, unsuccessfully, to wipe out a proud and ancient culture and replace it with an inflexible political doctrine. Now, 34 years later, she speaks with evident pride of the recent resurrection of a culture she has vividly recounted in such books as Grandmother of Time. The rhythm and landscape of the country that Budapest writes about still retains elements of its pre-Roman pagan origins. These memories were strongly embedded in the young refugee who arrived in the United States in 1958.

Then, in the sixties, a rising tide of feminism inspired her to look back to her roots to develop a female-centered theology that celebrated Mother Earth. By the early seventies, her bold political stances and unflagging energy had established her reputation as the "initiator of the women's spirituality movement."

In May 1980, Mayor Tom Bradley of Los Angeles awarded her with a special certificate of thanks for her instrumental participation in organizing the "Take Back the Night" marches against rape. Together with the National Organization for Women and local women's groups, she recruited thousands of men and women to march for women's safety.

In 1986, Z. Budapest founded the Women's Spirituality Forum, a non-profit organization dedicated to bringing women's spirituality to the forefront of feminist consciousness by honoring the Goddess experience in everyday life. Besides producing lecture series, classes, annual Spiral Dances and retreats, The Forum is working to end the cycle of child abuse by raising consciousness and funds and healing the spiritual hurts of individuals who are affected.

As an outspoken proponent of a Goddess-centered religion, Budapest has faced her share of persecution in this country, from personal insults to physical threats. When we interviewed her at her home in Berkeley, California, we half expected to find a hardened, battle-scarred revolutionary campaigner, but the woman we met seemed to take in stride the controversy that has surrounded her. Full of humor and brimming over with a contagious love of life, she spoke of her early years in Transylvania, her abiding love for her fiercely independent mother, her experiences as a political refugee in the late '50s, and her ongoing struggle for the full equality of women—an equality that includes the right to worship a female "Source," a deity whose body is nature itself. According to Budapest, we humans have all but forgotten nature. She believes it is time to "reinstate the natural holidays, to celebrate the changing of the seasons and the seasons of our lives, and to conduct rituals that speak to nature's passages in our lives." To Budapest, the goal of spirituality is ecstasy, and ecstasy, she says, can be reached in many ways. According to the Good Witch of the West, the secret lies in "making a big do about life, not a little do."

Z. Budapest's book *The Holy Book of Women's Mysteries* (Wingbow Press, Berkeley, CA) focuses on Dianic Wicca and the celebration of women's spirituality through ancient European traditions. *The Grandmother of Time* (Harper & Row), is a book of celebrations, spells and sacred objects for every month of the year. Her newest book, *Grandmother of the Moon*, to be published by Harper & Row and released in the Fall of 1991, serves as a follow-up to *The Grandmother of Time*, with an emphasis on lunar aspects of the year including lunar holidays, lunar diets, spells, and transitional stories about the moon.

In addition to her writings, Z. Budapest hosts a monthly cable TV program shown in Portland, Oregon, and the San Francisco Bay Area devoted to the many manifestations of the Goddess and Her history and celebrations.

In The Grandmother of Time, *you wrote about witnessing pagan rites as a child in Hungary. Was your own background pagan?*

Z. Budapest: In my family, we were witches, herbalists, and healers. Mother was an outstanding sculptress, but she never got the recognition she deserved because she was a witch. She was very much feared because of this in the art world. Mother talked to the ancestors if she wanted something, and she prayed on the winds. She had names for the winds. To her, every wind was a different entity.

A lot of my values were instilled just by watching her. She showed me that God is a source. I also got her outlook on life, which always included humor. Yes, I got witchcraft from my mother, and I also got laughter. If it wasn't for the laughter, I wouldn't be able to popularize the witchcraft, because humor is my tool. Every time I taught, I had to be funny; I had to be immediate; I had to be engaging, and what I taught had to make common sense in order to start up a viable Goddess movement.

So you were instilled with a lyrical appreciation of life at an early age?

Z. Budapest: Yes. I got it from my mother, who was also a great poet and storyteller. In Hungarian, which is an old language, there is no "he, she, it." It is a nonsexist language. And my mother showed me that we are surrounded by invisible worlds; the dead are not dead, and the newborn are ancient travelers who have been here before.

When you came to the United States in the sixties, what were some of the obstacles that confronted you as a pagan and as a woman?

Z. Budapest: One thing that astonished me happened at the end of high school. I was one of a large group of political refugees. We were favored refugees then, sort of like the Contras were favored refugees in the eighties. As soon as we finished high school, the boys started to be awarded scholarships, Rockefeller grants, and Ford grants, but the girls were given very, very little. So, I said, "How come? My grades are better than theirs." Then, little by little I started to understand the answer: "Because you are a girl; you will get married." It did not really become clear how unfair this was until I grew up. I didn't question it then because I actually was planning to get married. When you are an immigrant, you want to make roots as fast as you can. And if you are a female, you already know how to make roots: You make children, and "Voila!" You got roots. It was not until around 1967 that I started to appreciate the unfairness and rebel. By the time I was thirty, the Saturn cycle was putting incredible psychic pressure on me. I wanted to die. I thought, "If I cannot become myself, whatever it might be, I don't want to go on." Kids mean nothing if you don't have yourself. It was the Hungarian maid my mother had sent me who told me that I would have to follow my heart. She supported me to leave my split-level existence, and so I asked her if I decided to go, would she make sure the kids were all right. At first, I thought I'd just take a three-week vacation, but I'm still on that vacation.

What happened next was a total change. Everything suddenly fell in place. Everything was happening like a dizzying speedball. I hitch-hiked from New York to Los Angeles in three rides. As one ride left me, the other one was coming like it was put down on schedule. I had the hand of the Goddess on me. It was moving me where I was supposed to be.

I arrived in L.A. and within two weeks went to my first Women's Liberation march. I became a staffer at the Women's Center and started raising my consciousness about feminist issues. As that happened, all the memories about the old religion came back. Suddenly, it was easy to put the two together and I said to my friends in the women's move-ment, "Look, you haven't got cosmology here. You don't have a revo-lution without cosmology." So, I told them about earlier religions and witch burning and how the goddess was everywhere. They gave me a very cool reception at first, but they allowed me to follow through with my first Sabbat because I was a staffer and had earned my stripes as an activist. I told the six friends who came, "I know enough to begin it. The rest of it, we have to invent."

As I describe in my book *The Grandmother of Time*, we gathered, and I evoked the four corners just as my mother used to evoke the four winds. I called the Goddess to help us recreate the old religion because we had so little to go on. I called on Her to give me strength. One of the women who was studying shamanism and possession at the university went into trance. She rhymed for four hours. My other guests included a cab driver, a socialist, and two lesbians. All I knew was that I had to keep the group moving, and I had to make sure that everyone was safe in whatever they had to do. That was my first lesson as a high priestess, how to manage this energy.

Afterwards a sprinkle of rain came outside. It was the first rain that year, and we ran out into it. As we were running underneath the palm trees, I heard an owl hooting. I stopped, first because it's very rare to hear an owl in Hollywood and secondly, because I knew my mytholo-gy; the owl is the sacred bird of Athena. So I told everybody to stop and ask the Goddess whether our movement would catch on. I was a femi-nist, and I wanted to see women empower themselves from the center, not just by changing laws. I think revolution comes from the middle and goes out, instead of the other way. So I asked the Goddess to prophesy through the owl. I asked for the owl to hoot seven times if the movement would catch on and five times if it would not. When she hooted seven times, we got goose bumps.

The next Sabbat was double the size because every friend brought another friend. It just snowballed afterwards. Suddenly, everybody wanted to have Goddess rituals, probably because the word got out that witches gave the best parties. I let it be like that because ecstasy is the purpose of the old religion.

Finding a safe place where we could make noise and play the drums as loud as we wanted, and could take our clothes off if we wanted, was a constant problem. We moved around a lot until we found a mountain top in Malibu which became known as the "Old Covenstead," where we worshipped the Goddess something like five years. I developed a small group of priestesses. Then I got arrested for Tarot reading, which sort of surfaced me from the feminist underground into the pagan underground and mainstream visibility. At the time, nobody had heard of a feminist witch. The pagan community was just as sexist as the regular community. But I was glad to find out there were men who loved the Goddess, and it didn't take too long for a more egalitarian approach. The result was a great cross-fertilization.

During that time, you worked with Starhawk, another woman who became a strong influence on spiritual alternatives.

Z. Budapest: Starhawk was one of my first great students. I've had many others since—writers, teachers, psychologists, ecologists. Starhawk became an ice-breaker. Americans cannot always hear me because I talk with an accent and teach about the native European tradition, which is white people's roots. But Starhawk gave the Goddess message a twist and a turn and suddenly plugged it into the psychology community and the peace movement and spread it out to the heterosexual community. She opened audiences for the Goddess that were not opened before and took the movement into the mainstream.

As I said, my focus is the European tradition; it's memories are in my genes. Europeans are a tribal people who have totems, just like the native Americans. I'm writing about the wolf totem in my new book, *Transylvanian Blood Memories.* I'm uncovering a great deal about the wolf as image, and how we have emulated its society, which is a very noble society: no orphans, the sick are fed and taken care of. Every member cooperates in the hunt. Pups are cared for by one female while the rest of the females go off with the males to hunt. The division of labor is totally equal up until the time the mother has the baby, and then the male feeds and takes care of the pups. The wolves have a lot of noble features that we emulated. Europeans respected the wolf. And then Christianity arrived. Around 500 A.D. Constantine decided to have a state religion, and he forced it on all his subjects. Europeans were part of the Roman empire at that time, so we fell into it.

The Christians sent missionaries to clear the forests, and when the forests were cleared, a little bit of desert religion began to be established. A desert religion is very extreme. It was "water or die," "an eye for an eye, tooth for a tooth." This desperate environment gave birth to the Bible. At the time, we Europeans were a forest religion people, but as the desert religion was brought in by missionaries and mercenaries, the forest was pushed away. The temple, which was our forests, was removed from around us and our spirituality collapsed. We were no longer learning from other species like the wolf, who is thirty million years old. Now there are only a few forests left.

White people were Christianized by force, not by cooperation. Their spirituality collapsed when the environment that supported it was removed. And so, for over six hundred years, Europeans killed other Europeans over a book imported from the Middle East with no white people in it. After creating a lot of pain in our own culture, we went to Africa and kidnapped the natives and took them for slaves. With the book still in hand, we confronted the Native Americans. We ignored their high morality and superior religion and told them they were savages.Europeans have a lot of soul-searching to do as a race. We are an abused race, and we have abused ourselves because our spiritual center was taken away from us by force. We were forced to turn on each other during the witch burning times; we accused our neighbors; we accused each other to escape the tortures and the burnings. Our ancestors killed each other repeatedly. We carry a deep psychic wound. Just as an abused child often grows up to be an abusive parent, the abused European grew up to abuse Blacks and Indians. The Goddess movement serves to heal these ancient wounds.

Many people would agree with your objectives but would argue that the same goals can be accomplished through Christianity.

Z. Budapest: I don't see how. My objective does not allow for sin, guilt, judgment, or blaming women for the ills in the world. If you take these out of Christianity, what have you got left?

But the power structure of the Western world is predominantly Chris-
tian, and it doesn't seem likely that Christianity is ready to replace the Father
and the Son with the Goddess.

Z. Budapest: I think I know how it's going to be. I started seeing glim-
mers of it. Suddenly, the Goddess will just be in the grassroots. There
won't be any storming of the bastions. There won't be any impeaching
of Bishops. The Goddess will just suddenly be there. Masses of women
and men will simply relate to her and not the male gods. She's the only
unifying image we have. She is the only archetype that we all have in
our souls that unites us. The all-male archetypes divide us. The sexes
need a unification, and the Goddess image with Her nature religion
and Her focus on the land is the one that can do that. The Christians are
losing believers left and right. Women are dropping out by the droves.
Very few nuns are entering to do the free labor of the Church.

Eastern Europe is a very good example of collective consciousness
suddenly clicking in. One day the Communist leaders looked out and
found out they had no more support. The grassroots movements have
turned the tides of history. That's when bloodless revolutions can happen.

When I look at the crises in the Middle-East, I think that the only
way to find a solution is to have the women do the negotiating. The
men are locked in their roles. It's almost that their "manhood" demands that they act in a death-oriented way. Wars should go the way
of the dodo birds.

In this country, we're breaking down some of the borders of sexism. Wom-
en are getting elected, and are breaking up that "old boy" network.

Z. Budapest: I'm cheering for them, even though I wish we could have
a better selection of female leaders worldwide. I believe it will take at
least three generations of women leaders to see truly inspiring women
leaders. That's because what they have to go on is so little. They have
to invent their role.

It seems like part of the education of this entire generation, male and fe-
male alike, is learning how to adjust to our transitional role.

Z. Budapest: The very fact that you're aware of this is already a change.
Already you can accept it, let it in, let it out whenever you want to. No
generation was in this much control before. But once the consciousness
is freed up, then there is a thought form that flows through us. I notice

it in people very much unlike me, people who dress very conservative-
ly, for instance. I look at them and think, "No, I would not get along
with those people. They are too uptight. They are too structured for
me." And yet, when I talk to them, I realize that the trappings are only
on the outside; on the inside they are already different. And that's all it
takes. It doesn't matter what clothes you wear. History has been the
great costume war. If you were a warrior, you looked it, and if you were
a woman, you looked it. That is changing. The outerscape of costuming
is being replaced with an innerscape of spirit.

And we don't need to have everything planned out. We don't require a complete vision of where we are going. All we need is the next
step. If we get to that next step, then that step will be the mother of the
steps to come. It doesn't matter if you don't have the vision of where
you are going. You'll still get there.

*I think a lot of people feel lost today because of uncertainty. It's as if we
are stranded on a road without a map, and a lot of people think that means we
don't know where we are. What you seem to be saying is that it's quite clear
where we are; we're on the road. The only thing we don't know is where that
road is going to take us.*

Z. Budapest: Right. It's like, what's the rush? The life that flows through
us knows the agenda already. Let me give you an example. In star cast-
ing I always teach women to have an open-ended spell, even if it's a
love spell. Let's say they are lonely and they really want a lover. They
know what they want. They want somebody that's compatible, who
loves them back, who is emotionally available. But they get hooked on
Joe Doe or Mary Doe. Those two individuals are not available, but they
just put everything in that direction and they cast spells until they turn
blue in the face. And I keep telling them, "No, no, no." Because life
works out of abundance, and Joe Doe and Mary Doe are not the point.
The point is the abundance and to get your needs met. So you need to
have faith in the picture you don't see, in the invisible world. I always
have them base their spell by quality, no names. So Mother Nature can
take a look at the possibilities: "Oh, we have somebody down the block
they never met. Maybe they'll bump into each other." I think nature
works with us if we don't tie her hands.

*You've given us some of your views on the past and present; what about
the future?*

Z. Budapest: Consciousness-raising is the main job of our generation; it's also the source of our power. I'd like to tell people to take heart; things are changing. From what we've seen, when change occurs, it happens suddenly, but the preparation for it may take a very long time. The generation that we call The Baby Boomers is very large and has a very unique opportunity to change the world. Astrologically, a generation is defined by Pluto, and in this generation, Pluto was in Leo. That means we naturally think about power—how to use it, and when. That's our destiny. And it's a good destiny.

I'd like to have our generation come to a "generational" consciousness that would unite this large group of people and help us overcome the hatred and distrust that we inherited from the past. I would like us to just dispense with hate.

And I would like to see men become more vocal in support of women. Women want to hear that men do not condone violence against them. It is cowardice to attack women, and I would like that to be seen as an unmanly thing to do. I'd like to see men stand up for women in the company of men. That's what defines a brother for me.

The definition of a sister to me is somebody who stands up for herself and for all women in the company of others of both sexes. A sister does not let any racism, sexism, or homophobia go by without her standing up and saying, "Not in my presence. If you are a sexist, I'm walking. If you are putting down somebody about race, I'm walking." I think that's a good way to teach groups that women and men will not tolerate this in their presence.

I would like to see these social barriers crumble just like the Berlin wall. What we need to do as a race, more than anything, is to recognize our potential and commit ourselves to being the generation that woke up. I want us to be able to say, "This is the generation that stopped wars between men and between the sexes. This is the generation that will bring in the splendid 21st century."

For more information, contact: The Women's Spirituality Forum, P.O. Box 11363, Oakland, CA 94611, (415) 444-7724.

Spirituality
The Shamanic Revival

Alberto Villoldo: The Shamanic Tools

with Michael Langevin and Richard Daab

Psychologist Alberto Villoldo traveled to Peru to research the effects of the jungle plant *ayahuasca*, known by natives as "the Vine of Death." It was used by shamans to lead them to a place of power and ancient knowledge. Through ritual, ceremony, and the use of mind-wrenching potions, a renowned Incan shaman known to the Indians as Don Jicaram ushered the psychologist into a dangerous and fantastic realm of mind and body. Villoldo's book, *The Four Winds*, provides a riveting personal account of this shamanic initiation.

Alberto Villoldo established the Biological Self-Regulation Laboratory at San Francisco State University to investigate the neuropsychology of healing. In addition to *The Four Winds*, (Harper & Row), he is the author of *Millennium: Glimpses into the Twenty-First Century, Healing States*, and *Realms of Healing*. In this interview, Alberto Villoldo reveals the mythic journey through four cardinal points of the Medicine Wheel.

Why is it that suddenly we are digging into our past to find techniques like shamanism to help us face our future?

Alberto Villoldo: If you look at times when humanity has taken evolutionary quantum leaps, these leaps have always occurred when we were faced with possible extinction. When things are going great there's no need to change. It is out of the threat of extinction that humanity makes quantum leaps, and I think we're at the threshold of one again today. And we are rediscovering the neurological tools to do what the medicine man or visionary was able to do so elegantly—to quantum leap into the future.

About a hundred thousand years ago the human brain nearly doubled in size. We acquired a new neural computer that we are still learning how to use. I'm talking about the neocortex that's divided into the left and right brain hemispheres. I believe that the awakening of the neocortex has been the driving force of prophets, visionaries, great scientists, and great medicine men and women. Once awakened, this new brain is not bound by the ordinary definitions of time and space. This new brain is awakening in humanity at large today, and unless we learn how to master its capabilities, it begins to turn against us, creating psychosomatic disease and psychosomatic disorders. It is also giving us the ability to heal ourselves (creating psychosomatic health) and to choose our individual destinies. But above all, it's giving us the power to engage the *totality* of human knowledge—through computers, through the media, through observing nature. Shamanism is but an ancient map for mastering these capabilities.

In the meantime, we are in the process of gaining access to all the information of mankind through our computers. The access to that information in a time of crisis could propel us into a fundamental shift in the myths we live by.

How can shamanism aid in shifting our mythologies?

Alberto Villoldo: Shamanism offers a different mythology of our origins. One shift that's taking place in our mythologies right now involves renouncing the myth that we are outcast from nature. The Judeo-Christian mythology is not one of liberation but of atonement. As far as I know, it is the only mythology to kick its people out of paradise and make them win their way back through penance. Ecology comes naturally to the Native American and to the shaman because they were never cast out from the garden. It's not something you have to do. It's something you live. It's the principle of "walking with beauty" on the earth. What's happening is that we're breaking out of a mythology of control and repression into one of liberation. One of the reasons that church and state have, for centuries, hunted down shamanism is that it expounds a mythology of liberation. Shamanism offers a direct communion with the divine and the possibility to influence the course of one's own destiny. Shamanism is not a religion. There is no Christ, no Buddha, nobody who says, "Follow my footsteps." Shamanism demands that you take your own steps with courage, compassion, and vision. It requires that you learn how to learn from nature. It teaches you to meet power directly, embrace it, and claim it.

Surely shamanism offers a guide.

Alberto Villoldo: the Medicine Wheel is such a guide. It presents the four steps to power and knowledge and ways to access the abilities of our neocortex. Each direction has a specific theme associated with it.

The South is the place of the serpent—the way of the healer. The work here is shedding the past. You shed the past the same way the serpent sheds his skin—all at once. For the shaman this is an act of power. You let go not only of the pain but also of the joy of your past. In shedding the past you acknowledge and forgive those who have wronged you and whom you have wronged. Psychology attempts to free you from the past by dissecting the traumatic experiences of your life. In shamanism you set free all at once the spirits from the past that are haunting you. These spirits are not necessarily people who have died. They may be people who are alive that you've trapped in some way in your psyche, and who continue to haunt you in the present.

The next direction is the West—the way of the warrior—represented by the jaguar, the abilities of cunning, stealth, and total relaxation, and the ability to strike instantaneously. When I first began the work of the West, the medicine man I was studying with, Don Ramon, assigned me a task. He told me he wanted me to walk into the Amazon without having all the sounds of the jungle stop. That wasn't an easy thing to do. The first time I tried, I was only into the jungle two feet when the parrots stopped singing and the monkeys stopped screeching. Everything stopped. Ramon said that this was because the animals could smell the violence in me. He walked into the Amazon, and the noise continued; the animals took no notice. I told him it was because he smelled like the jungle and that if I smelled like he did, the animals wouldn't notice me either. Later we happened upon two Indians by the edge of a stream who were melting the fat of an animal. I asked them for some of the fat and rubbed it all over my body. I stank. There was no way you could smell any vestiges of underarm deodorant, shaving cream, or shampoo. I got up and walked into the jungle. I took the first step, and the animals took no notice. I took a second step, and everything was still all right. But when I took the third step, every sound stopped. It was not until about five years later that I succeeded in that task. Ramon and I had been walking in the jungle for about an hour and a half and he said, "Listen." The jungle was filled with noise, and I could finally walk in the Amazon without making the animals silent.

The third step in the Medicine Wheel is the North, which is the way of mastery. It's represented by the white buffalo, by the snow leopard, and by the dragon. In the North the shaman understands the workings of Heaven and Earth. According to legend, the mastery teachings give you power with the forces of nature and the ability to influence the course of our collective destinies. Rolling Thunder, the Shoshone medicine man, was known for his ability to influence the weather—I saw him produce a thunderstorm that drenched us in the desert during dry season. The North-South axis is the axis that most readily lends itself to abuse for the sake of power.

The East is the direction of healing through vision. It emphasizes the possible—not the probable, but the possible. Its animal is the eagle, and it teaches the shaman the use of vision. To the medicine person vision is more precious than sight. It has to do with placing the cart way before the horse and seeing what you are trying to accomplish before looking at the limitations. It is an act of creation, of forging the kind of future we want our children to inherit. the Medicine Wheel is described in detail in my book, *The Four Winds.*

The East-West axis is the axis of compassion and vision, and is the horizon on which the shaman operates. It has direct access of power, but it is tempered by compassion and service. In Castaneda's tradition, for example, you find that dimension missing completely. Castaneda's Don Juan was a sorcerer, not a shaman. There is no instance of healing in any of the Castaneda books at all.

You have to admit that Castaneda caught the public imagination and foreshadowed much of the current interest in shamanism.

Alberto Villoldo: I certainly admire his writings. He's a good storyteller, but what he's writing about is not strictly shamanism. Don Juan is a sorcerer. Sorcery is the gathering and accumulation of power. Shamanism is the exercise of power with the goal of service and compassion. I think that Castaneda's writings are extraordinary even though he might have construed a lot that he wrote about. It's sad that he's not accessible and is unwilling to have his material verified. My gripe with Castaneda is that anybody who has credentials like he has, or like I do, has to make his work verifiable by others. If you don't, then it's a figment of your imagination. It becomes just another hallucinatory experience. Yes, he has opened the doorways into domains of mystery for many people, but it's sad that he has personally not been more accountable for his experiences. All of the shamans I work with are real flesh and blood—you can meet them in one of the expeditions that I lead through the Four Winds Society.

If Don Juan is not a shaman, what is?

Alberto Villoldo: The role of the shaman is split up into four different roles: healer, sorcerer, priest, and myth maker. Narrowly defined, the priest repeats the old stories and keeps the mythology going, whereas the shaman links us directly to the knowledge contained in the myth. When the priest sits at the top of the hierarchy and withholds knowledge from the people, the shaman ceases to be a viable part of the society. That's when the shamans begin to disappear. There are some tribes in North America in which the role of the shaman is still intact, but you are more likely to find them in the Amazon and the Andes in South America where the people have not been confined to reservations for 200 years. In the classical sense, shamans are the intermediaries between Heaven and Earth. They do not dispense healing. That's the role of the healer. The shaman says you can't heal yourself until you become a healer, until you become a person of power. If you are unable or unwilling to do that, then you go see the healer and he or she will give you the herbs. The shaman is more of an instigator who brings you directly into contact with your own power. The priest is interested in the answers; the shaman is more interested in provoking you to ask the questions that will lead you into paradox and duality. The shaman helps you to learn how to step out of the monochronic time—the linear time that we're familiar with—into a polychronic time that may look linear but really folds forward upon itself.

In most non-Western cultures, you see time and history repeating itself. If you understand the cycles of history, you understand the future. If you're in tune with the seasons, you know that spring follows winter and that winter is a time of going within. Once you are able to bring yourself into tune with the cycles of nature, you can begin to learn how to step outside ordinary time into dream-time. You cannot take your ego into the dream-time, only your intent. Personality has no place there. Many of the techniques of shamanism are designed to strengthen and empower the intent so that you can move into domains with two or three coordinates in time rather than just one. These are domains that exist parallel to ours and where you have access to knowledge and information directly. You don't have to depend on narrative, be it storytelling or the printed word.

In the Amazon, before you begin certain ceremonies, everybody gets a chance to share who they are and what they're there for—what they're looking for. The interesting thing is that everybody does it all at once. Everybody talks simultaneously. The goal is to tune into the flow of information to get an impression of the totality of the group's purpose. You're not allowed to begin the ceremony until you know exactly what each person is saying without listening to them individually.

So it's a matter of retraining your senses?

Alberto Villoldo: I look at it as a way of developing a kind of common sense. It's not a matter of bridging ordinary senses, but of developing crossover senses so that, for example, I can hear something I see. What happens is that the five senses begin to meld into a common sense. Musicians often develop this. They see a flight of geese three miles away and can hear the flapping of their wings, or they hear music, and they can see eagles soaring. With this common sense you can learn to literally see with your skin. For example, when I look at you in the dream-time, I'm not just looking at your face as I am now. I'm looking at you from the front, the back, and the sides simultaneously. In the dream-time, you perceive globally. It's an oceanic kind of perception that is totally disorienting until you learn to focus your intent. Once you learn how to decipher that common sense into your other senses, you begin to perceive outside ordinary time. You can hear voices that were spoken 2000 years ago. You're sensitive to this flow of information that is all around you. I think it's a sense that's dormant in everybody.

It sounds similar to lucid dreaming, of learning to maintain a point of consciousness in the dream state?

Alberto Villoldo: That's the first stage of it. Shamans say that there are two kinds of people: people that dream and people that are being dreamt. The dreamers are those who can consciously guide their dreams. Lucid dreaming is an excellent way to enter the dream-time. In shamanic traditions you are taught to see, to use your vision to see into these realities. In seeing them, you enter them, you're in dual realities simultaneously. You do that through learning to see concurrent realities. If you can teach yourself to develop the common sense perception that we were speaking about before, then you can hear twelve conversations at the same time. Perception is really the key to entering these realities. You learn to perceive and recognize what's happening concurrently all around you all the time.

How do you go about entering the dream-time?

Alberto Villoldo: I used lucid dreaming to become aware of myself in my dreams. Castaneda wrote about achieving this awareness by looking at his hands while in the dream state. What I did was to bring a small crystal I owned with me into dream-time. When that crystal appeared to me in my dream, I became conscious that I was dreaming. Then my task became to will myself to places of power I had visited, such as Machu Picchu or the Anazasi cliff dwellings in Arizona. In the dream state, one has access to teachers who are not in the flesh. They are not even in our time frame. If you can cross the curtain of time, you can sit at the feet of ancient Mayan masters and hear their stories.

What about time in the shamanic realms?

Alberto Villoldo: The shaman's perspective of time is not strictly linear. One of my interests is how shamanism looks at the future, which you can influence in the same way the chaos theory claims that a tornado ripping through Texas may have been started by a butterfly flapping its wings in Beijing. The same concept applies across time. The master shaman who has completed the journey through the Medicine Wheel can call forth a higher destiny for his/her people. Those who have completed this journey have predicted many of the crises and challenges that we face today. Their prophecies include the return of the jaguar people and the return of Quetzlcoatl, Lord of the Dawn to the Mayans.

What are these prophecies?

Alberto Villoldo: A Mayan prophecy goes like this: Seven heavens of decreasing choice, and nine hells of increasing doom, and then the Lord of the Dawn shall return. Each of these heavens or hells is a 52- year cycle of the Aztec calendar. At the end of the seventh heaven of decreasing choice, the conquistadors came to Mexico, and the Aztecs thought it was the god Quetzlcoatl coming from the East. That was the beginning of the nine hells of increasing doom. The last hell started in 1942 with the detonation of the first atomic bomb in Almogordo, New Mexico. The end of the ninth hell is 1994. The Inca prophecies speak about the return of the jaguar people, people who have gone beyond death, violence, and territorial conflicts. The jaguar people are no longer burdened with or hunted by death. They do not need to bring death to others to placate the hungry gods that live within them.

What about history after these nine hells?

Alberto Villoldo: They speak about the return of Viracocha, the creator god that walked among men. They talk about a time of peace, prosperity, and the return of the god of the Sun, the Lord of Light. Once we conquer death, once death no longer lives in us, it will be a time of long-lasting peace.

You mean fear of death, or death itself?

Alberto Villoldo: They prophesy the end of death. I can't be any more succinct than that. That lends itself to many different interpretations. Whether we should read that as symbolic or literal, I can't say. Perhaps they are referring to a change in our perception of death. I read that prophecy as also heralding an end to violence.

As if we have been wearing blinders and are about to remove them?

Alberto Villoldo: That's what the rites of passage through the Medicine Wheel are: learning how to see when the blinders are removed without being overwhelmed. And that's where shamanism can help. The blinders are off for us as a species and we are overwhelmed. It used to take years of training to be a yogi, or a medicine man or woman, or a shaman. Many people alive today were born with those faculties fully awakened, yet poorly trained and developed, and so all they can do is inhibit them. The brain is masterful at inhibition. When you put your shoes on in the morning, you don't want to be reminded all day that your shoes are on, so you inhibit that signal. You inhibit everything you don't want to be bothered with, whether its wind chimes or traffic noise.

When the blinders go off, fear rushes in. For example, sometimes when I'm going to sleep, I start going into sort of an out-of-body experience, and my immediate response is intense fear or panic. It feels like a very primitive, animal-like fear of going into these other states.

Alberto Villoldo: Yes, I know that fear. Some psychologists have speculated that it might be a response to an old genetic memory from when our ancestors lived in trees. If we fell to the ground in our sleep, we might be devoured by animals. A medicine woman or man will say that your task is eventually to learn how to leave the physical body gracefully. Then, when the time comes, your departure is an act of courage that will lead you to the land of the ancestors.

In the shamanic traditions that I was trained in, fear is the great enemy. You learn to use fear as an early warning system rather than as a response mechanism. When this happens, the centers of the brain associated with violent response are disengaged. One of the key teachings of the shamanic tradition is that you cannot free yourself from the grip of fear until you exorcise violence from yourself. The fear that lives within us is basically the fear of death, but we don't die all at once. We die a little bit at a time. So, by exorcising fear you are exorcising death. You will die, but you won't be claimed by death if you've already been claimed by life. In shamanism, fear and violence are denials of life. They are two harsh sides of the same coin.

Could you address the role of hallucinogens in shamanic practices? Some people think that's the only way you can reliably get to these other spaces, and others think they're something you should never touch.

Alberto Villoldo: In my training I have used the *ayahuasca*, a very powerful hallucinogen. It's not the sort of thing I recommend. The name *ayahuasca* means the rope of the dead. It takes you beyond death to face every fear that you ever had. It's not easy. I didn't know what I was getting into when I first started working with the plant. Personal and collective horrors came to me, and my worst dread at the moment was that I would not die. Definitely not a good high. I was terrified that I would continue to live seeing this horror. My training was to learn to observe both horror and beauty and neither deny nor identify with them. Then when you look at the horrors around you they become a very small and encapsulated part of one reality that coexists with many others.

I think that the medicines, as they're called, are valuable and powerful when used in the right context. I have seen much abuse of hallucinogens, and I don't advise anybody to work with them unless they're working with a master. Otherwise, I think it's a lot of escapism. I know so many people who have extraordinary mystical visions and communion with the divine, but their lives are a dysfunctional mess. They're struggling to survive doing something they don't like. Their relationships aren't working. They're living in adversity. To me hallucinogenic escapades are a pseudo knowledge that mimics but forestalls the kind of knowledge that a shaman truly seeks; it is the greatest trap in the shamanic training.

What about teachers? Is it necessary to study with a medicine person?

Alberto Villoldo: I don't necessarily advise people to find a medicine man. I do encourage them to go to nature and learn from nature. There are many great teachers around today, both native and non-native. But above all, you must know yourself. Lao Tsu, talking about the art of war, said that if you know yourself and you don't know your enemies you will be victorious in half your battles, but if you know yourself and your enemy, you will be victorious in all your battles. Well, if you don't know yourself *and* you don't know your adversary in the shamanic sense of calling out the best in you—then you will lose all your battles.

I tell people I'm working with on a one-on-one basis to change nothing in their lives. I think we're addicted to change. The only thing we need to change is our perception. It's like the story of the two six-teenth century stone masons that are chipping away at two stones. Asked "What are you doing?" the first mason says, "I'm squaring out this stone." When asked what he's doing, the other mason says, "I'm building a cathedral." They're both doing the same thing, but their per-spectives are totally different.

How does one go about developing and keeping that larger perspective?

Alberto Villoldo: I think it's vital to do your work of the South, to make an act of power with your own past, and to complete all the "I love you's," all the "I forgive you's." Come up with your own rite of passage for shedding the skin of the past, but make sure that it's more than just a mental exercise. Go through your rite of passage—design it, devise it, and do it. That's what brings the sacred into your life. The task of the shaman is not to pursue meaning but to create it, to bring the sacred to an otherwise profane and mundane reality. That takes a daily act of courage and a willingness to make mistakes.

You need to live your life with power, honor, and dignity. To do that may be as simple as placing yourself ten years from now and ask-ing yourself: What is it that I wish I had attempted—not necessarily at-tained but attempted—in those ten years? What would make you the type of human being that you want to grow into?

Shamans say that everybody has a future, but only a few people have a destiny. A destiny is something you have to summon. You do this by embracing a mythology where you're never cast out from par-adise, where you still walk with beauty on Earth. You do this by living your life with mastery and vision, seeing what everybody else sees and thinking something different about it. This is a personal ecology; this is the practice of shamanism.

(Magical Blend issue #45)

Spirituality
The Shamanic Revival

Lynn Andrews: Enlightenment—"Drug" of Choice

I have often wondered why the entire generation of the sixties seemed to make such a radical change in direction. I remember an age of instant delights of the senses—you drop acid and you're an instant shaman or are instantly enlightened. During the sixties, important gateways were approached. We started doing our homework, unwittingly in many cases. We are, for the most part, a privileged society. We had the opportunity to have love-ins. We had the time. We had the tremendous luxury to read and to learn. As a result, we now are reaping what we started in the sixties.

In the sixties, there appeared an opening in the lens of consciousness. We developed the desire to open the third eye. We realized there was more to life than what we were seeing. We didn't exactly know what that was, but we were going to find it. For some people, it was the beginning of understanding what gateways really are—those places of luminosity and power that appear to people who have strengthened their intent and their dream bodies to the point where they can actually see them. Gateways are places of luminosity that are very seductive. Some are good gateways some are not.

It is very important if ever you come across a gateway, a passage place that provides the possibility for higher teaching and higher learning, that you are accompanied by "one-who-knows-how," someone who has walked that trail before you. Gateways are way beyond your ordinary knowing and not unlike dropping acid in the sixties. LSD provided a gateway for many people, but it was an unknown world, and it blew a lot of people's minds completely. They were not ready for what they saw. Had they been able to join with a teacher at that time, maybe they could have used their vision and their experience in a different way.

In my book *Dark Sister, A Sorcerer's Love Story,* Jaguar Woman took me on a journey to meet my own aspects of darkness. I learned much about myself. Jaguar Woman told me she was using the smoke of a very magical and powerful herb to induce the trance state within me. When I came out of the experience, she told me the sacred smoke was a combination of only cedar and plain tobacco. The power of our mind can take us anywhere we choose. In truth, Jaguar Woman knows how to literally put her will inside you and tug those places where your luminous fibers attach, where all of your knowing gathers and is secured. She can juggle them around and move you from one level of consciousness to another. She can help you to physically go through a gateway.

A good shaman teacher understands the workings of the mind. She understands how fear works and how intent works. I have often said that sorcerers never kill you—they make you kill yourself. And the reverse is also true. You can become a powerful seer and traveler of the dimensions, if you believe that you can do that, if you can will yourself into that experience through practice and commitment. You have to prepare the body, and when you move into those events, remember that you can literally burn the myelin sheathing around the nerves, because there is a heat that's involved with this process. It's not just something you drop into.

So you must look with careful discernment at what your choices are, looking at your choices every day and taking stock of what consequence each and every choice is in your life. Enlightenment is one of those choices. If you realize that this is an Earthwalk that is really about enlightenment, then you realize that life is really about nothing else. Power always tests us in a personal way, and power always tests a society as well. We often make choices out of greed, out of envy, out of very limited vision. And I think that is our tragedy, because we as human beings have the ability to truly see and experience all of the dimensions in the universe. And if for some reason, whether it is because of our terror of change or fear of the unknown, we choose to be limited in our ability to feel and to create, then so be it. But instead of choosing to sit in tiny spaces of limited awareness, we could instead be reaching out our arms and embracing that very thing that could heal us. We could be sitting in the realm of the gods. But, of course, that is part of the unknown. We have to let go of what we know to move into the Great Mystery. That's what is so difficult for us.

Spirituality
The Shamanic Revival

Merilyn Tunneshende: War of the Wizards

Introduction by Jerry Snider

When we released an issue of *Magical Blend* with its sub-theme of nagualism, we expected controversy, but we were not prepared for what ensued. Originally, we sought to interview Carlos Castaneda for that issue, but were unable to acquire it. Then, *Body Mind Spirit* ran an interview with Castaneda in which the elusive sorcerer flatly denied that don Juan Matus ever had any disciples that he himself had not previously mentioned.

This was disconcerting to us because it appeared to invalidate claims made by Merilyn Tunneshende in these pages. When we asked Merilyn to respond, she did so with the following article, in which she tells more of the story than she was previously inclined. Although no names are mentioned, we think readers can interpret for themselves the identities of the Old Nagual, The Dreamer and the unfortunate sorcerer who crossed them.

In 1980 there was a battle of sorcerers in Mexico. By this time, the Old Nagual and The Dreamer had moved into other realms; however, it is not true that they could not get out of them. This battle was so intense that it parted the whole world of sorcery, and even aligned curers, herbalists and other types of spiritual healers with one of the two energetic movements.

One of the main focuses of the battle was over ancient immortality teachings The Old Nagual possessed. He was extremely concerned about the misuse and misrepresentation of those teachings, and in 1980, he definitely turned his back on certain members of his old party. The Dreamer was a little more patient. He remained in contact with some of the members who had been expelled by the Old

Nagual for about six more months. Then he, too, turned his back on them.

It was at that time, after 1980, that the quality of the explanations of the teachings began to deteriorate. It was also at that time that references to The Old Nagual's party of original apprentices began to disappear and a new group of individuals began to appear. The resulting split formed a division in the world of energy work very akin to the division between the ancient Toltecs and the Maya.

Nagualism has been traced to the Maya, but it is much older. The knowledge of the naguals has its ancient roots in pre-Tibetan occultism. Tibetan Buddhism contains some of the most advanced occult knowledge on the planet, but much of their knowledge precedes Buddhism. The Tibetans gleaned their wisdom from the same source that ancient naguals gleaned theirs, which explains some amazing similarities between the two cultures. Both had highly advanced astronomy. Both were able to make in-depth and extremely accurate predictions of future events. And both cultures shared an understanding of the clockwork structure of energies, certain transformational teachings, dreaming practices, as well as transmutational and healing knowledge. But again, I must stress the root of this knowledge comes from a culture that predates both Tibetan and Central Mexican cultures.

The Toltecs appeared much later. They were a military/religious culture that ravaged the world of the Maya in about 1200 AD. It was from the Maya that the Toltecs learned their energy practices, but they did not learn them all. They promised the miracles the Maya had been able to produce, but were unable to. The Toltecs stressed energy draining practices, and what you got when you arrived at the end of the Toltec labyrinth was human sacrifice. Their practice of ripping out the heart of a sacrificial victim on top of the Temple of the Warriors goes a long way to explain what happened to the path with heart—the Toltecs sacrificed it.

Toltec practitioners in this century indicate they are much too abstract for practices of that nature. However, the labyrinth of illusion is still there. One wanders endlessly in it, looking for the promise of genuine revelation of power, but one does not find it. One just finds more of the labyrinth of illusion. Once in the labyrinth, the unused portion of one's energy—the energy that would actually manifest the totality of these ancient teachings—is drained and utilized by others, who feed off of it in classic Toltec fashion.

It was the Toltec approach that precipitated the battle of the sorcerers in 1980. A major portion of this battle is over one of the immortality
practices called "The Fire Within." This is not the only immortality
practice. There are actually four, but this is the one that was beginning
to be taught to a particular segment of the Old Nagual's group before
it was subverted and created the split. The fact is, the individuals currently representing the Fire Within do not understand it. They don't
know how to perform it, although they may say they do. What con-
cerns me is that in the strategic inner workings of their inaccessibility,
it would be highly possible to fake.

The Fire Within, when executed, can have multiple effects. Imagine a supernova. The light is so bright and the transformation so rapid
you can't even look at it. And that light expands everywhere. It's like
going into warp speed hyper-drive. Following this, matter is scattered
everywhere and it may appear that nothing is left of the individual ex-
ecuting the Fire Within. Another thing that can happen is that some
vestige of the body may be left, like an old cocoon left by a butterfly.
Another possibility is the entirety of the energy can be taken, but this is
a great art. It requires absolutely the most scrupulous intention.

At the moment of death for an ordinary person, the energy leaks
out gradually. If it is a conscious, peaceful death, it is a very soft and
gentle process of energy slowing moving up through one's internal energy column, having that energy resonate to a degree that it expands itself and recollects outside the body. It appears, to an individual who
doesn't have total Seeing, that the energy is seeping away.

The way a nagual moves into the death experience is entirely different from this gentle, extraction process. At the moment of death, or
before, the nagual ignites the luminosity and moves out of the body
with intent, unleashing transfigurational energies that have been
stored in the body for an entire lifetime, for just this purpose. It is a very
individual thing. It is the destiny and design of each individual as to
how much of that energy they will take with them and where they will
go with it. Some people choose to leave something behind as a gift of
thanks for the people of the Earth. Some people need to take what energy they have with them.

The teachings of the Fire Within come from Mayan nagualism. The
original term for the nagual is *Uay Kin*. It essentially means nagual of
the Sun or Sun nagual. Nagual, of course, is the being who has the capacity to transmute and transfigure across species and into higher and
lower vibrational realms. *Kin* means light, the sun, and this term refers

to the explosive, supernova type transformation of moving into the realms of light energy.

When it was seen by the Old Nagual that these teachings were going to be subverted, the teachings were stopped. Essentially, the group that fell on the negative side of the split was taught an illusion. What they are seeking is similar to looking for how to control the bizarre phenomenon of spontaneous combustion. In other words, they are wandering in a world of lesser realities in a trap, a labyrinth, constructed by the Old Nagual himself to keep them from being able to do harm.

The Old Nagual essentially blasted the individuals that fell on the negative side of the split into a nether realm. How could such a blasting into another realm be done? The nagual, or Uay Kin, has the capacity to transmit energy and knowledge through light. It is a direct transmission. Again, we have many references to this in the original practices of the Tibetans. In the light comes all the coding, all the sequencing, the sounds—everything that is necessary for the light to enter into the totality of the being.

If it is necessary to blast, then one does the exact opposite. One reflects the absence of light, extracting light from the iris. After having witnessed such a phenomenon, the individual finds him or herself in a lower astral abyss, in which everyone has had their light extracted, too. If any being with any light is dumb enough to wander into this realm, they become prey to hungry ghosts who feed off whatever light energy there is. These hungry ghosts don't understand that if they protect the light and honor it, the light will grow and extend to them through their kindness. Instead, they feel the hungry void within themselves and they feed.

The abyss is a mini-dimension. It is not a totality of the hierarchical universal structure. It is like a psychotic split in the fabric of the sacred, beautiful wholeness. It is caused by misunderstanding and ignorance. It is caused by misappropriation of energy. And once in the abyss, one cannot get out, unless one passes through to a stage of understanding and can slowly be lifted through appropriate dreaming practices and other energetic work.

So now we know what happened when the Old Nagual saw his teachings were being misused. He blasted certain members of his original party into the abyss. What happened to those who were left on the positive side of the split? Some are working with the potential healing of the AIDS virus. Viruses and cancer cells have the missing genetic encoding, and they can reproduce themselves infinitely. The problem is they do it in a chaotic way, so they cannot be aligned with the matrix of creation. Nagualism, or the work with the transmutational energies relating to creation, is an excellent way to approach this virus. Of course, we won't know until it manifests in its totality as an absolute, tangible, reality-based, physical form that people can feel and see. A full manifestation of these energies on Earth, to be shared with everyone, has the potential to bring about one portion of a series of prophesied headings and transformations that are to take place as we move into the potential for a new energetic dimension.

The universe is evolving. The energies are evolving and growing, living and pulsing. And transformations are happening. I can absolutely state this is a fact, from my own personal reality. I absolutely wish you well.

(Magical Blend issue #48)

Merilyn Tunneshende is the author of Medicine Dream: A Nagual Woman's Energetic Healing, *Hampton Roads Publishing Company, Charlottesville, VA 22902.*

Culture

Culture

Culture can be thought of as the integrated pattern of human behavior appearing at one particular time in one particular place. In our own era, both time and place have ceased to be local affairs. The evolution of a vast network of planetary communication and international commerce has turned local time and place into a 24-hour global gestalt, and the rapidly developing Internet seems to signal a final fusion of world culture. The more time we spend on the Internet (and make no mistake, we will), the more we become accustomed to a borderless world, for in cyberspace geography is a state of mind and local custom is a matter of personal choice.

As the tools change, the rules change, and the tools are changing fast. But although we may no longer be bound by a cultural identity, we are still shaped by it. For thousands of years we have bred cultures the way we have bred dogs—attempting to strengthen and stabilize desirable traits and discourage and eliminate undesirable ones. Considering that what is desirable in one culture may be undesirable in another, our global society presents us with an identity crisis of unparalleled proportions. Our conditioning puts us at odds with the reality we live in. No wonder societies worldwide seem to be in a state of disequilibrium and chaos.

But chaos, like cyberspace, is a state of mind. As the science of chaos theory reminds us, the more complex the pattern and the more disequilibrium it displays, the more likely it is to jump the tracks into a totally new pattern with a higher state of order. Since Darwin, the model of human society has been evolution, a gradual process of natural selection. If chaos theory turns out to be a more appropriate model, linear history may give way to something entirely new. As the symbolic year 2000 approaches, millennial fever has gripped popular imagination. As Robert Anton Wilson points out, the year 2000 may be an arbitrary choice for an epochal movement, since our calendar is a Christian device. But the Gregorian calendar is not the only epochal indicator; the Mayan calendar assigns the equivalent of 2012 as the end of history, a nice coincidence for the millenialists among us.

Whether or not history flowers into a timeless, placeless eternity, events have brought us to an unprecedented nexus of historical trends and a high degree of cultural confusion. In a world as complex as ours, prophecy is a sucker's game. The best we can do is to try to stay sane and observe events as they unfold, hoping against hope that our current state of chaos is about to phase into a reintegrated pattern of human behavior, preferably at a higher level. In the meantime, we do what we can to absorb diverse traditions and learn from the past. That seems as good a policy as any. And while we wait and watch, a sense of humor can be an indispensable ally, for we are in a ludicrous position. Although we have serious problems to contend with and sometimes we can even agree over what they are, we cannot seem to reach a consensus about what to do about them. The more we try to push our way through the chaos, the more problems we seem to create. Old approaches must give way to new ones, and discovering new approaches in our chaotic world is an anything-goes proposition.

From its beginning, Magical Blend *has looked at culture as an adventure in chaos. Rather than trying to tie the frayed ends of modern society into a neat hypothesis of who we are and what we are becoming, it has viewed these frayed ends as powerful crosscurrents of cultural electricity, often touching the wires together just to see it spark. As cultures collide and ideologies clash,* Magical Blend *has sought to use the outer confusion to jolt an inner experience. Sensing that any attempt to define our current state of cultural chaos is a step in the wrong direction, the editors have presented the social montage the way a movie presents a visual narrative, hoping that the mind will fill in the gaps between separate and distinct images and establish a sense of movement and continuity.*

The trend so far suggests popular culture is stuck in a stage of deconstruction. The old cliché that everyone complains about the weather but nobody does anything about it seems as good a description as any for our current cultural climate. With a world of ideas to choose from, we have exhausted ourselves trying them on, and yet nothing seems to fit. Discarding ideas has become a cultural obsession. Habit is a powerful force, and it seems as if we are growing accustomed to a meaningless universe. But perhaps therein lies our salvation. The concept of the Void is a rich tradition in both magic and mysticism. It is nothing and yet it is everything, for in its emptiness is ultimate potential. Maybe, just maybe, once we stop looking for what is not there, we will discover what is.

The message of the Magical Universe is that reality is largely a social creation. Considering the ebb and flow of our cultural patterns could shed new light on both our past and our present, especially if Malidoma Patrice Somé ("Of Water and the Spirit") is correct in his observation that much of our modern cultural alienation is a result of having cut ourselves off from our ancestors. Somé, a Dagara tribesman from Western Africa, forecasts a gradual rebirth of indigenous energy in the West, and youth culture trends like the Rave certainly stress a modern tribal approach. The coming of age of Generation X has placed alienation center stage, and that, too, may be more of a blessing than it first appears. To quote Malidoma Somé, "People who are stuck in…nowhereness need each other to ease the alienation…. When people who are longing for the same thing come together, a new community gets created. When I realize that you long for the same thing that I do, my longing diminishes. And so the two of us will start to create a world that is more conducive to what our souls want."

Discovering what our souls truly want from the vast array of available cultural traditions and modern innovations is an epic task, but it is the task of our times. Whether or not we rise to the challenge remains to be seen. If we do succeed in pulling together a consensus out of chaos, the resulting "reality" will be a magical blend of the human spirit in which our highest aspirations are the only ones worth following.

Culture

The Presence of the Past

Malidoma Somé—Of Water & Spirit

with Jerry Snider

Malidoma, whose name means "Be friends with the stranger/ene-my," was born under the shadow of French colonial rule in Upper Vol-ta, West Africa. When he was four years old, he was kidnapped by a Jesuit Father and imprisoned in a seminary built for the training of a new generation of "black" Catholic priests. This was the beginning of a 15-year nightmare, during which Malidoma was abused and intimidat-ed into forgetting everything "tribal," and indoctrinated into seeing the world through the lens of French language and culture—and into envi-sioning a white God through the white man's religion.

In spite of his isolation from his tribe and his village, Malidoma stubbornly refused to forget where he had come from and who he was. With the help of the spirit of his grandfather Bakhye—his teacher, guide, and constant companion in childhood—Malidoma resisted the brainwashing he and his fellow students were exposed to daily.

Finally, a decade and a half later, Malidoma escaped from the sem-inary and walked 125 miles through the jungle, back to his own people, the Dagara. Once home, however, he received a mixed welcome. He could not remember enough Dagara to speak to his own mother and fa-ther. Worst of all, many people in the tribe regarded him as a "white black," a person to be looked on with suspicion and fear because he had been contaminated by the "sickness" of the colonial world.

Over the next year he came to realize that his only hope of recon-necting with his people was to undergo the traditional Dagara initia-tion ritual, even if that meant risking death. His month-long ordeal in a wilderness camp with elders resulted in a dramatic meeting with mag-ic, the forces of the supernatural, and his own personal power.

The fascinating life of Malidoma Patrice Somé is the subject of his autobiography, *Of Water and the Spirit* (G. P. Putnam's Sons, May 1994). Today, Malidoma lives as a man of two worlds, flying the jetways and writing on his laptop computer, and sharing the ancient wisdom of the Dagara with thousands of people around the globe. He is also learning more about the Western perspective and bringing an understanding of this way of life back to his village. In this manner he hopes his people can avoid the fate of many indigenous cultures that have been destroyed by the incursions of colonialism and the modern world.

Malidoma holds three master's degrees, as well as doctorates from the Sorbonne and Brandeis, and for three years he taught literature at the University of Michigan. A popular speaker at men's movement meetings across the country, he is also the author of *Ritual: Power, Healing and Community* (Swan•Raven & Co., an imprint of Blue Water Publishing, Inc., Mill Spring NC)

One of the first things you discuss in Of Water and the Spirit *is the difficulty you experienced translating an indigenous worldview into the English language.*

Malidoma Patrice Somé: It was difficult because the things I was writing about did not happen in English; they happened in a language that has a very different mindset about reality. The Dagara view of reality is large. We do not make distinctions between reality and imagination. If one can imagine something, then it has at least the potential to exist. In Western reality there is a clear split between the spiritual and the material. This concept is alien to the Dagara. For us, as for many indigenous cultures, the supernatural is just part of everyday life. The material is just the spiritual taking on form. The closest we come to the concept of supernatural is *yielbongura*—"the thing that knowledge can't eat." This word suggests that the life and power of certain things depend upon their resistance to the very kind of categorizing on which the English language is based.

You write about how your connection to both tribal and Western ways makes you feel stuck between worlds. Many of us brought up solely in the West feel the same way. What do you make of our particular brand of cultural alienation?

Malidoma Patrice Somé: It has been an interesting discovery for me. I used to think that a person who was born and raised in a specifically defined culture could not feel in between worlds or trapped without a sense of belonging. The discovery that this is not so has caused me to consider the whole issue further. What I now think is that the restlessness that traps the modern individual has its roots in a dysfunctional relationship with the ancestors.

To the Dagara, the ancestors have an intimate and absolutely vital connection to the world of the living. They represent one of the pathways between the knowledge of this world and the next. Unless the relationship between the living and the dead is in balance, chaos results. So when you grow up in a culture that does not have a connection with its ancestors, you are forced to deal with issues by yourself individually.

Some individuals hear the cry of the ancestors much louder than others, but how do you respond when your culture says that the voices you're hearing do not exist? Trying to heed their call only increases the alienation, and this alienation puts a person into a neutral zone. You haven't switched from one world to another, you have switched from one world into no world. So you long for a renewed sense of belonging.

The people who are stuck in this nowhereness need each other to ease their alienation, and this is where the possibility for a new tribal order becomes possible. When people who are longing for the same thing come together, a new community gets created. When I realize that you long for the same thing that I do, my longing diminishes. And so the two of us together will start to create a world that is more conducive to what our souls want.

Tell me more about this new tribal order.

Malidoma Patrice Somé: You know it has become popular for people in the West to defend tribal people, their worldview, and their lifeways. But while the West is engaged in a great debate about what it means to preserve culture, the indigenous world is aware that it has already lost the battle. In many cultures, the Dagara included, it is no longer a question of preservation but of survival in some form or another.

At the same time the indigenous cultures are disappearing, the West is discovering the staggering implications of its own profound spiritual alienation. What I see happening is a coming together of needs, a gradual rebirth of indigenous energy in the heart and soul of people who are born in the West. This is a modern tribal order that can survive because it is invisible to modern destructive tendencies. In other words, when indigenous beliefs look modern to the eyes of the modern, it outwits the modern destructive instinct.

So our alienation is actually the beginning of a healing?

Malidoma Patrice Somé: In order to qualify for healing, one has to be alienated. There has to be a moment of separation. If you are too much in the middle of something, you cannot act positively. There's got to be a detachment first, and then a return. That's what initiation is—a separation followed by a return.

Lack of initiation has been blamed for a number of our social ills.

Malidoma Patrice Somé: It's not so much a lack of initiation as a lack of framework. When I look at all the violence that happens, the abuses that go on, the individual's massive challenge in the face of life—I see these things as initiatory experiences. But there isn't a context. When initiation happens out of context, it becomes more painful and more lethal than an initiation that happens within a framework that is supervised by the wisdom of the ancients.

If there is a Western cultural disregard for ancestors, then it seems to me that this may shed some light on why elders have been denied a meaningful role in our society.

Malidoma Patrice Somé: That's right. And not just the elders, but the children too. In a Dagara village, it is the infants and elders who are closest to the ancestral energy and wisdom. The Dagara recognizes that our true nature is spiritual. Every person is a spirit who has taken on a body. This world is where one comes to carry out specific projects. A birth is therefore the arrival of someone, usually an ancestor that somebody already knows, who has important tasks to do here. So the ancestors are the real school of the living. Grandparents become involved with a new life practically from the moment of conception because that unborn child has just come from the place they are going to.

As I understand it, grandparents actually converse with the incoming soul before it is born.

Malidoma Patrice Somé: A few months before birth, when the grandchild is still a fetus, a ritual called a "hearing" is held. The pregnant mother, her brothers, the grandfather, and the officiating priest are the participants. The child's father is not present for the ritual, but merely prepares the space. Afterward, he is informed about what happened. During the ritual, the incoming soul takes the voice of the mother (some say the soul takes the whole body of the mother, which is why the mother falls into trance and does not remember anything afterward) and answers every question the priest asks.

This way the living find out who is being reborn, where the soul is from, why it chose to come here, and what gender it has chosen. Even the name of the newborn is based upon the results of these communications. For the Dagara, a name is the life program of its bearer. They become a constant reminder of what you are here in this world to do. For example, my Dagara name, Malidoma, means "be friends with the stranger/enemy." As my name implies, I am here in the West to tell the world about my people in any way I can, and to take back to my people the knowledge I gain about this world. So reflecting on my name reminds me of my purpose.

I think this is the kind of area in which indigenous wisdom has something significant to offer to a modern culture that is probably too fixed in thinking that you come here as someone who knows nothing, so everything must be loaded on like a software file. In Dagara culture, it is the incoming soul who tells the living about its role rather than the tribe telling the soul what its purpose is. That makes a lot of difference.

How do we reestablish contact with the ancestors?

Malidoma Patrice Somé: I think that the problem calls for a solution that offers situational context. I have found that every time even a minor context is created, such as a week-long ritual workshop, the creation of a sacred space causes the indigenous instinct to rise instantly in the modern soul. There is an unbelievable propensity for the Western soul to connect with the great beyond. The slightest sacred space opened allows the person to encounter so many baffling things, including images, visions, and unnameable geographies. But this is only the beginning. It is the start of a process and of a relationship. Now what a person does with the relationship is up to that person. In the village it's the same thing. What you do with your relationship with the ancestors is up to you, but at least you get the chance in the proper context to make a link, a hookup. I believe that if that hookup happens we don't need to lay out a plan. It will work out itself, because when the ancestors are allowed to take over, they know best. They know how to make this thing happen much more than we do.

Your book emphasizes the community preparations that are required before one enters into magical space. In this culture we tend to jump into things headfirst. What risks do we take when we practice magic without a license, so to speak?

Malidoma Patrice Somé: Magical experiences that happen in a context of unpreparedness can be lethal. My elders didn't tell me what exact logistics to expect in handling situations in the West. All they said was, "Go and talk to them about us. Show us the way. Show them what we have." Now I'm discovering the consequences of that. People want to have a deep sip of the other worlds, but when I tell them what they have to go through to prepare themselves, I can see the impatience and the disappointment in their faces. In this culture there is always this intense need for immediacy. People don't care what the experience is going to do to them as long as they can get it now. This eagerness and passion to jump into another world only tells me that you're not ready. Just as death can occur in the physical world, death can happen in these other worlds. So if I help someone enter these other realms who is not ready and they die, then I am responsible for that death.

So how can one monitor this whole thing so that the acquisition of the other world does not become lethal to the receiver but permits that receiver to eventually heal and grow?

Malidoma Patrice Somé: That's a big question. It's an unpredictable thing, and I have to admit that I don't have all the competence it takes to do that in the safest and most secure way. I've noticed in the village that they don't either because every time there's some kind of initiatory experience, there is, at one point or another, some incident that is either lethal or very damaging. The reason for this danger is that the other world is constantly shifting. To act as a guide to that other world, I have to have the ability to time its different seasons to find out how the person who is longing for that world can be made to move a little closer to it and eventually become fully part of it without any kind of unfortunate incident occurring. When a person is slowly introduced to it, they can be led into a magical experience without even realizing it.

While you were saying that, it struck me that you could easily have been talking about modern culture itself. It's almost as if we've constructed our own magical world that keeps shifting before us.

Malidoma Patrice Somé: That's true. Technology is something you cannot be on the neck of because the moment you think you've caught up, you're outdated. The moment after that you're obsolete. It's all a matter of timing.

When I look at modern technology, I see it as a very rustic path to the same magical experience that indigenous people are using a backdoor to access. So the feeling for me is that where indigenous people can go into some kind of time shift to move into a magical realm, the modern world wants to cover millions and billions of miles to get there. I suppose that if you go far enough you can reach west by going east, but why do that if you can just turn around and face west?

There's also the ecological consequences of taking the long road.

Malidoma Patrice Somé: When you are going in the opposite direction that you meant to go, you will find a lot of things along the road standing in your way. It may be that these obstacles are really allies trying to tell you that you're going in the wrong direction and that you need to turn around and go backward. But if you are too stubborn to listen, you will see them as standing in your way and will probably destroy them. This gives you the sense of having covered some kind of ground when, in fact, you didn't go anywhere. You're just struggling in the same place and creating more and more dirt, more and more pollution, and alienating yourself from the very world that you're living in.

But we don't need to see the world as something we necessarily need to protect, as if the Earth was some kind of helpless being in our hands. The Earth can decide to take three or four million years to take care of herself. Whether we have three or four million years to wait until the Earth rebalances herself is another question.

So when we talk about saving the planet, what we're really talking about is saving ourselves?

Malidoma Patrice Somé: Right. Instead of trying to save the planet, we need to stop and listen to the message the Earth is trying to tell us. To hear that message you have to shift hierarchies from one that talks about saving the planet to one that is willing to listen. It's the same problem one encounters when one talks about saving indigenous cultures—the savior is always above the saved. The inflated ego has no room for help from spirit, the ancestors, or the Earth; it has to take care of everything itself.

Any person brought up in the Western culture who has gone through any form of Western education has been conditioned to fixate on the ego. So, every time there is a need to do something new—something besides the quick fix—there's always going to be the nagging voice of the inflated ego. It will always find a way to make you question what you are doing. I'm not saying that you have to silence it, but you have to learn to use it as a yardstick to measure the appropriateness of the direction you are heading. The indigenous view sees humanity as a part of the natural order instead of somehow above it looking down. Learning to see things that way may just deflate the ego enough so that the healing, or the real magic that we're talking about, has room to happen. Spirit wants to come into our lives; they want to help us do things that are magical. If we don't allow them, they're not going to force themselves on us, because they respect us more than we do them. But if we make room for them, then we will see the direct result of a self that has opened its ears, its soul, and its heart to the vibration of the Earth.

Sort of a soft revolution?

Malidoma Patrice Somé: The most far-reaching transformation is very discreet. It is seemingly amorphous, as if there's nothing happening until eventually the ego is challenged. Your ego will argue that you're accomplishing nothing, but there's another part of you that well knows that you're sending energy out there to join other minute energies until it eventually becomes a huge ball that will someday explode and spread its healing energy all around. That, to me, is the most far-reaching initiative. It's much more profound than this youthful energy that sends troops, planes, tankers, and so forth out there to fix something now, even if it sets everything ablaze within a matter of days.

In other words the history of Western civilization?

Malidoma Patrice Somé: That's right. You have the evidence; it's right there. Drop the bomb and you see the whole area in flames. That's evidence that you've done something, whereas the most lasting magical healing is one that starts at the ground. By the time it takes effect, you don't even know when it started; you don't even know what the exact process has been. All you sense is a certain breeze of peace, a healing breeze that really feels appropriate.

Most shifts, be they cultural, philosophical, or spiritual, start at the bottom, grow like a flame and burn all the ego and infected energies all the way up. Without that energy we find ourselves constantly depending on empty symbols as yardsticks to measure the worth of our lives, when in fact those empty symbols contain nothing. They're useless.

They don't contain soul. These symbols can come in the form of a huge car or a private jet or a million-dollar house—the ways are endless.

It almost seems that these things are our form of talismans. Our private airplanes are power objects.

Malidoma Patrice Somé: That's exactly right. They're illusionary power objects. They could be just the same thing as the little talisman a person in the African desert wears. But the difference is the kind of service or the kind of energy that this huge talismanic object demands from us. It's got to be maintained, and the energy that takes is amazing. So we end up becoming servants to our power objects rather than having these power objects serve our needs. That's the irony involved. The indigenous person would say that whatever spirit is behind this is extremely greedy. The more you give to it, the more it's going to ask of you until it sucks you completely dry.

That brings up an interesting question. Is the West contacting different spirits than the indigenous cultures?

Malidoma Patrice Somé: That's what they say. There are certain worlds or galaxies or subspace regions whose energy is incompatible with the kind of energy we're vibrating, and so the spirits who live there don't ordinarily notice us. But suppose there's a certain frequency both worlds vibrate to, and in our world that frequency becomes amplified to the point that the spirits living in these other worlds begin to notice us. It's like they're suddenly picking us up on their visual screen, and they see that we have a lot of things to give them. It's not that they have bad intentions, it's just that they'll use us as long as we'll let them. They'll suck us dry if we allow it.

The indigenous world's ability to help the modern world could very well come in the form of the indigenous world managing to cut off that channel or scrambling it so that all of a sudden, from the other side, we blip off their screen. Then the spirits from that world will simply look somewhere else. But until that happens, there will be the feeling that what we are doing is righteous, adequate, and good. We just think that we have to go a little further along in the same direction to fix the little problem that we've created. In fact, that's not what it is. The problems are meant to become deeper and deeper. Can we wake up before we hit the deadly line? That's the question, and that's where the indigenous world wants to come in, and it must do so quickly before that line of no return is reached.

That's something that requires a great deal of underground work, because in a situation like this, you cannot be frontal with respect to the person who is going through this kind of habit. Such a person doesn't have the right kind of ears that can hear what is going on. So you've got to go underneath and talk directly to their souls.

How do you do that?

Malidoma Patrice Somé: That is going to happen through the creation of ritual space, because in ritual space there is no arguing You put a person in there and that person is met by spirit. Usually the mental self doesn't know where to fit in, so it becomes confused and then blacks out.

I think ritual space is going to allow people to stop their rhetorical compulsiveness in order to be able to move into that place where, at least, they can allow themselves to be disconnected from the negative orbit they're in. Ultimately that will only happen when the indigenous spirit takes on a white skin or modern status that is supportive.

In a way it's almost like what the Jesuits were trying to do in Africa.

Malidoma Patrice Somé: That's exactly right. They knew that colonizing works better when the colonizer has taken on the local color. Then it becomes a family matter. It's not the other anymore.

And then what happens?

Malidoma Patrice Somé: When one has been opened to the magic of spirit encounter or the vision of another world, he doesn't have to convince that person to take it out and share it with others. So the first practical teaching, I believe, will have to come by putting people right in the middle of this kind of space where they can experience the magic.

The creation of the proper link with spirit, the creation of ritual spaces, communities, the rethinking or reinventing of initiation—these are the things that are going to help fix the kind of crises that modern culture is experiencing. I think that the modern world is very ready. The timing could not be any better. We're all gradually moving into a different century and a different millennium. It's just about time that the fire sparks before we enter that space.

(Magical Blend issue #43)

Culture
A Culture in Search of Itself

⬯⬤⬯

Jean Houston—Gold of the Psyche

with Jerry Snider

Just as a magnet passed over iron filings attracts them, causing the filings to take on the shape of the magnet, so, too, does myth attract and repattern human consciousness. Jean Houston, through a pioneering blend of mythology, psychology, anthropology, history, and new physics, has studied humanity's dominant myths in more than 35 traditional cultures from India and Mexico to Australia. As founder of a discipline she calls "sacred psychology," Dr. Houston serves as a kind of cultural psychoanalyst helping world leaders to define and refine both positive and negative aspects of their culture's unique "leading myths."

In this interview, Dr. Houston discusses the current world-wide repatterning of humanity by its "mythic magnets," and suggests where they may be leading, and how they may help us to learn to live our lives more consciously and dramatically.

Jean Houston is an internationally renowned psychologist, scholar, philosopher and teacher, and the bestselling author of fifteen books, including *The Possible Human* and *The Search for the Beloved*. She is also co-director of the Foundation for Mind Research in Pomona, New York, and founder and director of the Mystery School—an institution dedicated to teaching history, philosophy, the new physics, psychology, anthropology, myth, and the many dimensions of our human potential. A consultant to the United Nations, UNICEF, and other international agencies, Dr. Houston presents transformational workshops to people and organizations all over the world.

Your discussions of mythic realms have a feel similar to what we refer to as "dreamtime." Both note a prevailing sense of disjointedness in terms of time and space perception—a sort of overlapping of realities.

Jean Houston: What you are calling dreamtime belongs to the archetypal realm which is unbound by time and space. We are always influenced by the archetypal realm whether we are aware of it or not, for even when archetypes are repressed, they bleed through into other areas of human experience. I believe we are living in a time when the psyche is rising to reveal this transcendent realm. Perhaps the disjointedness you speak of merely represents a focus on the separateness of things in local-historical-personal time, instead of recognizing that in the archetypal realm, everything is dynamically and creatively related to everything else. That is why the rediscovery of myth is so important to us today. When we tell our great stories, we reach across barriers of consciousness and bridge the gap between local, personal consciousness and the *mysterium tremendum et fascinans* of the universe—the vast, overwhelming environment of human being. By becoming aware we exist both here and in that other order, we turn a corner on our existence, and, instead of feeling disconnected and disjointed, we discover a sense of deep belonging to all of life and the eternal patterns of creation.

In the practice of what you call "sacred psychology," you outline several specific realms of experience. What are they?

Jean Houston: I talk about four realms. There are probably many more. Buddhism talks about hundreds, if not thousands, of realms. I have settled on the four major constellations of the psyche that I have delineated from my work over many years. There is the realm of the senses, or the physical realm. Then there is the psychological and recollective realm. In addition there are the mythic and spiritual realms. In sacred psychology, one is essentially operating on all four levels all the time.

What is the difference between psychology and sacred psychology?

Jean Houston: Sacred psychology essentially asks certain kinds of questions that regular psychology generally does not. Among those questions are: How do you put the regular personal-historical-psychological self in the service of the larger mythic and spiritual self? How do you gain enough passion for the possible when you're not feeling any particular passion yourself? How do you begin to break out of normative limits and begin to realize that the human being is by nature transparent to transcendence? Asking these questions assumes that the whole body-mind system is a great deal more complex than we have given it credit for. Or, if you will, it is as complex as the ancients gave it credit for.

In The Hero and the Goddess *you write, "Whenever a society is in a state of break down...it often requires a new social alignment that only the complex and comprehensive understanding of myth can bring." Could you elaborate?*

Jean Houston: All over the world, we are experiencing a radical breakdown of virtually everything in terms of the way things work. Standard brand religions, cultures, governments, ways of being, politics, family, sexuality, sociology—all of these things are losing the glue, the congruence, that had kept them together for so many hundreds and thousands of years. As these more recent patterns are coming unglued, deeper patterns are emerging from what you are referring to as the dreamtime and what I call the mythic and archetypal realm. In these hyperdimensional mindfields, one feels one's own particular way of being pulsed and repatterned by larger patterns. Bateson referred to it as the "pattern that connects." One comes back from these states and these knowings in a state of what seems to be new knowledge. Or, let's say knowledge put together in remarkably innovative ways. At that point, I think there are very critical changes in the system and one becomes much more available to these nested realities. Along with the rising of those mythic structures, I think we will see larger domains for art, for religion, for science, and for culture. A whole new order of society may begin to emerge. It's not guaranteed, but it seems to me that the potential is clearly there.

In other words, a certain amount of breakdown has to occur for breakthrough?

Jean Houston: In a way, but what I'm finding around the world is that it's much more than breakthrough. Breakthrough suggests just emergence of the depth to no particular purpose. I think it is a co-creative process in which many of us are feeling these shifting realities, not just in society but in ourselves. We are living in a time in which archetypes are literally being re-grown.

Why now?

Jean Houston: The wider use of the self has been the dream for millennia, but only in our time do we have access to the findings of many cultures as well as scientific studies concerning the nature and variety of this potential. At the same time, both of these factors are creating enormous confusion. Even as technology has enabled the cross-fertilization of cultures, so has it also pulled our focus away from the mystery of life. One of the reasons that myth is rising so much in our time is that suddenly we're without a road map. In the past people had definitive maps as to what they would do in their lives, what their roles were, what their parents' roles were, what they would tell the children, how they would punish the criminals, what they could expect in the seasons of life. Now, suddenly, we are without maps just at a time when we need them most to cope with the complexity of modern life.

In terms of sheer experience and events, our lives are five times as long as those of our forebears living a hundred years ago. Along with all that experience there comes a certain vulnerability that comes of having been wounded so many times. It's as if we are so full of holes, we have become holy. These holes, if you will, are giving us access to much deeper source levels and patterns. I can't tell you how many people around the world are hounded and haunted by the sense of their own inadequacy as to preparation. What I think is happening is that we are beginning to recognize that we have begun a process of regenesis. There is a sense of urgency to reprepare, to regestate, and reweave. Worldwide, we are responding to patterns that I think are coming from these depth realities that we're calling hyperdimensional space and time, or dreamtime.

What concerns me is the possibility of getting so confused, we don't recognize the deeper patterns and get stuck in the chaos.

Jean Houston: Yes, you could get stuck. These patterns exist deep within the psyche, and when the psyche rises, so do all its shadows. When you study the phenomenology of meditatively altered states, for example, it's very interesting to see how many shadows rise. I think one of the things that's happening all over the world is that memories that had been caught in a sort of tribal matrix of things that happened but weren't talked about are rising. Memories of transgressions and taboos like incest and other forms of abuse are rising. Many kinds of memories having to do with parents' effect on us are coming to the surface. The shadows are rising up all over the place to a degree that's probably unequaled in human history. It's almost as if they're rising up not just for a kind of general catharsis, but as energy systems to be reorchestrated and applied differently.

So, the dreamlike quality of life is the result of our encounters with our shadows?

Jean Houston: Look at the presidential elections. The more sordid aspects of candidates' private lives are rising. Everybody attributes the phenomenon to the media, but I think there are deeper reasons. The obvious reason is that people want a candidate who walks his talk and who has had a kind of noble life, but I believe it's still more than that. I think President Clinton is just the latest victim in the rise of the shadows of dreamtime. Simply put, nothing will go away anymore. It's part of a shift in consciousness in which anything that was suppressed is now coming up.

In The Hero and the Goddess, *you use* The Odyssey *to help people see their own lives as a mythic journey. Is it necessary to reach that far back into history to find a relevant myth? As powerful as* The Odyssey *may be, I suspect many people would have trouble relating it to what's happening in America today.*

Jean Houston: That's not been my experience. My experience is that the Greco-Roman and Middle Eastern myths are as powerful as any modern American myths, and sometimes more so because we don't face ourselves quite so cruelly. But if you're asking about modern American myths, one of the ones that speaks deeply to people and is now getting an awful lot of mileage is *The Wizard of Oz.*

At its deepest level, *The Wizard of Oz* is the story of the disempowered heart, the disempowered mind, and disempowered courage. It is the quest for the green land in the midst of the wasteland of Kansas. Frank Baum was actually writing, in part, a parable about William Jennings Bryan's 19th century crusade to abandon the silver standard, but it's obviously deeper than that. In a sense, it's the core American myth because it addresses the yearning behind the creation of the Americas. It evokes the longing of millions of people over thousands of years mythically for Oz— the land beyond the Western waters where it was thought there would be a kind of land of opportunity in real space and time providing what had been thought to belong only to vertical space and time in paradise. As a myth, *The Wizard of Oz* promises that, once you go to Oz, you can then finally come home deeply. Once you enter into the mythic space of your home, you can then remythologize and green dreary, gray Kansas in real space and time.

Also, in talking about America, one has to acknowledge the enormously heavy facts of our existence. This country was created by the millennial hopes and dreams of millions of people. If you can talk about a continent or country having a psyche, this dream of millions has stocked our collective psyche. We have this incredibly rich, potent, multi-leveled psyche that got objectified by a historical event whose development paralleled America's growth as a nation. That event was the industrial revolution. What happened was that we objectified the psyche's longing for Oz into automobiles and highways and an endless parade of consumer goods.

One of the things that is unique about America is that the longing for Oz by the deep psyche kept us relatively protected. Unlike other countries, we had only one great national tragedy—the Civil War. But now that first level of the country's psyche has been exhausted. What is now rising are deeper, more organic mythic structures from the deeper dreamtime of the American psyche. What we're seeing now is the catharsis of surface levels before other domains of other psyches rise. I think that's one of the reasons for the fascination with myth all over the Americas. Just look at America's growing fascination with depths and dimensions of consciousness. What is the New Age at its best but a reflection of the fascination—and the sense of commitment to—these depths? I think it's all a part of that deeper psyche made available to all.

After several hundred years, cultures around the world are reclaiming their identities. Rather than being repressed by dominant economic cultures, individual cultures are flourishing. They are recovering their myths. They are recovering their dances. They are recovering their rituals. They are looking to find patterns of journey and transition that simply were not there before. One of the contributing factors to the collapse of the Soviet Union was that it tried to subsume within its giant maw so many subcultures that simply refused to be digested into a single homogenized entity. Now they are rediscovering their own unique identities. All over the world cultures are rising. It's as if this incredible individuation of cultures is occurring in preparation for a planetary society which clearly is not going to be a big Japanese or American homogenization of the world.

Even this country is no longer the melting pot it was in the 19th and throughout most of the 20th century. What we see instead is growing multiculturalism. The Vietnamese are not becoming Americanized. The Koreans are not becoming Americanized. What we have are enclaves that are both American and Korean. Everything is a hyphen.

We're about to become a society in which we are Korean-American-transcendentalist shoemaking-tapdancers.

We have moved away from homogenization. Instead, there is a gestalt of factors coming together that suggests the creation of an essentially new organic society that is made up of patterns of relatedness rather than patterns that are one homogenized whole. Maybe this is happening because the planet requires more species. In the Cenozoic era, which was the era of the last hundreds of millions of years, there was a tremendous proliferation of species. Now, we have killed off many of those species, and watch others disappear on an hourly basis. To use my friend Tom Berry's term, we're no longer in the Cenozoic, we're in the Ecozoic era in which the dominant species becomes responsible for evolutionary governance. Within a very few years we will probably be creating new species, but in the interim what is occurring, I think, is that speciation (the creating of species) is happening through the development of many subcultures.

How does myth help to guide us through the rising shadows of the dream-time?

Jean Houston: For one thing, it makes us become part of a larger story—a larger domain. We are no longer caught in our own literalness, our own historical past-present-future. In the mythic realm, we connect not just with the past-present-future of our own life, but the past-present-future of many lives and of what we call great lives. What the mythical being, or god, or archetype, represents is our selves writ large—our selves if we had access to many more dimensions of our own minds, brains, psyches, and historical systems. In other words, the myth is always anticipatory of the possible human that we really could be.

Cultures in which myth plays an important role understand this. I've worked with aboriginal peoples all over the world, and I have found most of them to have a complex and sophisticated sense of the nested realities in which we live. About a year and a half ago, for example, I asked an aboriginal woman in Australia, "How do humans differ from animals, from the wallaby and the kangaroo and koala?" She replied, with some astonishment at my naïveté, "Why, we are the ones who can tell the stories about all the others."

This may be our human condition, that we are able to tell the stories about the others. We are able to reflect their pattern and their process. In doing so, we're able to deepen our own. It was Walt Whitman who said, "I become what I behold." I would extend that to say, "I'm able to incarnate what I'm able to talk about." When we tell our great stories, we exhibit our species' genius for empathy and for incarnation. That's why worldwide myths of incarnation are so popular. They speak to something more than just one person who resurrects or one god who comes down and becomes a human. They speak to us all because we all have psyches that are subtle enough to take on an immense amount of empathy. We relate to the lives, the passions, and the feelings of other people. Now we're in a time when the people we empathize with are not just of our own tribe, or our own racial or genetic or cultural group. We are becoming empathic with the stories of people across the globe. What happens is that in incarnating these great lives, be they legendary or historical, we are able to take the personal particular incidents of our own lives and see them in a larger context of the personal universals of great life.

When we enter what I refer to as the strange and beautiful country of myth, we get to source patterns that originate in the ground of our being. These patterns are the keys to our personal, historical existence. They give us access to the next patterns of our lives, guiding and nurturing us into these new patterns.

The myth uniquely speaks to the personal *entelechy* in each person. Entelechy is the Greek-derived word which means the dynamic pattern of purpose. It is the entelechy of an acorn to be an oak tree. It's the entelechy of a popcorn kernel to be a fully popped entity. It's the entelechy of a baby to be a grown-up being. It's the entelechy of you and me to be that something and someone which myth serves to evoke. So, myth works in curious, quixotic ways to give us this larger story and give us the pattern that we can begin to unfold. That's what people deeply want. They want the recognition, quickening, and empowerment to be part of a larger story.

Clearly, we are in the most interesting time in human history. The sheer fascinating-absurd-paradoxical complexity of it all creates this dreamlike atmosphere you are talking about. But it's precisely because the responsibility is much larger for us in our time, that we are getting much more help. We're getting many more ideas. We are blending and accessing levels and patterns of self and society that, hitherto in human history, we never had to assume. We've never had to deal with the amount of accumulated culture and psyche as we do now. Faced with the necessary alchemy of blending so many different patterns that have never had to be blended before, we are now creating, hopefully, out of the alembic of our time, a new gold of the psyche.

Sidebar

In earlier times, the family used to sit around the hearth and listen to stories. Much of the wisdom of the elders was dispensed through these tales. Then, for a long while, we lost our hearth. It could be argued that maybe television has now replaced the hearth and is giving us the grand stories back again. And perhaps these great stories are activating the deep story in ourselves.

Clearly television plays an important part in the cross-fertilization of cultures. Now-a-days, every little village everywhere has a television set. I've been in countless villages in India where the people have nothing, but they do have one television set that the whole village shares. For example, every Sunday in India the villagers come in from their water buffaloes, put down their water jugs, and sit down in front of the one television set in the village to watch *The Ramayana*. *The Ramayana* is the great mythic journey of Rama in a search to recover his beloved wife Sita, among other things. It's one of the great guiding myths of India, and it contains the whole constellation of Indian culture.

As a program, it's gorgeous, full of beautiful dancing, art, and culture. As I was watching the program in this one tiny village in rural India, a little old lady sitting next to me remarked, "Oh! I don't like Sita."

"What do you mean you don't like Sita?" I asked.

She said, "Sita, she is too weak. She is locked up by the demon waiting to be rescued. Well, my name is Sita and my husband's name is Rama. They are very common names in India. My husband, he's a lazy bum. I do all the work. I should have a greater part of the story!"

The amazing thing about this exchange was that, even as she spoke, you could see the myth changing.

The program that followed *The Ramayana* was *Dynasty*. I was quite embarrassed, but every one else was watching it with the same passion and intensity that they were watching *The Ramayana*. Apparently, the little old lady recognized my discomfort and asked, "Sister, why are you worried."

I said, "I'm worried because it's so embarrassing, this terrible American show after *The Ramayana*."

She patted my hand and said, "Oh! Sister don't you see? It's the same story. You got the good lady. You got the bad lady. You got the beautiful house. You got the good against the evil. It's the same story." And, of course she's right, but I didn't see it until she pointed it out.

In the past, the stories people told were about people essentially like themselves or else faerie stories. Now, our electronic hearth is conditioning us to respond to cross-cultural patterns. For example, I watched two television programs last night. One was a nature show about animals' deep and intense struggle for survival, and one was an English drama about the life of the British gentry. In the span of two hours, my empathy pulled me into two entirely different worlds, uniting me not only with a different culture, but also a different species.

Our own recent history has demonstrated the enormous cultural influence of television. Despite its limitations, TV has somehow managed to unite us in times of national tragedy and need, perhaps because it has helped us to see the other person's point of view. Now, the other person's point of view is not just our neighbor's, but a little old lady watching *Dynasty* in a rural village in India.

(Magical Blend issue #35)

Culture
A Culture in Search of Itself

---○---

Douglas Rushkoff—Generation X

with Mike Gorman and DNA

Illiterate channel surfers? Couch potatoes? Apathetic video junkies? Socially alienated ciphers? Journalists, college professors, avatars of popular culture, parents, marketing experts and twenty-somethings, themselves, have been trying to define the post-Baby Boomer generation since hippies turned into yuppies and the bloated eighties gave way to the more sedate nineties. GenXers are too young to remember the assassination of Kennedy, and just old enough to remember the embarrassing end of disco. They didn't profit from the excesses of the eighties, but they are guaranteed to pay for them. For a long time, Generation X was defined more by what it was not than what it was.

Ironically, out of this "vacuum of identity" came a steady stream of hip, smart, insightful words and images that both reflected and formed new attitudes. Emerging form the margins of society, twenty-something voices encroached on mainstream society making Bart Simpson, Ren and Stempy, Cyberspace and MTV part of our common vocabulary.

Douglas Rushkoff, himself a GenXer, is among the first mainstream journalists to cover favorite topics like virtual reality, cyberpunks, the psychedelic revival and rave culture for publications as diverse as *Vibe* magazine, *The Whole Earth, Miami Herald, Wall Street Journal, The Boston Globe* and *GQ*. His books, including *Free Rides* (Dell), *Cyberia: Life in the Trenches of Hyperspace* (HarperSanFrancisco), *The GenX Reader* and *Media Virus!: Hidden Agendas in Popular Culture* (both by Ballantine), are witty explorations of his generation's attempt to find a future of their own in the nether regions of the Baby Boomer's high-tech society. Rushkoff's intimate portraits reveal a generation of social theorists: kids who dropped out of consensus culture and slid into a subversive subculture wise beyond its years.

In the book Media Virus! *you state that "the loudest battle cry against the media comes from the New Age community." Is this because they are fearful of technology, or do you think they believe that this is the coming of the apocalypse?*

Douglas Rushkoff: A lot of New Age people seem suspicious of technology. They see it as somehow unnatural and something that really needs to be reversed in order to return us to a natural state. Personally, I think this is a sixties' paranoid view. I look at everything as ultimately natural. If we are in a technological morass, then the only way to get through it is to push through it, not to reverse it.

Do you believe that technology is serving to link us with nature and one another?

Douglas Rushkoff: Ultimately, yes. Technology is part of nature. It's an extension of human consciousness. Ironically the portals that technology opens to us are generally portals that we could open without technology, if we knew how. I think that we are fully capable as human beings of having a global brain and of communicating with each other as parts of a single great organism. But either we really haven't developed those skills, or else we've lost the ability to use them. Back in tribal days, people didn't see themselves as individuals; they saw themselves as parts of a little organism. Well, being one part of an eight-billion-part organism is much harder to come to grips with. In a way, technology is a test run.

So the Internet is the first test run of a process that will eventually hard-wire us together as a single great organism?

Douglas Rushkoff: It is a hardwiring, but I think if, and when, it succeeds in linking up planetary consciousness, we'll realize we had that ability all along.

The hype word of today is "interactivity," which generally suggests a person interacting with machines. But I was talking to Timothy Leary a couple of weeks ago, and he told me about a conversation he had with Albert Einstein, about the coming age of computers. Timothy Leary was talking about interconnectivity and interactivity, and Einstein said, "No, the real significance and the real word to use for what's going to happen isn't just interactivity, it's interpersonal connections."

Einstein looked at everything in terms of relativity. And he's right. It's not a matter of individuals relating to a machine, it's individuals relating to each other. It's truly an interpersonal technology rather than an interactive technology.

You talk about computer viruses and media viruses. Is there a real scare that the whole Internet will be infiltrated by these viruses?

Doug Rushkoff: Well, I think the threat and efficacy of media viruses to destabilize or screw up is vastly overrated. The truth is, when you hear a news report about a computer virus, nine times out of ten you'll hear in the same newscast an advertisement about a seminar that will help rid your company's computers of viruses. In other words, the press release originated from the computer-virus-extinguishing companies. And why? To get people to spend money on unnecessary computer security.

There are some bad trips people get on about the mediaspace. If they're not afraid of catching computer viruses by spending too much time on the Internet, they're afraid their children are going to jack themselves into the matrix and get addicted to virtual sex. Let's face the facts—people are afraid of intimacy, period. AIDS has become the latest excuse for people not to have sex. I mean we should be careful and all that, but it's one thing to be afraid of AIDS and quite another to be afraid of sex. It's the same thing with computer viruses. If you're afraid of computer viruses that's one thing—you can deal with that by being careful about what you download—but if you're talking about fear of empowerment and fear of the kind of intimacy that immersion in the Internet creates, that's another thing entirely.

You cite one example of a media virus being the Salmon Rushdie affair, in which the Ayatollah reacted to Rushdie's Satanic Verses *with an assassination edict. Could you talk a little bit about that?*

Douglas Rushkoff: The spread of a global culture through media is most threatening to fundamentalists. That's because fundamentalism is maintained by isolating your group from the general global wash of imagery. That's the way fundamentalism works. It tries to remain pure by isolating itself. What the Ayatollah did by launching the "Kill-Salmon-Rushdie-Virus" was to put his foot down and say that threatening ideas would be stomped out. In other words, he declared that memes are real. In his effort to stomp them out, he has admitted their potency and ability to cause damage through infiltration. So the Ayatollah treats the threat as real by declaring an ideological war.

What exactly are memes?

Douglas Rushkoff: I think Dawkin's coined the term in *The Selfish Gene.* Memes are the ideological equivalent of genes. A virus in the real world isn't a living thing; it's not like bacteria. It's protein wrapped around genes, wrapped around DNA. A media virus is an event or some sort of media shell wrapped around memes, around ideas.

You had a great example of Virus 23, *the zine, and* Boing! Boing! *being media viruses.*

Douglas Rushkoff: Even *Mondo 2000.* They're viral shells wrapped around memes. I mean *Magical Blend* is a virus of sorts. It's a blend of ideas, memes and techniques. It's a group of coherent, discreet, units of thought that, when absorbed by readers, is capable of changing the way they function.

Which is why fundamentalists don't much care for us.

Douglas Rushkoff: What fundamentalists are afraid of is a certain kind of change. In this country there are huge numbers of people who are afraid that their kids are going to disengage from the static moral templates that have traditionally defined and limited our behaviors. And they're quite right. Generation X doesn't see moral templates, father figures and all that patriarchal, hierarchical stuff as real. They don't see the two-party system as real. They realize it's the vestiges of old static systems that don't adequately express the modern human experience.

You write that "a generation that has disconnected itself from the propaganda machine can no longer be controlled by it." I thought that was really a key to the twenty-something perspective. Maybe the GenXers are disconnecting themselves from the media because the content really isn't there.

Douglas Rushkoff: They are reconnecting to media in other ways. I mean, they're watching *Mystery Science Theater* and *Beavis and Butthead,* because that's all media commentary. It's television's version of Brecht's alienation, where you are constantly made aware that you are watching television and that viruses are being shot out at you.

Do you find within Generation X a different concept of spiritual beliefs that separate them from the sixties' model?

Douglas Rushkoff: As a broad categorization, I would say that a unique contribution that Generation X has made to the cultural conversation about religion and spirituality is that they don't feel the same need to have a religion of tenets or a system of beliefs to go by. Instead, I think they're moving toward more direct experiential forms of spirituality. The real religious interface is no longer between the individual and God the Father, but between the individual and everything else. I think, for example, that one way to experience the connection to the higher heartbeat, or the great pulse of the universe, is through activities like the rave.

People keep harping about the collapse of the family and the loss of family values, but that's not the problem. The problem is the loss of community values. We lost our community values. We don't know our neighbors. We moved into a suburban life-style where each family was a separate unit and was being asked to serve the function of an entire community. No family can do that. The two-parent/1.5-children nuclear family is not enough to create a sense of connection to the world and to the higher power, if you can call it that. The family has collapsed because it's been asked to do more than it should do. What we do need to do, if we want to restore the sense of family, is to learn how to live as what we are, which is a colonial organism, a huge mass of individuals.

In Cyberia *you talk about two kids dropping in on the net while taking ecstasy. Is this one way people get connected?*

Douglas Rushkoff: Psychedelics, be they natural or synthetic, are a valuable cultural medicine for a society that has lost its connection to itself. In a world of all-too-discrete individuals, it helps to break down the illusion of separateness. That's why the rave experience is so popular. Kids coming out of our very ego-based culture need a medicine to create that feeling of connection that breaks down walls and allows the animal to rise up. Medicinally or technologically generated communities are valuable, and are an important stage for a society that really needs remedial help, because we seem to have lost the ability to do it in any other way.

I wrote about the drug war in my first book, *Free Rides.* What I said was that the war is not against drugs, but against the states of consciousness they offer, because they are threatening to those who would keep things the way they are.

If in fact we are moving into different levels of reality, will the future be more user-friendly to those with broader experiences?

Douglas Rushkoff: You know that most of the people in the research and development departments of the computer industry had to have experienced hallucinatory realities. That's what the computer reality was at the beginning—people charting a totally new region of consciousness. Naturally, the people who felt comfortable doing that were people who had already done it with chemicals.

The Internet is currently multidimensional in its consciousness. What will happen when the government steps in? Will there be toll gates at each node? Will it get swallowed up?

Douglas Rushkoff: It can't get swallowed up. It was conceived by the Rand Corporation and was brilliantly constructed to avoid that kind of control. The smartest minds figured out that if you created a natural chaotic system, no one will be able to censor it. They've created the beehive, ant nest, networked grass-roots subculture. They can't take it back. This is the best war machine they have ever made.

It's so ironic in that sense.

Douglas Rushkoff: That's the thing, everyone considers the cold war and the industrial revolution to be all bad. They weren't bad, they just got us to a stage. A little kid, when he's two or three years old, starts saying no to his parents and turns into a little brat. That's what we did as a baby civilization growing up. We kept crying, No! Like a little baby, we were angry that we weren't one with the mother any more. But what does a baby do as it grows up? It fights for its individuality. Then, when it becomes an adolescent, it says, "OK, I'm going to drop some of my ego, because I want to get laid." That's what we're doing. We decided it's more valuable to have intimacy than some notion of this separate self.

It seems that now, more than ever, writers of science fiction like William Gibson, Phillip K. Dick and Terence McKenna should be known as the prophets of the future. Do you think they're correct in their views?

Douglas Rushkoff: Sometimes I get the feeling that they all lack faith in human nature. McKenna says we've gone down a dead end, and we need to back up and go out the way we came in. I say absolutely not! We need to push through. McKenna believes there's a bottleneck effect, and people who have had the DMT experience and other realizations are going to make it through the attractor at the end of time, while the vast majority will not. The way I see it, either we all make it or none of us will. It's one organism, one thing. Dick and Gibson say that technology is going to change and get better, but human nature is going to stay the same. In other words, human nature is bad, and we're just going to use our new technology to do mean things to each other. I just don't believe that's true. Human nature changes, and I believe that it's basically good, not bad. Technology is inherently liberating, ultimately. Renaissances don't happen overnight.

When we look to the future of cyberspace, what's the warning sign up ahead?

Douglas Rushkoff: If we are derailed from the optimistic vision of a technologically mediated global organism, it's going to be because we're afraid of it. If we start to believe that this kind of intimacy is bad for us, then we will convince ourselves that we need toll booths and policemen, because we can't be trusted. Or else we'll get distracted. We might, for example, end up choosing a system that provides Sylvester Stallone movies on demand, over a system that gives us an opportunity to feedback. So we can get derailed. It's sort of like the bardo thing in *The Tibetan Book of the Dead*, where you move through layers of distraction. You get distracted by Bardo sex, and you end up being reincarnated. In the same way, we can get distracted by the *Pizza* button on the remote control. It all depends on how we choose to spend our time with this great gift of technology. If it turns out we want to spend our time absorbing *90210,* then we're going to get derailed, because people just won't be involved the way they could be.

(Magical Blend issue #46)

Culture
Problems and Solutions

—————————◉—————————

Andrew Weil: Why We Are All Addicted

I recently ran across an article that appeared in *Science* back in 1961. The senior author was a man named Heinz von Forster, who's an electrical engineer at MIT. The title of the article was "Doomsday, Friday the 13th, 2026." Von Forster, who was not a population biologist, and as a result of that the article outraged population biologists, did an analysis of the increase in world population and developed a new mathematical model to account for and predict the way the population was increasing. His conclusion was that the population curve was following what he called "super exponential growth," that the expansion of population was proportional to the square of the growth rate. He was concerned with the doubling time of the human population. In other words, the time it took for the human population to go from small numbers to one billion was a very, very long time. From one billion to two billion was a tiny fraction of that time, but still long.

When I was growing up, the population of the world was two billion. From two billion to four billion has occurred within my lifetime; it took about 30 years. Von Forster's prediction is that from four billion to eight billion will be about 15 years, from eight billion to 16 billion around seven and a half years, and so forth. On the basis of this, he drew a curve that described this expansion and concluded that somewhere around the year 2026, plus or minus five years, the population of the world would reach infinity—that is all the mass of the earth would have been converted to people. Therefore, the end of the world would be by squeezing to death. Obviously, long before the population of the world got near infinity, there would be disasters of one sort or another—epidemics, wars, famines, or whatever.

When the article appeared in 1961 it was roundly denounced in subsequent issues of *Science* by mathematicians and population biologists. The theme of population biologists at that time was that the rate of increase of population was slowing, and therefore population biologists were putting out an optimistic message. However, a long letter appeared in *Science* in April of last year by a population biologist who urged readers to remember von Forster and the doomsday curve, and pointed out that the actual increase in world population since 1961 has not only conformed to von Forster's prediction, but in fact is slightly ahead of it. That means that the end of the world, or at least the end of civilization as we know it, is really not far off—I would assume that the disasters that will come in the wake of this population increase will happen much before 2026. It could happen within 20 years—well within our lifetimes.

The reasons for the global catastrophes that are coming have a lot to do with addictive behavior. The world population increase has a lot to do with addiction to sex, for example. The destruction of rain forests and the pollution of oceans and atmospheres has a lot to do with addiction to power and to money. The subject of addiction cannot be taken out of the context of the imminence of the end of life as we know it.

Roger Walsh has said that he thinks that addiction is the fundamental problem. I could not agree with that more. It's fundamental in every sense of the word. It is a deep core problem. It is at the core of being human. It's also at the core of all of the specific problems that we have in the world today. I can think of no area in which it is more important to try to get help for ourselves and for everyone.

I also feel very strongly that addiction is a universal problem. All of us are taken up in addictive behavior. Hopefully, we are in a process of change now where we are beginning to see the universality of addiction. But still there is a tendency to focus on some kinds of addictions as the ones that are serious and to ignore others either because they are socially acceptable or because they don't fit our conceptual model of what addiction is.

I watched a movie the other night that was made in 1934 in black and white. All of the characters in the movie smoked. No wonder that generations of Americans were fascinated by smoking! We are living at a time when that social consensus is changing. Smoking is becoming unfashionable. If you talk to any smoker you will hear how irritated they are about how unfashionable it is becoming. It's a very different situation from the thirties. But that legacy of the thirties and the years before conditioned our thinking about tobacco addiction.

In World War II soldiers were issued cigarettes in their rations. There was a tendency in the twenties and thirties to encourage people to smoke in the belief that smoking facilitated concentration. You only have to look back to the fifties to *Life* magazine to find doctors selling cigarettes. You will find full page ads of doctors in white coats with mirrors on their heads, holding out packages of Old Golds saying, "I recommend these to all my patients because they're soothing to the throat." Imagine. That was 40 years ago. It was only within the past ten years that the American Medical Association was forced to divest itself of tobacco stock by voices of protest from its constituents.

When I was a student in Harvard Medical School between 1964 and 1968, I was taught that tobacco was not addictive. I was taught that it was a health problem in that it led to emphysema and lung cancer, but there was not a word about it being addictive. It was a psychological habit and therefore unimportant. So it was not discussed. We didn't hear much about what they considered real addictions either. Basically we heard a little bit about heroin addiction, which was the model or prototype of addiction. Tobacco did not fit that model so it wasn't taken seriously. Nobody paid any attention to it, and that consensus was so strong and it so affected American science that no one even did research to find out why that substance had such a powerful control over people's behavior.

For years I have urged people to look at smoking for what it is. Heroin addicts only have to get a fix once, twice, or three times a day. Tobacco addicts have to fix up every twenty minutes. Every twenty minutes the brain demands a discrete pulse of a high dose of nicotine coming through the arterial system. Why didn't anyone do research on that? Why didn't anyone look to see how nicotine caused such a profound influence on brain physiology? They didn't do it because it didn't fit the conceptual model and because it was a socially acceptable addiction. Well, there are many other socially acceptable addictions today that we don't take very seriously. It's awfully difficult in mainstream America to talk about sexual addiction as a concept. We live in a culture that tells us that it is desirable to have as many orgasms as possible all the time. When I ask people, as part of my medical history taking, if they have any sexual difficulties, the most common answer I get is that they aren't getting enough. In the cultural context in which we live, sexual addiction is invisible. Or take addiction to work or addiction to making money. These are both things that our culture tells us are good. So it is not seen in the same way that addiction to an unpopular drug is seen.

I think that many of our theories of addiction and our ways of looking at addiction are limited because they don't take into account the full spectrum of addictive behavior. As an example, let me read you a definition of addiction from this conference. After talking about how addiction extends far beyond the realm of chemical dependence, it then says, "In the broadest sense, *addiction* can be defined as an attitude that sees various aspects of the material world as exclusive sources of satisfaction. Addiction, understood in this way, represents a prominent feature of the entire Western civilization, which has lost the connection with its inner resources."

That, to my mind, is far from being a broad conception of addiction. And it surely does not involve just the Western world. That's a very limited view. First of all, if it's the attitude that various aspects of the material world make us feel all right, what about sexual addiction? Is that an addiction? I mean it may involve physical organs and other people, but what we're really talking about is an addiction to an inner experience. What about addiction to thought? That's something hardly ever discussed in the Western world. It is discussed in Buddhism. In Buddhist psychology, addiction to thought is seen as a serious impediment to enlightenment. That's one of the reasons you meditate—to try and get some freedom from thought. So you could look at universities as monuments to thought addiction where you are rewarded for the beauty or complexity or novelty of the thoughts that you produce. Given that social context, with those social rewards, why would you ever even think that thought could be addictive? And if your conception is that addiction involves something material and external, then that doesn't fit, so you don't pay attention to it.

I maintain that the essence of addiction is craving for an experience or object to make yourself feel all right. It's the craving for something other than the self, even if that's within the realm of the mind. I also feel that addiction is something that's fundamentally human; it affects everybody.

It's very easy to feel special about our addictions. That's an attitude that I run into a lot. One of the things that in the past has put me off about some of the 12-step programs is that they tend to regard certain addictions as more important than others, that alcohol addiction is somehow fundamentally worse, more difficult, than coffee addiction. I love to talk about coffee addiction. My new book has an entire section on coffee addiction. To me, that's the most interesting drug at the moment, because it's a hidden addiction in our culture. So I don't agree that alcoholism is somehow more important than coffee addiction. On the level that I'm talking about, on the level that we have to look at addiction, it is the same thing. It's the same process. It's the same craving for something apart from yourself to make you feel OK. What I'm most interested in is that process. What is the origin of craving? And what is the solution to the craving?

I had a patient come to me about four or five years ago who was shooting five to six grams of cocaine a day intravenously. I had never encountered cocaine use on that scale. She had been doing that for six months and had gotten into it after several years of snorting vast amounts of cocaine. When she moved in with a man who was dealing cocaine, he introduced her to using it intravenously and her usage quickly escalated. Remarkably, given the nature of that drug and the nature of her usage, she was in good health. She actually held a job. She was a single mother, and at the moment she was doing a fantastic juggling act of keeping her life together despite her drug usage. I didn't know how much longer she would be able to do that.

I learned a number of things just in listening to her talk about her addiction. First of all, in describing the experience that she had from using cocaine in this way, she said that the first few minutes after the first injection of the day, she felt an overwhelming pleasure and rush. But that was it for pleasure. The rest of the time—five or six hours—was filled with paranoia, violent shaking, insomnia, and palpitations. I find this interesting because many people think that people get involved with addictions because they're sources of pleasure, but when you look at people caught up in extreme forms of addiction, especially with substances and food, the percentage of pleasure relative to the percentage of distress is minimal. There's not that much pleasure there, so the pleasure is certainly not the thing that keeps the addiction going. So after going on very articulately about how awful her life had become being a slave to this compulsion, she looked off and said something that was just a beautiful expression of the plight of the addict. She said, "I want not to want it."

If you want not to want things, how do you achieve that? What is this problem of craving? Where does it come from? What is the origin?

It seems to me that the Eastern spiritual philosophies, especially Buddhism, have the most to say on the subject. The first noble truth of Buddha is that life is somehow incomplete and unfulfilled, so that in anything you do there is something missing. There's a sense that there should be more, and it's not supplied by the things of this world and the things of life. It's often translated as life is suffering—and I suppose there is certainly a suffering that comes out of that—but suffering is very easily misunderstood by speakers of English. That's not the sense of it; it's that life is incomplete; it's unfulfilled. The second noble truth is that the cause of this incompleteness is craving and attachment. But the Buddha has nothing to say about where craving comes from. That's the question that has always interested me. Why do we crave? Why does everyone crave? Why aren't we content to just be as we are? If, in fact, our core essence of being is pure self-luminous consciousness, why do we have to go outside of that? That's not an easy question to answer.

The prevailing view in psychiatry and medicine and science today is that consciousness is an epiphenomenon that happens to arise out of the chance circuitry of the brain or biochemical interactions in the brain. In other words, consciousness is incidental. It's a product of matter arranged in certain ways. There is, however, a minority opinion—call it the mystical view—that consciousness precedes matter. In other words, consciousness is what's primary, and consciousness initiated the evolution of energy and matter into more and more complex forms, seemingly with the purpose of knowing itself better. At the moment, human consciousness is the form where that process has reached its highest expression. But why does consciousness need to know itself in this roundabout way? Why can't it just sit in its own being's awareness of bliss and self knowledge? The whole paradox of existence is tied up with that question.

The most frustrating and interesting aspect of quantum physics and the quantum view of reality is the paradoxes that are revealed by it. If you push knowledge inquiry in any direction, you run into the limit of paradox. And the essence of paradox is self reference. The reason you get into paradox is because you're trying somehow to refer to the thing that you're part of. So the old view that we are passive observers of a mechanistic universe doesn't work anymore. We're connected; we're part of the universe that is trying to understand itself. So you get into that endless loop of paradox like a dog chasing its tail. And all of that was initiated by consciousness attempting to know itself and in the process initiating a cycle of manifested existence. So the big bang was not the initiating event. The big bang was an effect of what I'd call the little itch.

What is that little itch? What is that disturbed consciousness that led to all this? It was the primal craving. To me, if you try to trace the root of craving, you literally get tied up with the origins of the universe and the evolution of human consciousness. It's that fundamental. It's that much a part of our humanness. Not only is addiction universal—not only are all of us in it—but it's the essence of our being as humans. It's not something to be disowned. You can't do that, because addiction is part of our core being. It's part of who we are. Given that, what can we do about addictive behavior? I can think of only two things to do about it. The first is to try to move it, to try and shift it so that the forms of its expression are less harmful rather than more harmful. It is better to be addicted to a 12-step program than to be addicted to alcohol. It is better to be addicted to exercise than it is to be addicted to smoking. You can make those value judgments about addictive behavior. And that approach to addiction should not be discounted because, in fact, maybe that's the only thing that most of us can do.

The only other strategy is to try to get at the root of craving. The Oriental religions would have us believe that this is possible through intense introspection and meditation and practice. I'm not so sure of that. I think maybe you can go a long way—you can get way down there—but if the origin of craving is indeed tied up with the origin of the universe, then I'm not so sure that it can be uprooted. I think all you can do is do the best you can. I mean, go after it; try to contain it and understand it. The biggest mistake we can make is trying to disown it.

I don't think addiction is curable until the expansion of the universe reverses and we begin going back to a single point. But that should not be a source of despair. That's part of who we are. What we need to do is to accept that aspect of our humanness and work with it so that it's not destructive to ourselves or to other people. We also need to celebrate it for what it is. Because it connects us with all other people, it's a source of great compassion and great empathy. It's a motivation to work with others to try to halt the kinds of destructive behavior that are happening today. I can think of nothing more important than that.

So don't let your perspective about addiction be limited by one group's definition of it. It is the broadest and most important problem we face. It's something that all of us share, and it's what connects us to everybody and to the higher power. That's how it is.

(Magical Blend issue #43)

Andrew Weil is a botanist, physician, and author of numerous books about consciousness and healing, including Spontaneous Healing *(Alfred A. Knopf Publishing). This article is an edited version of a talk Dr. Weil gave at the 1994 International Transpersonal Conference in Eugene, Oregon.*

Culture
Problems and Solutions

David Kyle: A Call for Elder Leaders

The role of the elder woman and man traditionally has been that of a person with authority and dignity within the community who carries the values, traditions, and experiential wisdom of the people. Elders can help balance, heal, and restore the constant strain of interaction between people, environmental conditions, and the relationship to the spiritual world. Being in a different stage of life, elders are slower to action, more cautious in their decisions, and most importantly, are more willing to take the longer view on issues. They have fewer pressures generally and no deadlines to meet. In the life of the community, elders can act as a balance to the impetuousness, heat, and quickness of youth. But true elders do not squash and control the energy and dynamics of youth. The elder's role is to channel, focus, bless, and encourage youthful energy toward constructive and creative ends in society. There is a direct link between elders and youth. If the elders are doing their job appropriately, youths move into adulthood contributing to the community. From the elders they can learn how to temper their youthful fire. Elders give guidance through adulthood and help to sustain a balanced life of economic fulfillment, artistic and creative expression, along with spiritual and political governance within the community.

Over the past 100 years, elder leadership has waned and all but been destroyed in Western culture. Rather than being given dignity and authority, our elders are often separated from families and put into retirement compounds. Rather than observing youngsters in their communities and helping to guide, initiate, and mentor them, our elders often sit and watch the problems of youth played out on *Days of Our Lives* or other soap operas and sitcoms. Until 75 to 100 years ago, there was no retirement for older people. Their role was to focus on the children, share their wisdom and insight, and prepare for their own crossing through the portals of death. It was acknowledged by society that, as older people, they were at a different stage of activity and purpose in their lives, but clearly there was a role for them.

Our current idea of retirement is associated with the release from the daily job as if it were a prison. Retirement is the release from the isolation, alienation, and fragmentation of a life compartmentalized between work and what we call our "real" life of family, hobbies, or recreation. Retirement means we can have our own lives back once again. Retirement means we no longer have a boss telling us what to do. The problem is that, by the time we reach retirement age, we have been so conditioned by our jobs and hypnotic consumption that we don't know how to reclaim our lives for ourselves. We replace the time we spent at our jobs with more of the consumption and recreation pattern rather than learning to grow and change into a different role as a responsible elder in the community.

Within the fragmentation that occurs between work obligations and personal fulfillment, we have lost a sense of individual and collective purpose and direction. Our formal education hasn't taught us about the stages of life and initiations that humans need to go through. And our parents and grandparents were removed far enough from this knowledge themselves that they couldn't articulate it to us. Without this elder wisdom, community and society no longer provide us with the wider vision and context in which to develop and grow as a human being. Without this context we are cast into life alone, without an operating manual that can show us the connection between the beginning of life and its end.

Out of our loss of a meaningful, sacred connection to life, we became frightened of death. We lost the sense of the stage in human development that death plays in each of our lives. As a result, we have lost meaningful rituals for those who die. Our only alternative for those who are dying is to try to keep them medically alive, often far beyond the wishes of the ill person and the family members.

We are taught to fear aging and death, so we create a cultural facade and pretend that we never get old. Our facade is eternal youthfulness. Beauty is defined as a certain age, a certain physical look, and a certain style of living. To preserve youth we create the need for "things," from hair dye to face-lifts to tummy tucks. In the disconnection from both the sacred and the purposefulness of old age, our older leaders learned to copy the media hype—the youthful patterns. Our older leaders are dieting, jogging, often wearing the most youthful fashions; many participate in senior-level marathons and so on. In the most basic way, those who should be our elder-leaders are unwilling to accept their natural stage in life; they use their energy in trying to look and be younger. Our cultural taboo of growing old is robbing us of the human resource that is most needed at this time.

My call is for us to recover elder-leadership in a youth-dominated culture. Young people often turn toward novelty, and challenge the structure and dynamics of current values and traditions. With this natural challenge, society needs to have a big enough container so that the living essence of those values and traditions aren't destroyed. Because young people lack groundedness as they work and play and experiment, elder-leaders can provide the context, the experimental ground, the depth of perspective, and the boundaries that help not only young people but the culture itself to stay healthy and in balance.

Carl Jung, in his classic essay "The Stages of Life," submits this question of culture to us: "Could by any chance culture be the meaning and purpose of the second half of life?" He goes on to observe that old people in tribal cultures were always the guardians of the mysteries and laws of the people. He then says, "How does the matter stand with us? Where is the wisdom of our old people, where are their precious secrets and their visions? For the most part our old people try to compete with the young." Jung tells us that the confusion and fear about old age and the "cult of youth" occurs because the only purpose that is taught older people is to keep expanding what they did through the first half of their lives: making money, increasing position in society, and continuing to expand personal prestige. "The afternoon of human life must also have a significance of its own and cannot be merely a pitiful appendage of life's morning." Jung says that the reason for this failure of having few wise elders is that we now "have no schools for forty-years-olds. That is not quite true. Our religions were always such schools in the past, but how many people regard them as such today?"

Many of the older cultures gave men and women a second initiation around the age of fifty. Even today there are indigenous peoples who initiate a person at different periods in his or her life. The Dagara people in West Africa initiate boys and girls between thirteen and seventeen with rites of adulthood. This initiation gives them direct connection to the sacredness of the Otherworld of the Ancestors and a larger spiritual reality. The rites also give them a deep respect and clear knowledge of the cosmology of their tribe.

Malidoma Somé went through the last officially sanctioned initiation as a Dagara in his African village at the age of twenty-two. Although Malidoma completed a master's degree at the national University in Burkina Faso, a master's and a doctorate from the Sorbonne in Paris, and another master's and doctorate from Brandeis University in New York state, he asserts that it was his six weeks of being initiated into the realities of the Otherworld by the Ancestors in the African bush that taught him real knowledge.

Malidoma recognizes that Westerners can't be initiated as he and his wife, Sobonfu, were initiated in Africa. But he says that we must be *responsible* to ourselves and to this Western world in a different way than we have been up to now. He says, "To be responsible is to *remember*. In Africa, initiation is a process of recalling and reactivating lost memories." Within us are 40,000 to 60,000 years of memories about how to live in relationship to nature, to spiritual reality, and to each other.

In responding to the question of how we can be initiated into remembering, Malidoma acknowledges that we need elders who have themselves remembered. Remembering means having gained knowledge and wisdom, and having been given techniques from the Otherworld in how to initiate young people into the sacredness of this world.

The initiation of men and women around fifty years of age in Malidoma's village gives them direct knowledge and communication between the world of spirits and the physical world. In this initiation they are given the knowledge and power of the *primary* language. This is the language of the spiritual world that can create unexpected events in the physical world. Basic to being given the primary language is the understanding of how to initiate boys into manhood and girls into womanhood; how to keep balance and harmony between the natural world and the unseen world; and how to resolve emotional and physical sickness through ritual and ceremony. The initiated men and women have their own family and day-to-day living responsibilities, but they also do physical and spiritual healing and survival work together as critical situations occur in the village. Most of their days are spent talking together, doing artistic and ritual work together, singing and playing, and, as a sacred obligation, holding together a sense of responsibility for their community and people.

It is this communal initiation that we have missed as women and men moving into our fifties and sixties. This is an initiation in which we come to know the language and road maps of moving between the

Otherworld of animistic and spiritual complexity and this physical one. Some of us have had spontaneous experiences of the Otherworld and feel connected to it, but we don't seem to have a common experience or language in order for us to work together in channeling the power of the nonmaterial world into this one. We seem to do well at diagnosing problems here, but we don't seem to know how to get power from "over there."

Mircea Eliade, the great mythologist, believed that myth, ritual, and power were linked together. In fact, all ancient cultures have known for thousands of years that power was an interaction between the seen and unseen. Power came from outside the material world, and myth (the cultural story that links the Spirit world to this one) provided the understanding of the power. Myth gave the boundaries, conditions, and approaches to the power. Ritual was a technique for using and determining how the power could be used. Ritual protected us from the power. Ritual proscribed the conduit through which power could be channeled safely.

Rediscovering the relationship between myth, ritual, and power may be one of the paths back to our ancient roots. We need to regain a myth—a story—that can channel the power of our lives at this time.

Without healthy, mature elders to help raise up new images at the center of our world community, we will continue to live in a narrow economic definition of reality that excludes, or minimizes, the importance of an inner spiritual world. Without new forms of leadership there may well be no elders to teach the rituals and the various stages of life; none to teach how to be truly human, none to bring us into contact and balance with the natural world, and none to show us the inner guide that can help us redefine a new world. Without this kind of elder leadership in our families and communities, we will increasingly drift away from life's deepest knowing and greatest joys.

Yes, it is true that our initiation as elders will not be easy. In a youth culture we have relegated older people to the role of useless parts. And most people who have aged have, themselves, not learned how to tap the sources of wisdom that come through consistent contact with the natural world. We who are in our fifties and sixties must learn to reclaim the role of elder in our culture. One of the first steps of initiation is learning to be quiet. We need to spend as much time as we can in natural settings and listen to what nature will teach us. Slowing down, being quiet, and listening are, in my view, the first initiation steps to becoming an elder-leader.

Leadership from those of us in our fifties and sixties must take both old and new forms if we are to get through our current crisis. We have some work to do individually and collectively:

• We must return to the past of our distant ancestors and find the images of the ancient power that comes from outside and beyond the material world.

• We must understand anew the value and power of myths and how they create boundaries for the choices we make in the world.

• As elder-leaders we must discover the potent use of ritual that creates a conduit through which power for healing can be safely channeled.

• We must also explore the forward flow of today's circumstances to find the elder-leader pattern that best works for us now.

In small and large groups and with great intensity, we must call forth together for a new direction and leadership. Our challenge is to find the way to reinitiate our elders so that healing and help can come to our wounded brothers and sisters and to our wounded communities. This call and challenge is to each of us individually who have arrived at this elder-leader stage of life.

(Magical Blend issue #40)

Reprinted from *Human Robots & Holy Mechanics* by David T. Kyle, with permission from Swan•Raven & Co., an imprint of Blue Water Publishing, Inc. (Mill Spring, NC).

Culture
Problems and Solutions

———◯———

Riane Eisler: Sex, Myth and Body Politics

with Jerry Snider

As a child, Riane Eisler barely escaped the horror of the Nazi holocaust—this century's graphic and ghastly reminder of what happens when society divides itself into *us* vs. *them*. Later, as a pioneer in the women's movement, she saw this same "dominator" model continuing to pit one half of humanity against the other.

Searching for an alternative to a social structure built on senseless fear and violence, Eisler found it in the work of UCLA anthropologist Marija Gimbutas, whose work suggested a prehistoric society based on partnership rather than domination.

Rethinking history, Eisler developed an entirely new theory of cultural evolution, which she presented in *The Chalice and the Blade: Our History, Our Future,* a book that Princeton anthropologist Ashley Montague hailed as "the most important book since Darwin's *Origin of Species.*" Since its publication in 1987, *The Chalice and the Blade* has been translated into nine languages, sparking worldwide discussion and debate.

Riane Eisler is also the author of *The Partnership Way* and *Sacred Pleasure: Sex, Myth and the Politics of the Body.* Her multi-disciplinary work in evolutionary studies, human rights and peace, feminist and environmental issues is internationally recognized. She is a cultural historian, lecturer and codirector of the Center for Partnership Studies in Pacific Grove, California.

I have heard you comment that we often blame the tools the dominator model has used. You seem to feel that as a result such things as rationalism, the Enlightenment and technology get a bad rap.

Riane Eisler: I think it's very important to emphasize the fact that so much of what one reads or hears in the so-called New Age movement is a rejecting of the rationalism that we've inherited. It's understandable because of the fact that science and technology, and even "reason" in the service of goals that are antihuman, have indeed caused enormous pain. But it's like throwing out the baby with the bath water and not really understanding what the problem is. The problem is the guiding ethos and not reason, science and technology, *per se.*

And yet there seems to be something in human nature looking for that scapegoat to blame things on, as opposed to our own ethos.

Riane Eisler: Well, is it really our own ethos or is it something that we have been taught and that we are beginning to re-examine? The point of this is that if we re-examine the ethos, rather than reject it and blame science, then reason and technology (which are simply the tools, how those tools are shaped and the uses to which they are put) are not inherent in the tools, *per se.* So we're back to the same distinction. I'm trying to find a way—and maybe you can help me and we can make this more of a dialogue—to express this, because I think it's enormously important. The anti-technology fervor, the anti-reason fervor, is very dangerous to us, and it defeats the very purposes that we're trying to achieve. People say, "What's wrong is this rationalist approach...." Well, reason happens to be one of the evolutionary gifts that we have received as a species—the capacity to think, the capacity to reason. It is true that we are so used to thinking of reason as something detached from empathy, but it doesn't have to be, does it? It can be informed by empathy. So the problem isn't using our capacity to reason. The problem is the deadening of empathy, which is culturally induced.

But it's difficult to get beyond that point until people become aware that much of what we're taught is culturally inspired and can, at times, lead us in the wrong direction. I think it was Buckminster Fuller who outlined the cultural development of technology. In his scenario, each significant technology starts off in the military and takes 50 years for the technology to filter down into our everyday lives.

Riane Eisler: It does not have to be that way. The reason is a very simple one: the reason is that in societies that orient closely to what I call a dominator model, funding for weapons, for the military, is a top priority, as it must be, because it's a system that is basically one of ranking, be it man over woman, man over man or nation over nation, ultimately backed up by fear of force. So, if you have that kind of a system, then you're going to see a great deal of allocation of money and resources for military research. Then you'll get a little of the trickle down affect, won't you?

A militia, like a sports team, needs to practice. A lot of little wars can take place over the 50 years that it takes technology to get to the masses....

Riane Eisler: That's right. And of course, one of the problems that we're seeing writ large today with that allocation of funding is that the high-tech age is bankrupting the world, because the weapons systems become more and more complex and more and more expensive. Not only is it bankrupting the world by siphoning off more and more money from pro-human uses, but the weapons become obsolete almost by the time they are delivered. Look at what's happening right now with these giant aircraft that the Pentagon doesn't even want but that Congress is allocating seven billion dollars for it. What's going to happen with them? They're going to be sold to some other nation, aren't they? And the nations we sell them to may end up using them against us, as happened with Iraq. It's a totally irrational system, isn't it?

Let's look at the other side of that. Take Japan, for example. It would seem they are following a dominator model as much as the US is. Yet they don't...

Riane Eisler: Ah! But you know what happens with Japan? I use Japan in my analysis as an example of precisely what can happen economically. Japan and Germany were the great postwar World War II economic miracles. Why? Because as part of the peace treaty under which they were defeated, Japan and Germany could not have armament allocations of any significance whatsoever. But that came from the outside. It was an arbitrary modification of the structure. If they had been left to their own devices, that would never have happened. And they also wouldn't have had the phenomenal recovery that they did.

But in that economic recovery, do you see the uses of their billions as being any more humanitarian or partnership oriented than ours?

Riane Eisler: To some extent, yes. In all fairness, Germany has a much better safety net, social and economic, than this country. That's very shocking to Americans. Both Germany and Japan have a national health care system, which we lack. So there are differences, but the point is that they are still societies that orient to a large extent to the dominator model. The fact that they are not allocating to armaments is an historical accident. It wasn't part of the organic truth to the specter of the society.

But if it steered them in the right direction, we need to look at that.

Riane Eisler: Well, it did steer them in the right direction. Obviously there was more money left for economic development. There was more money left for some of the social services. But there's more. Neither Japanese nor German executives make nearly as much money as executives in this country. It's not even close in terms of haves and have-nots, but they still very much embrace a ranking system, especially in Japan. The point is that they're not really examples of partnership societies. I'd say for that, you'd have to look to the Scandinavian nations.

Let's go there, then.

Riane Eisler: There it happened organically. There, what happened is that you have societies where you have a deliberate attempt—the first peace academies came out of the Scandinavian world. Some of the very first experimentation with what American companies today call team work, came out of a Volvo plant in the 1960s, came out of Sweden and Norway. That's part of the partnership movement, changing from the worker as a cog in a giant assembly line machine to what they did in that Volvo plant where workers basically made their own decisions and worked together rather than just being part of an assembly line. But the most significant thing about the Scandinavian nations is in terms of the configuration of a more equal partnership between women and men, which they've been moving toward not only in the political democracy, where you have about 30% of the national legislature female, but also in their more stereotypically feminine social priorities. They are the home of the welfare state, and a lot of what we see in Japan or a lot of what we see in Germany really were innovations first used in the Scandinavian world. The idea that the function of government is not just to inflict pain—to have armies and prisons—but that the function of government is a care-taking one, a more stereotypically feminine function. Of course I hope to make it very clear that we're talking about stereotypes here.

Or archetypes?

Riane Eisler: Well, I prefer stereotypes, because the word "archetype" takes on a sense of inevitability for people, whereas what we're talking about is the social construction of masculinity and femininity, which we're seeing deconstructed and reconstructed before our very eyes in our times. So it's obviously not a fixed archetype. I don't think of archetypes in the Jungian sense; I think of archetypes as being culturally embedded, but I'm afraid that for some people who are into Jungian thought, there is indication that that's just "human nature."

The closest I have been to a welfare state was a month I spent in the Netherlands, and I must say there was a very pleasant difference in the "feel of the streets." I walked all over Amsterdam, often late at night, and never encountered the toughs or threatening situations a midnight stroll though any American city would be sure to elicit.

Riane Eisler: Part of that is television. Most television in the Netherlands is public television, and there isn't as much violence on it. The social structure is different.

Even the scale is different. It's much more modest, more of a human scale, than what you see here.

Riane Eisler: You say it's very modest. It's interesting that what you don't see in the Scandinavian world is the enormous disparity between the haves and the have-nots. You see a much more even, but still high, standard of living. Half the country is not living in a third- world situation, as is beginning to happen in this country during this period of dominator regression.

You say the partnership model developed organically in the Scandinavian countries. Obviously that's the only way it's going to happen here, as well. We aren't going to be able to impose a different set of values.

Riane Eisler: When I say organically, I meant it happened because people organized to make it happen. Let's be very clear, here. It didn't happen by itself. What I meant by saying it happened organically is that it happened systemically. It didn't happen as an artificial add-on to a system that was oriented more toward a dominator model. I did not mean to imply that it didn't happen through human agency, because it most certainly did.

Let's look at that human agency. If we want to re-evaluate a little bit about where we're heading in our country, it's obviously going to behoove us to learn how it was done elsewhere. We're talking about two different sets of basic values. In this country, it seems that the majority of people who hold partnership values have become so discouraged that a lot of them have dropped out of the political system because they feel there is no hope of changing anything.

That is a very political act, to drop off, because you're basically, then, handing the society over to the very people that you're trying to get away from. That's obvious. So what can we learn from these systemic changes that have occurred in other countries that I assume were also resistant to change?

Riane Eisler: They were certainly resistant. And what we can learn is to hang in there. That's the first thing we can learn. I think you know that in my work I present a very different perspective on history, not only on prehistory—in other words the knowledge that what I call the dominator system is a relatively recent development. In terms of evolutionary time, in terms of the cultural evolution, we're talking about 30,000 years, and it's only about 5,000 years of that.

But I also present a much more realistic view of modern history and a much more integrated view of modern history than what we get in most accounts of it, which are at best fragmentary and at worst focus only, or primarily, on the wars and revolutions rather than on the social reform movements.

If we focus on these social-reform movements, what we see is that during the last 300 years, beginning in the West with the 18th century Enlightenment, we have seen one progressive social movement after another challenging entrenched patterns of domination. In other words, one challenge after another to what I call the dominator system. This began with the challenge to the so-called divinely ordained right of kings to rule over their subjects in the 18th century and at the same time the fledgling challenge, heightening in the 19th century, of the feminist movement against the so-called divinely ordained right of men to rule over women and children in the "castles" of their homes, the abolitionist movement challenging the domination of one race over another, even the enslavement of one race of another, culminating in the civil rights movement of the 20th century, the 19th century pacifist movement becoming the peace movement, challenging violence as a legitimate tool for imposing domination by one tribe or one nation, even the ecology movement is really a movement against the ethos of the idealized, so-called conquest of nature. Today that struggle is beginning to go to the basics.

As you know, the basis of my book, *Sacred Pleasure*, is that if you look at politics now in an integrated way, you not only focus on the so-called public sphere, which used to be only relations among men, because women and children were not supposed to be part of that "men's world," you also focus on the private sphere of relations between men, women and children, where you see that what our time brings is a mounting, organized challenge— for the first time really— against entrenched patterns of domination and violence in intimate relations. The laws criminalizing rape are one example. Basically it used to be considered the woman's fault. You know— she provoked it. Or even the laws against domestic violence. It used to be that if a man beat a stranger, he went straight to jail, but if he beat someone he had sex with, someone he said he loved, they at best walked him around the block. And of course we saw that still happening in the O.J. Simpson case. But at least, people are no longer accepting it. We used to say "spare the rod and spoil the child." Today we call it what it is—child abuse.

So look at modern history as a spiral movement upward toward partnership from domination, with a lot of dips, OK? Nazi Germany was a dip; Stalin's Russia was a major dip; and what we're seeing today, the so-called rightist fundamentalist movement—it has nothing to do with religion—is pure dominator regression time. So we see that there are dips in the spiral. That doesn't mean that the spiral will continue to go up. It could have a massive breakdown.

It's very dangerous at this point to have these dominator regressions for a number of reasons, one being the capability of our technology. We have a technology now, where we're beginning to see bacteriological terrorism, for goodness sake, like what we saw recently in Japan. So *dominator regressions* are periods where the idealization of the use of violence as manly and heroic, which we get all around us, is very dangerous. It could mean breakdown in terms of survival, and not just because of the environmental problems at this state of high technology. It isn't that this is the first time that whole forests were felled; this isn't the first time that whole populations were massacred. It's just that…you have gas chambers this time; you can get rid of whole rain forests, which you could not do so easily before. So it's very dangerous. I'm not saying that it will inevitably happen, but I am saying that these politics of intimate relations are very important, and if we get a better understanding of where some of the important intervention points are, and if we are politically active, instead of withdrawing to play in what one writer called the "New Age sand box," then we have a chance.

Listening to you, I keep thinking of the educational system. There's always a bit of a flurry and a fuss, but you've basically got the same model—the dominator model—being taught because it rests on certain assumptions. I guess that's where you start off, with the assumptions. It seems to me that that's where the danger is, it's simply the realization that there has been that movement, that it has been an uphill spiral, where those who would like to stop it are not going to picture it that way. We still have the history books that write the human story in terms of conquests and wars.

Riane Eisler: Absolutely. Well, my books have been adopted for many types of classes at the university level, but it's also exciting that I'm beginning to have a dialogue with educators about peer teaching, the teacher as facilitator, team teaching both in the corporation and the school—these ideas are beginning to seep in. You see there's been a lot of movement in the progressive education field toward what we might call partnership process. But there's a lot of confusion, because people tend to mistake giving up rules for different kinds of rules, so…it's the same confusion of the sixties, to some extent, of rebellion instead of reconstruction. But the movement is there for partnership processing, a cooperative learning movement—I'm sure you know about some of these movements, where it's been much slower in terms of partnership content, which is what you're bringing up.

I'm beginning to have dialogues with educators about that and I'm basically saying, "Look, you can teach kids, and peer teaching is very important. You can help them and empower them, but if you're still teaching them history the same way, that the wars are so much more important than the reform movements that you never even read about the reform movements, at best you get cognitive dissonance and confusion, and at worst you don't get any kind of lasting change. I was asked, for example, to do some consulting for a private school, setting up a new curriculum. Also I was recently invited to a conference on science and education and future generations. And though some people don't understand what I'm advocating, for the most part my ideas are well received, especially by teachers, many of whom are very receptive because they are becoming aware of the problem.

I don't mean to drive a stake in here, but I'm wondering how much of that is due to the influence of the professions. In education, you are probably going to find a larger percentage of women, for example, in higher places of authority than you would in the military or even in industry, at this point.

Riane Eisler: Yes, although I must say that there are women who are just as embedded in the dominator model as men and who have accepted it just as much as men. As I said, this is really not an issue of women against men and men against women, but you are quite right, and sometimes that can be a help.

In politics, one set of agendas has been described among the politicians as "women's issues."

Riane Eisler: That's still one of the big obstacles. In a society like the one we've grown up in, one half of humanity—the male half and anything associated with it—is simply given more importance, more funding, more attention, more coverage, be it in history books or newspapers, than anything associated with the female half of humanity, which become secondary issues. So, instead of talking about human rights, we talk of women's rights, and of course we have to at this point, because human rights became a code word for men's rights.

It's not that simple to change things, but it is fascinating once you become involved in this, because it brings up the whole hidden subtext of gender that really colors so much in our lives. I think we spoke about that the last time we spoke, about the insanity of what's happening in Washington today, that basically they're saying they want to balance the budget, but at the same time they want to give the Pentagon seven billion dollars more than the Pentagon wants for obsolete aircraft that are only going to be used against us. Then they turn around and say, "We don't have enough money for taking care of children, for taking care of people's health, the elderly and programs aimed at so-called minorities." And who does the care-taking work?

Who, stereotypically, is associated with taking care of kids, people's health and the environment? It's women. So it colors our thinking in the most bizarre ways. In times of dominator regression, it becomes almost a caricature in its irrationality. We can talk about anti-intellectualism and anti-rationalism. We can also talk about irrational behavior, and a lot of what's happening in Washington is irrational. These top-down programs—whether it's a top-down bureaucracy in the government or a top-down bureaucracy in a big organization—don't work very well. It's no wonder some of the Great Society programs have failed. There was corruption; they were top-down; the people involved never were really participants; and there was no partnership. But that doesn't mean that you can't devise programs that empower people to help themselves and that it should not be a major social priority.

What programs out there do you see that are doing that?

Riane Eisler: I see in my own community where there are programs that are more participatory, where people are basically becoming involved. It's small; it's grassroots organizations, and at this point it's mostly nongovernmental, but there are programs. For example…I'm thinking of a program that's not in the United States, but of a program that's been very successful—the village loan programs. I'm sure you've heard of them, where women who are small entrepreneurs are given loans, rather than giving money to some big corporate entity. There's no trickle down; it's there. I write about some of the those programs in the last few chapters of *Sacred Pleasure*, about programs where people on the grassroots level all over the world, not just in the United States, are forming cooperatives, but it doesn't have to be just cooperatives. One of the ones I'm thinking about in this country are the so-called garden projects. There is one in New York, where a wonderful Black woman is basically trying to get people involved and also get funding for the reclamation of these terribly neglected inner city areas and get people involved in creating gardens there.

Especially in the ecology movement, everything that seems to be getting done is getting done at the grassroots level, although the EPA gave them a tool to work with.

Riane Eisler: That's it. I'm so glad you said that, because you see all this emphasis on where the private sector will do, the private sector can't do anything unless there is a public policy that supports what's they're doing, and then you're back to government. And now we're back to the issue of voting again. You're not going to get the ideal representative or the ideal president, and sometimes it truly is voting for the lesser of two evils.

But isn't that better than what we've got?

Riane Eisler: In my mind, it is, what with our embassies being closed down because of the irrational thinking of one man who was elected only by the electorate of one state. I mean, how the hell did we get Jesse Helms deciding our foreign policy? It's amazing isn't it? Mr. Helms, who has the audacity to complain about government handouts, gives government subsidies to grow tobacco which kills people.

For those who are open to it, it's very easy to embrace the need for a different system. But how do those who embrace a partnership model get their message across to others in a meaningful way?

Riane Eisler: There is a movement that is beginning to grow. It's a small organization called The International Partnership Network. It's aimed at linking partnership educators—people like you, who find that having a systems view clarifies. People say to me when they read my work that it's full of "Aha!" experiences. Well, that's what the research was like, because once you have those baskets in which to sort—which is what the partnership and dominator models really are—then it's no longer this random jumble, and you don't feel so helpless.

Back to the ecology movement, when you're speaking of a partnership model, nothing is more basic than a partnership between the people who are producing goods and the Earth that is providing the materials. Yet, the Gross National Product doesn't even take into account the environmental costs of producing more and more material goods to keep the economic numbers high. In other words, what's being lost has no value assigned to it.

Riane Eisler: And that's dominator economics, because what's valued is the exploitation.... That's very important to realize. Today we realize that this is something bad. In the 19th century, they wrote about it as if were something terrific. In economic models, women's life-supporting, life-giving, life-nurturing services, within a male dominator family, within a dominator society, are considered men's due. So men expect that women are supposed to do it for free, right? Women might be given privileges, but they won't have rights in that system. In the same way, nature's life-supporting, life-giving services are supposed to be men's due, and you don't have to give anything back. Everything is there to be exploited. So it's all of one cloth, isn't it? We can't change one without changing the other. That's really the moral of the whole story.

Economics seems to be the big stumbling point. I am convinced that the worship of the almighty dollar has become the state religion.

Riane Eisler: Absolutely. And we have seen in recent history times bubble up where that consciousness tries to surface. Remember the Equal Rights Amendment? It seems to me that the reason things like that tend not to get off the ground is because the economic system just won't allow it.

But the economic system is composed of people. There is a movement afoot right now, of which our organization, The Center for Partnership Studies, is a part. We just published a study called "Women and the Global Quality of Life," which calls for a revision of the models. What are the models? The models are what is considered to be a measure of economic productivity and economic well-being, and the GNP is not an adequate measure. You just pointed out the basic reason.

Let's take a very silly example that's also a very good example. Part of the GNP is Mr. Helms getting his subsidy for his tobacco farmers, the sale of that tobacco in cigarettes to people who then get sick, the cost of taking care of those people when they get sick—the medical bills, the pharmacy bills and the undertaking bills. So here you have a totally negative transaction—negative from A to Z—that, by current measures of economic well being, is considered a plus rather than a minus. That's crazy isn't it?

We have to start with different models, but one of the problems is that unless we also start factoring in the non-monetized contribution of community work, of women's work, women will end up with very inadequate indicators. It's one of those times when there is a growing perception that GNP is not an accurate indicator, but we have to be very careful that we don't end up with something that is just as inadequate, because it leaves out the whole issue of what is really productive work. But we're getting into a very complex issue here. The economic issue for right now is that we are in a time of tremendous dislocation, as we move from industrial to a so-called post-industrial age of electronic, nuclear and biochemical technology.

What we're finding is that work, as traditionally defined, is beginning to disappear. It's just like agriculture during the industrial revolution. Prior to the industrial revolution, agriculture was a huge part of the employment base. It's gone, right? A very small percentage of the population is employed in agriculture now. The same thing is beginning to happen with most conventional work. The blue collar jobs are going, due to automation. Telephone operators are going, bank tellers are going. In other words, there is shrinking base of work, as traditionally defined.

So, the question for us is: How do we define what is productive work? That's where the hidden subtext of gender comes in. When we talk about the most important work in this society, I think it comes down to two types of work—one is the care of people and the second is the preservation of our natural habitat. The two are completely related, and both have been considered basically valueless, or very low pay work. So that, I think, is one of the major economic issues. If we can redefine what is productive work, then we completely change the reward system in this society, and we don't have the mess we have now, where people are rewarded for precisely the meanest kinds of behaviors. It's a big conflict, but I think we need to work on it.

Let's get back to the subject of anti-intellectualism. Again, you seem to see it most strongly in the arena of politics. There are all these arguments that are passed off as logical arguments that rest on a whole set of assumptions that are, as you say, anti-nurturing, anti-partnership and...

Riane Eisler: Antihuman. We're really talking about anti-welfare of human beings and of other life forms we share our planet with. They are totally irrational.

We're back to values again, aren't we? If we're talking intellectualism, we're basically talking academia, and the structures of academia would seem to be anything but the partnership model with their rigid hierarchies.

Riane Eisler: Absolutely, but there are also within those structures people who really have very sound pro-human values. We're having a heck of a time in those structures, as we are everywhere else. The issue is really trying to change both the culture and the structure. It's not going to happen overnight, but some of it has begun to happen, slowly, gradually, and as I say, if you really look at it during the last few hundred years—which is nothing in terms of human cultural evolution—we've seen some enormous changes. I keep coming back to the hopeful part, because it is very important to us at this very difficult and regressive time to know that we should hang in there, that if we really keep working at it, we may be able to shorten the dip of dominator regression, see that it doesn't go quite as deep and doesn't cause as much human suffering as it is already causing. We're talking about thinking things through, and that's why it's so important to talk about reason and to talk about using our natural capacity to reason.

You mentioned the whole New Age anti-intellectualism. It's basically the other side. It's a reasoning process, but it's a reasoning process where the assumptions start out wrong.

Riane Eisler: I think that's very true, and I think that one of the greatest forces for change could be from people within the New Age movement who are obviously dissatisfied with a lot of the conventional ways of doing things. If, instead of escaping into concepts, they take a proactive approach, then I think the New Age movement will be a much more potent force for change than it is. Otherwise, New Age approaches become a way of avoiding responsibility and avoiding reasoning, too. We have to be careful not to keep returning to the same set of assumptions. Embedded in a lot of these "alternatives," is the dominator model. One place in society where I can see that changing, although the results are still pretty sketchy, is in the Internet. It's a partnership-oriented technology. There are nodes of influence. There is really no hierarchy. The amount of information you can already get from people who are feeding it in but who are not associated with any particular corporate structure or political structure....

There's that, too, but there's also an awful lot of input from your regular, ordinary person, as well.

Riane Eisler: I think the technology offers us a tremendous opportunity. It's a toy right now. We are just playing with it, but it does seem to be one of those hopeful signs, because without a typical hierarchical structure, the information content changes subtly, but, I think, profoundly. Our concept of what constitutes an authority is changing. On the Internet, more than anywhere else, information stands by itself. If it resonates with enough people, it gains influence, without having to have the authorized blessing of some recognized institution or résumé. On the Internet, there is no way of knowing, unless the person offers the information, whether you're corresponding with a man or a woman, a teenager or a septuagenarian, a black or a white.

There is an equality of information, which is hopeful, as long as people who take it in are capable of reasoning and weighing the information's worth.

Riane Eisler: That's right. It levels some of these immediate status issues. I think it's fascinating. It would be very interesting to have a conversation on the Internet about what the culture wars are really about, and what we mean by such things as family values, what kind of family do we really want to value? We're searching for new standards to replace some of the old ones—not all of them. Not everything we were taught was necessarily part of the dominator model. Partnership relations have to be co-opted. They have to be subsumed by the system. Otherwise we wouldn't have survived.

So, in the process of searching for clarification of values, of standards, we're looking for criteria, for ways of substituting for the old rules and principals. I think that's what this work offers, doesn't it? It's a way of re-examining and revaluing what's important to us, what we value, what we want to leave behind. This encompasses sex, economics, politics and family life. To do that, and this is where we come back to the issue of anti-rationalism or anti-intellectualism, we do need to use the intellect. When we say something doesn't feel good, that's very important that feelings of some kind inform our thinking, that it not be this detached thinking. But our feelings have been so manipulated by images, by the myths, by the dominator archetypes, that we can't completely trust them, either. It's a balancing act.

The first step is awareness, but it has to be somewhat of a detached awareness, because we get so involved in our particular school of concepts.

Riane Eisler: To me, the word "detached" has a sense of abandoning empathy. If by detached, however, you mean stepping back a few steps and looking at things from fresh eyes, then absolutely. That's exactly what is required. Looking at your own viewpoint with the same kind of criteria you use to look at your so-called enemy's viewpoint.

One of the basic problems I talk about in my work is that those who are trying to pull us back recognize (because it's so central to their belief system) the centrality of so-called women's issues: that women have their roles and they have to be in families where men call the shots. We have all grown up with these attitudes. We have to bring back to a central focus these things we have shunted off to the side as "women's issues." We have to overcome the idea that what happens to women and children is secondary to more important things. This is at the heart of the debate over family values. After all, a certain type of family has been the lynch pin of the dominator model, a certain type of gender hierarchy. It's really fascinating, isn't it, once you start stepping back a little bit from the old assumptions?

It is enlightening. Sometimes it's hard to feel empowered, but as you say, most of the early work is going to take place on the grassroots level and then will catch the attention those who set policy.

Riane Eisler: We also need to recognize that social change entails changes in consciousness, and these things start with a small group— usually a highly unpopular small minority. And if we're willing to be that minority and to have a good time while we're at it, and if we are able to keep ourselves buoyed up by the recent spiral of history, then we stand a good chance. The point that we've made time and time again is that people who consider themselves a part of the New Age movement need to take a holistic view. Rather than saying, "The only thing good is emotions," or "The only thing good is some kind of mystical experience," we need to look at the whole picture, including our capacity to think things through, using our capacity to step back and letting the boxes shift in our head to get that new consciousness, which is so exciting.

Culture
Problems and Solutions

---⊙---

Michael Peter Langevin: Healing With Chocolate Milk and Magic

Adolescence is a difficult time for most of us. Reality is unclear. You want to be a child and an adult at the same time, yet you don't feel comfortable as either. And everything that happens seems like the end of the world. If this difficulty intensifies to the degree that you cannot function in society, you then become labeled emotionally disturbed.

Adolescents so labeled are usually placed in institutions for treatment. The closer to functional are placed in group homes; the most extreme are placed in juvenile halls and mental hospitals. In between there exists a little known institution called residential treatment. These facilities are unlocked and intensively staffed with professionals, social workers, therapists, counselors, etc. with the hope that, in these settings, children and adolescents can be treated and taught to better function in society.

Fred Finch Youth Center is a special residential treatment facility located in Oakland, CA. Over the last two years I have been allowed the unique privilege of attempting different New Age techniques as healing tools at Fred Finch.

There is a cottage at Fred Finch called Tahoe where adolescent, emotionally disturbed boys from the ages of eleven to nineteen live. In my tenure there as a supervisor I have had the honor to work with the highest quality counselors, social worker, chaplain, program director, and support staff. We have all worked hard to bring in new healing approaches to give these boys a better chance.

The key to dealing with emotionally disturbed adolescents is attitude—positivity, optimism and high expectations. The beauty of each individual involved in the healing process is the underlying factor that keeps it all unfolding. Adaptability, tolerance, and the fact that nothing is written in granite gives us the leeway to make mistakes, admit them and move on.

We use a Milieu model which stresses a team approach and a feeling of extended family. As a supervisor, I freely admit that I don't have all the answers, and I try to be comfortable with that. Indeed, no one person has all the answers. Instead, the process relies on the ideas and opinions of everyone involved. It is the potential to effect healing rather than who comes up with the idea that is of paramount consideration. As an example, one of the residents at Tahoe decided that the white walls were too institutional, and he was allowed to redo his room. The idea caught on, and now each room and each door to each room is done to the unique taste of the boy residing in it.

This change in the house interior decor illustrates how people's thoughts help to unfold their reality. The new image of the walls and doors is physical, but it also serves to reflect the theory we use in treatment.

They boys are encouraged to be in touch and aware of their problems and to gain understanding and control over them. However, the problems themselves are not overly accented. They are looked at as challenges. Instead, goals are accented. Where are they now? How do they want to be now? What improvements can they make? What are their short-term and long-range goals? Creativity is stressed through poetry, story writing and art. Such creativity is also required of all who work in the milieu with them. Every interaction between adult and resident is an opportunity for growth and healing. Most adolescents act out and challenge authority. Emotionally disturbed adolescents can do this with great intensity. To engage the youths in power conflicts is a losing situation all around. Rather than resorting to physical means of handling difficulties, the challenge is to use a type of judo of the mind. We try to see how their anger can be worked with or transmuted so that it is productive. Then, everyone wins. A very important part of this therapy is fun. If you can laugh at your problems then they are easier to leave behind, and one can then move from victory to victory.

However, when the prevalent mood is one of anger or frustration, the next step in a session is unclear. At this point it is often necessary for everyone to stop and catch their breath. This can serve to interrupt the incessant dialogue and sense of futility in the situation. The theory we utilize at this juncture is heavily influenced by R. D. Laing, Jung, A. S. Neill, and Maslow, and can be simply stated as "chocolate milk therapy." This means that when a session gets stalled, it is often helpful to talk about some totally unrelated and often absurd thing, i.e., chocolate milk. This invariably breaks up the rigid headset and brings things back to a fun place from which to relate. This also gives everyone the clear message that if you don't like the way your life is, you have the power to change it and to make it fun.

There is a gentle balance here of trust and unpredictability that is required to make it work. One must be comfortable with being involved in a process that might take varied forms. Mistakes are often made, but those mistakes can be the catalyst to further growth. Faith is a large part of the picture. Although situations are often difficult and the solutions not immediately apparent, it is necessary to believe that your knowledge, experience, healing intentions, and best efforts will bear fruit.

One such situation that was resolved satisfactorily involved the food sent to us from the kitchen. The boys and counselors felt that it was not as healthy and appealing as it might be. Joint research was done, menus were drawn up, and counselors and residents began buying their own health foods, vitamins, herbal supplements. Now the house cooks its own food. We all eat better and the boys' behavior reflects the extra involvement and care that has been taken.

One of the more interesting New Age techniques that has been employed is creative visualization. Periodically those interested gather together to sit in a circle or lie on the living room rug and meditate or pray. We have used guided relaxation imagery, crystal meditation, and subliminal tapes. Even adaptations of Christian and Pagan rituals have been included. Picture in your mind's eye ten adolescent boys—many inner city kids—and two to four counselors sitting in a circle passing a quartz crystal from one to another. As a person is passed the crystal he visualizes his wish—one specific thing that he feels has a fair chance to manifest. While the individual does this, everyone else concentrates their energy on that person's visualization coming true. When all have had their turn we do a closing prayer: "Oh higher selves, God, powers on high, please help what is right, best and healthiest for all concerned to come to pass." Then we blow out the candles and turn the lights back on. The conversation that follows often lasts far past bedtime and ranges in topic from the power of thought to the history of Tibet as the boys are eager to discover different theories of spirituality which are so often left out of psychological treatment. The responses to these visualizations vary, but most of the boys and counselors who participate are pleased with the results. Indeed, it seems that much of what is visualized comes into being, although I must admit that we were all disappointed when one of the youths visualized the cottage levitating off the campus.

Sometimes, however, a boy's grip on reality is weak and the spiritual aspects get out of hand. When I became supervisor there was a 17-year-old who believed the Devil told him to kill himself and hurt others. He was diagnosed as a paranoid schizophrenic. He had many serious attempted suicides and was on heavy medication. The chaplain, the counselors, the social worker, myself, and the other boys all set upon a program. We used his belief that the Devil spoke to him to set up a debate. We all joined in, asking such questions as: "What is evil?" "Does everyone hear voices?" "Are there people in the world who don't even believe in the Devil?" "Are we victims of fate, or can we take control of our own destiny?" And on and on…. That boy had a tumultuous time at Fred Finch with much progress and many back slides. But he is now living in the real world. He graduated from high school and is no longer on medication. The debate apparently widened his spiritual view of the world as he no longer hears voices and is a practicing Buddhist. He is trying hard to make a future for himself. He is just one boy in two years. We have had more than twenty pass through the house. Some stay, some go quickly. Some we never reached. Tragically they went on to locked institutions.

As a cottage, our track record is high. This is because people are encouraged to care for each other, to tell and show each other that they are important. Isn't this the basis of New Age thought—unconditional love?

All of the people involved at Tahoe House hope that this program will become the mainstay of Fred Finch youth center and became a trend-setter for institutions world wide. But even if the program ends tomorrow, seeds have been planted that will grow when the time is right. That is what those of us who believe in the New Age must do—plant seeds that manifest the future with love and healing.

(Magical Blend issue #11)

Culture
But Seriously, Folks...

John Cleese: The Importance of Being Offensive

However unintentionally Monty Python-ish family therapy meetings may get, rarely do they have a real, flesh-and-blood Monty Python in attendance. At the 1991 annual American Family Therapy Association meeting, however, actor, director, author, and celebrated Pythoner John Cleese gave the following address on the sanity-bestowing power of humor.

When I first came to America in 1964, to do a Broadway show, I was immediately struck by two things. The first was that if a New York couple were offered the choice between two tickets for a big hit that everybody knew wasn't really any good and two tickets for a non-hit that they knew was absolutely excellent, they would always choose the tickets for the hit. I realized this was because external, visible success mattered more than quality to an enormous number of people in America.

The opposite was true in Britain at the time, because we're terrible snobs. In Britain, it was felt that something was more likely to have real quality if it wasn't a success. Here in the States it seemed that success was all-important, and, of course, the thing that strikes an enormous number of visitors to America is your absolute obsession with show business. The amount of status that actors and anchor-men and TV personalities and weather forecasters have in this country is quite extraordinary.

Look at me, for example. You are a very respectable and, if I may say so, highly intelligent group of people. Yet you've asked me—typical show business rubbish—to come and talk to you. I mean, really, you should be ashamed.

Now, the second thing I noticed back in '64, and I think it's still true, was that, in America, the acquisition of staggering quantities of cash gave a person moral stature. It's not just importance, and it's not just respect based, perhaps, on fear, but a kind of ethical superiority. In the sixties, this shocked me rigid, because, back in England, making money was regarded as irredeemably vulgar. As a friend of mine, Tony Jay, once pointed out, it was all right to have money, it was just getting it that was totally unacceptable. But over here, any old crook that made it big stood out like a shining beacon, beckoning the huddled masses to a better way of life.

I was puzzled about this attitude to money and I thought about it for eighteen months. When I got back to London, the first week that I was back, there was an article in the newspaper by an English philosopher called Sir Alfred Ayer, a great friend of Bertrand Russell, and a very splendid man. He said that he noticed exactly the same thing and that he was inclined to think that it was because when the Puritans first arrived in this land and consulted their Bibles to see what they could do for fun, almost everything was ruled out. There was no singing, no dancing, no drinking, no making of graven images, no coveting neighbors' oxen. Nothing. But wait a moment...there in the Bible they found the parable of the ten talents. They read that the servant to whom the master entrusted five talents was congratulated by his master on his return. "Well done, good and faithful servant, come and share your master's happiness," whereas the servant entrusted with one talent who failed to increase his wealth is told, "Thou lazy, wicked servant," and has his talent taken away and given to the one who has ten.

So the guy given one talent, who buries it and doesn't make any more out of it, has it taken away from him, and it goes to the guy who has ten. The master in the parable gives a pretty clear message to the early Puritans, who were not without fundamentalist tendencies—and fundamentalism seems to me the determination to take literally what was supposed to be meant metaphorically. And they took it literally that the accumulation of staggering quantities of the old schlamoola was approved by God. In fact, it was just about the only thing approved by God, except, perhaps, burning witches. This belief that compulsively acquiring money gave one brownie points with God could only be made worse by the Calvinist idea that if you really were one of the elect, this might be indicated by your worldly prosperity—just might. Your accumulated riches might indicate that you were not to be stir-fried for eternity.

I believe that money is neutral. After all, the Bible doesn't say that money is the root of all evil. The Bible says that *love* of money is the root of all evil. Yet, here in America you have the country being founded by people whose love of money was regarded as sanctified by God himself. And it seems to me it's not such a big step from that to Gorden Gecko's philosophy in the movie *Wall Street*.

In the last 25 years, especially under Margaret Thatcher, the British have caught up with you in this respect. There are still some differences, nevertheless, between our attitudes toward making it and yours. Our thinking is not as dominated, I believe, by the idea of winning and losing. For example, when I was writing the part of Otto in *A Fish Called Wanda*, I found, to my surprise, that a lot of my American friends did not think it was very funny that I had found a book here in America, called, *Eat to Win*. I showed it to several of my American friends and they said, "So?"

Actually, there was one particular document that absolutely astounded me, but again, some of my American friends didn't quite see why I thought it was kind of funny, even though it gave me the clue to Otto's character. It was an advertisement in a Los Angeles magazine for a Zen Buddhist seminar under the heading "Zen gives you the competitive edge."

When I was being brought up in England during the fifties I was constantly being acculturated with an attitude that I genuinely believe is a very important one, which is that it's necessary to be able to be a good loser, which is, of course, allied to the idea that it's not all-important to win. But compare that with these quotes that I found in an American anthology of quotes that was published in the mid sixties:

"Winning is not everything, it's the only thing." We've all heard that one. Vince Lombardi.

"Nice guys finish last."

"Show me a good sportsman and I'll show you a player I'm going to trade."

"Show me a good loser and I'll show you an idiot."

"Without any winners, there wouldn't be a goddamn civilization."

And best of all, "Defeat is worse than death because you have to live with defeat."

All of those are from American folklore, and baseball and basketball coaches. And quite seriously, when I read that, I felt a little pang of sadness inside me, because the most wonderful moments that I've ever experienced at sporting events—and I'm not a great sports nut—are those moments when there is an act of sportsmanship by one of the players and the whole atmosphere in the stadium flips. It's no longer paranoid—them against us. Everybody knows at that moment that what is linking us is more important than what divides us.

I suppose that we have to put a lot of what I've been talking about down to rugged individualism, which after all has made many aspects of your country great. There's no doubt about that. But if you are all such rugged individualists, please explain this paradox to me: Why are you all so touchy? Now I've been making television and film programs for twenty-five years and they're shown almost all over the world. But every time something of mine surfaces in America, out come the protest groups. First of all, nobody would put the "Monty Python" television show on the air for about six years because they said there would be too many protests. Then, when *Life of Brian* came out, we had practically every religious group protesting, people walking up and down in front of the cinema holding placards saying "Monty Python is an agent of the devil." (I wish we had ten percent!) The film was condemned in a joint statement issued by the Lutherans, the Calvinists, the Catholics, the Orthodox Jews and the Liberal Jews. In fact, it was the first time in history, according to fellow Monty Pythoner Eric Idle, that they had ever been able to agree on anything. *Monty Python's Meaning of Life* brought huge protests from the Catholics, protests about violence, sexism, obesity, and people exploding in restaurants. And now *Wanda's* opening in the States, and the subsequent Oscar ceremonies, were dominated by protests from the stutterers.

The trouble with humor is that it is inevitably—and you can't get around this—critical. You can't make a joke without criticizing somebody, even if it's criticizing all of us, including ourselves. After I made *A Fish Called Wanda*, I had a terribly difficult time when interviewers would ask me, "Have you had any complaints from stutterers?" So I put it in a wider context by saying, "Yes, and we've also had a lot of complaints from members of the League of Stupid People about Kevin Kline's performance. We've had thousands of letters about Jamie Lee Curtis' performance from members of the American Association of Manipulative Women saying this is just the kind of portrayal of a manipulative woman that has given manipulative women a bad name, and I've had no less than four huge deputations from the British Society of Extremely Tall, Rather Skinny, Wimpy, Sexually Repressed, Hen-Pecked Barristers."

If you're going to cease making jokes about everyone who might protest, or if you're going to cease even making remarks that maybe will not be acceptable to everybody, what's going to happen to the culture?

Wherever I go in the world, people tell me racial jokes. I get in a cab in Stockholm and the cab driver says to me, right out of the blue, "Why do Norwegians have band-aids on their faces Monday morning?" I say, "I don't know." He says, "Because on Sunday they eat with a knife and a fork."

The French say, "Why do the Belgians have their windshield wipers on the inside of their cars?" For an answer: "They spit."

The Germans tell me that the Swiss take their own houses in at night.

The Spanish tell me about three men—two Spaniards and a Portuguese—who were due to face death by a firing squad. So on the first day they take the first Spaniard out, they line him up in front of the firing squad, and just as they're about to pull the trigger, he shouts "Tidal wave!" The firing squad runs away and he escapes. The second day they bring the second Spaniard out, line him up against the wall, and just as they are about to pull the trigger, he shouts, "Earthquake!" And they all run away and he escapes. On the third day, they bring out the Portuguese and they're just about to pull the trigger and he shouts, "Fire!"

The point I'm making is that I'm not telling any of these jokes because I hate the Norwegians, Belgians, or the Portuguese. Do we want to get the United Nations every year to vote one nation the butt of all the jokes? "How many Uruguayans does it take to screw in a light bulb?"

Perhaps the real problem is not that the groups are touchy—that's not so surprising—but that in America they're taken so seriously. I mean, if you were dealing with a smaller group of people, what would be the effect of allowing the weakest member of the group, the most sensitive, the most touchy, the most neurotic, to dictate everything that happened in that group? I think that the result would be to reduce the level of health in the group. Similarly, if you pander to protest groups, you're allowing the most oversensitive elements to impose their values on the culture. I'm not saying that you shouldn't listen to what they have to say, but you don't have to accept it automatically. Because if you do, the culture will become less robust, less spontaneous, less creative, and basically less interesting. And I think that's why your television is not as interesting as the television that we've had in England, where one famous director in the sixties, Graham Greene's brother, Sir Carlton Greene, said there are some people one would wish to offend.

Now I'm not saying, maybe, that that's the *right* attitude, but I think something a little closer to that is necessary.

I don't think people have a God-given right not to be offended, and I think that being offended can be enormously educative. So if any of you want to help me, I'll tell you how to offend me, because if you can listen to what people are teasing you about you learn an awful lot. There are two main ways. First of all, you can offend me by referring to me as an actor, which causes my hackles to rise faster than any other insult. It took me years to work out why I reacted like that, and I realized, of course, that all the other actors I knew spent their lives trying to impress other people. It took me many years before I could see that I was up to exactly the same thing, that I was devoting an absurd amount of energy to creating impressions. It was a very painful discovery. And the label still offends me in some extraordinary way, but it doesn't mean that people shouldn't go on calling me an actor. I can't stop them, and it wouldn't be right if I tried.

The other way to insult me is to ask me if I am in fact like Basil Fawlty, the character I played in *Fawlty Towers*, because I've been denying this for years to the British press who ask me nothing else. But as my friends will confirm, it is, of course, absolutely true. I am exactly like Basil. I am a snob. I'm depressive. I'm very frightened of anger, which therefore tends to come out of me in all sorts of dishonest and indirect ways, and not in the direct way that you use anger in this culture. I love people to think that I'm better educated and informed than, in fact, I am. And I'm very envious and competitive. In fact, there's really only one good thing to be said for me, and that is when I'm offended, I don't form a protest group.

(Magical Blend issue #31)

Conclusion

Michael Peter Langevin: A Magical Universe

The morning I was to finish this chapter I awoke with a dream of a UFO flying over my home: a huge red ball flying neither fast enough to be distinguished as much more than a jet, nor slow enough to discern it in its multiplicity. After it passed I saw myself go out to sleep in the old Chevy Van I had loved back in 1985. It was dilapidated, and I just couldn't get comfortable. It began changing around me: first into my present day pickup, then into an airplane. Finally it was a glorious futuristic home that flew. Then I saw myself fall asleep, and I woke up to the material world.

A Magical Universe is the manifestation of years of dreaming and working by many dozens of writers, editors, artists and staff. The honor falls to me to speak to the high points of over seventeen years of *Magical Blend* magazine by writing what can be viewed as a first chapter of the ongoing saga of humanity's transformative journey. In our first fifty issues we have created a vehicle that explores, explains and celebrates life, love, creativity, society's evolution and spirituality. We have viewed no aspect of life as too banal to pull back the curtains and veils from their mysteries.

Magical Blend started out as a vision with lots of love and hope. The first issue's volunteer staff and friends walked into Bay area bookstores and begged them to try selling it. Of the first seven issues three had no color printing and no advertising. The first eleven issues took five years to get out and were all done by volunteers who spent nights and weekends on the magazine. All of us put in our spare time and pocket money for a vision of a publication that would empower people and change the world.

The article I wrote, "Healing with Chocolate Milk," reprinted in this book, was written over eleven years ago. It describes the youth social work I was involved in before I became a full-time publisher. Soon after writing that article a conservative executive director was hired. She told me I had to repaint Tahoe House, which the kids who lived there had decorated to their own taste, and to start doing things by the hospital manual or leave. It broke my heart, but I left. As is often the case, when one door shuts another opens. Issue number eleven of *Magical Blend*, in which that article appeared, sold out in record time.

My partner and co-publisher, Jerry Snider, *Magical Blends'* managing editor is greatly responsible for the consistently high quality of this book and of our quarterly magazine. He often says, "If life gives you lemons, then make lemonade." That attitude has helped establish *Magical Blend* as a unique publication: imitated by many but surpassed by none. Once I could devote my full attention to the magazine, Jerry, some of the volunteer staff and I were then able to move toward unfolding a similar vision of my "Chocolate Milk"-style populist publishing in *Magical Blend*. Some of my former youth center colleagues eventually worked with or contributed articles and ideas to *Magical Blend*. I married Deborah Genito, the social worker I worked with to develop "Chocolate Milk Therapy." Today we have a seven year old daughter, Sophia, and an eight year old son, Henry, who are helping me refine my Chocolate Milk theory. It is a very Magical Universe.

Larry Dossey sums up the message when he says, "Prayer is a powerful, effective tool all of us can use." In the *Celestine Prophecy* interview James Redfield says, "There is a spiritual revolution going on on this planet that will create heaven on earth." Brian Eno says that what drives him on is "the desire to create beauty and add to the quality of our existence." Dr. Clarissa Pinkola Estes (Women Who Run with the Wolves), a contributor to *Magical Blend*, says, "Story brings the best of the past forward to our modern mundane world." Robin Williams sums it up: "Be here now or get here later."

Writing this book, like every issue of *Magical Blend* magazine, has been an organic process. It has had a life of its own and it has evolved as it has seen fit: not as we who co-created it wished, but as though by its own will. The creative process can be messy, filled with frustrations and roadblocks, tests, setbacks and mistakes. There never seems to be enough time, money or energy to do what any of us think we want to do. But it can be different if we accept all of that as part of life and the creative process and see each of those things as lesson-filled challenges. We each have the ability to transform limitations into unique advantages, or, at least, to incorporate these unplanned opportunities into our lives and creative projects in order to improve ourselves.

If you have read the last chapters of this book first, or if you are reading the whole book through to this final chapter, be aware that *Magical Blend* was created to map and explain the changes that are going on in our society. We strongly believe that people's thoughts are the most powerful element in creating and unfolding their reality. This material, if read in the right mindset, can help clarify the beginning-of-a-new-reality we as a species and Gaia as a planet are generating. It contains many clues and alternative views on how to control and focus your thoughts and empower yourself regardless of the radical crumbling of all aspects of life we have depended upon.

The question is being asked in a multitude of ways: "If everything is changing, then what do we hold on to? What do we use as a firm foundation, or even as a dependable life raft?" The answers come in many forms, but most are many centuries old: Believe in yourself. Love yourself. Have faith in yourself and those you touch. Have faith in a positive future. Use prayer and creativity to develop unselfishness, forgiveness, a willingness to laugh at yourself and the silly injustices and illogical ways things work or don't. Hold on to a belief in the powerful destiny of the human race, the healing energy of the planet Earth and the reality of a Magical Universe.

In the early issues of *Magical Blend*, poetry, comics, fantasy and black-and-white line art were important elements of the blend. The readers, through surveys, letters, and phone calls, requested that color art, articles and interviews take over. Alternative healing, technology, shamanism and music have been demanded as ways to explore and explain our world's changes. They provide the creative processes and self-empowerment which makes the nearly undefinable concepts we encounter comprehensible. This applies to all of us; even publishing a magazine must be an evolving, transformative experience.

We are at the threshold. A longtime reader and friend not long ago told me, "The early issues of *Magical Blend* seemed extreme and esoteric and almost unbelievable. Nowadays you are saying much the same things but it occurs as a comfortable, in-depth and positive exploration of the daily headlines." For over 17 years *Magical Blend* and its staff and contributors have attempted to explore and explain how the world is changing and how each individual can find their own answers, their own path and their own self-empowerment within a multitude of creative alternatives. This book contains the cream of the articles we have presented. It represents the best angles we have explored in our first 50 issues.

There are those who believe that orthodox religions hold the only spiritual truths worth practicing; that anything but orthodox religious practices are distractions to spiritual growth. *Magical Blend*'s contributing writers and editors come from all walks of life and all nature of belief systems and creative practices. We say anything that exists in reality or imagination can be a catalyst to an individual's growth, development and spiritual release. Sex shared with unselfish joy and reverence can be no less valid a path than prayer. If a piece of art catches a unique expression of spiritual potential it can be a stepping stone to higher consciousness. The computer technology which allows me to write this chapter faster and more meaningfully than my pen or typewriter is a spiritual tool worth exploring. Music can transform the listener and performer to higher levels of existence. Business, too, can be a transcendent art if viewed properly.

The thread that ties it all together is the process of exploring pathways. The world is changing radically around us. The Earth's population is speculating more each day what it all means and how to enjoy and benefit by these changes. *Magical Blend* never claims to have the answers. Most of those involved in creating it never agree on much but want to produce a quality publication consistent with our statement of purpose: "Before enlightenment: chopping wood and toting water. After enlightenment: chopping wood and toting water." Is it all perspective and attitude? It seems so.

The discussion of computer technology in this book speaks to creativity, spirituality and self-empowerment. Technology is but a material world manifestation of what we as individuals can and will do without machines in the future.

Music, like a smile, is a universal language. It takes us to other realms and dimensions. It gives feeling and insights in areas words and language cannot. It has the potential to be the clearest, purest creative process. Even a heroin junky can create blues music that quintessentially transforms.

Jerry Garcia appears in this book because he carried the banner of all that was best from the sixties revolution forward into the nineties. He is as important to history as is Mother Theresa. Mickey and Bob are redefining what The Dead are and where the dream might evolve. But The Dead cut across age, class and social structure. At their concerts young students and fifty year old executives grooved and felt a part of a transcendent experience. Whether on ecstasy, mushrooms, LSD, peyote, spinning or just a contact high, The Dead concerts spoke to a communal unselfish future and music as a extremely powerful positive social statement.

AIDs, herpes, and syphilis come to us now as unjust afflictions of the poor and disenfranchised: especially in the third world. Yet even STDs have a positive side. If an individual is mindful and not too risky with sexual sharing, that individual can stay healthy. The practice of indulging the wild abandon, coupling with anyone anytime, has mostly been replaced with quality, sensitive, creative sex with one partner.

That is where Tantra comes in. The ancients knew that sex with magical intent could raise your kundalini and spiritually advance those who practice it. Sex is addressed in *A Magical Universe* as an experience to be viewed for its potential for transcendence. When you share an orgasm with someone you love, who loves you, the two of you are one being at one with the Magical Universe's creative force. Was the Big Bang anything other than a godly orgasm? Is the process of change much different from the act of intercourse? All of existence is made up of wave patterns: in and out, up and down. Sex is a spiritual pathway to your higher vibration through increased awareness and attitude. Sex is great. Transform with it.

Sex is the perfect lead-in to health. We are born into and exist in material worlds. Our bodies are our tools for spiritual growth. If we do not stay in good health it is much harder to be creative, positive or to even grow and evolve spiritually.

My article, "Healing with Chocolate Milk," shows another side of mental health. Each emotionally disturbed adolescent was a difficult, draining individual for me to work with. Some made me crazy. Many made me cry. But never have I learned more about myself and my own demons or been helped to heal more than I did at that time with them. Mental health is an important goal, because by working to heal ourselves and others we learn to grasp the greater reasons we were born. We must stop building more prisons and each work to help heal more people in need.

Mental health leads to the Goddess. In the last 2000 years our world has been dominated by male gods. The 21st century will have a new balance of energies in which the feminine is slightly dominant. Riane Eisler and Jean Houston address this awareness and this need for every being to get in touch with the Goddess in each of us. As the Goddess rises we are able to end war and become a population of healers.The Goddess, as found and extolled in nature and ritual, are essential to our future. In the past these practices strengthened individuals. People who used them were persecuted because these practices validated strong, intelligent women who participated in social decision making enthusiastically. The Wiccan practices have much to offer in these changing times.

For centuries in the west spirituality has been viewed, practiced and expressed as the exclusive domain of organized religion. In this book we touch on Buddhism and Christianity. We say that if you belong to and/or believe in one religion that's fine; that's great; that's a perfect foundation to live from. But please work to remain open-minded, and experiment with alternative tools and paths that might complement your established beliefs. Question authority. Speak to God or the creative godhood inside yourself.

Shamanism is the area in which *Magical Blend* readers have consistently expressed the most interest. The indigenous peoples are vanishing. Their ways are vanishing. The secret to the smoothest transition as a planet into the 21st century is to bring the best of the old ways and make them stronger than ever. The writers in these articles are attempting to do that for us. When I read Carlos Castaneda in high school and college and searched for my power spots and attempted to recapitulate my energy and the experiences of my young life, never did I imagine that his unique shared knowledge represented a strong vein of spiritual practices passed down from the Toltecs, Aztecs, Mayans and Huichols. It didn't occur to me at that time that he was John the Baptist for a huge following of initiates that would teach and share these practices. These initiates help raise the vibration of the whole solar system so that we can better conquer death and time and create a beach head for an evolved, sorcerised society. Such practices can insure that the future is as magical and powerful as anything in myth and legend. I am thankful Carlos wrote his books and that more have come to spread and make this pathway more approachable.

Perhaps the inorganic beings and allies naguals communicate with are simply another form of UFO. If not, what are UFOs exactly? Ken Carey wrote this piece for us, but his millennium message is far more reality-shattering. Please read it. Whitley Strieber and Jacques Vallée have witnessed, experienced and grasped concepts and views of existence many of us may never consider. To speak to them is to wonder. Are UFOs faster-than-light starships from a federation of evolved planets? Are they the beings that seeded our human species? Are UFOs time travelers come back to observe this rarest event in history? Are they other-dimensional beings that share our planet yet remain unseen by us? Are they a future race of evolved sterile technical time-travelers using humans, sheep and cattle to reproduce and create hybrids? Are they our invisible government, controlling us through amazingly advanced social manipulation techniques? Are they in league with some members of the trilateral commission? Are they beyond beings as we know them? Are there celestial events along with our crop circles that are preparing us and even communicating to us about the coming magnetic and spiritual shifts? The possibilities are endless. Will an announcement be made in 1997 that world governments acknowledge that UFOs exist? If so, will what is revealed be factual and honest revelation or yet another level of manipulation? UFOs may hold all the secrets to humanity's future, or they may be only one possible future. They may be allies and catalysts for change; they may be deterrents or some of both. If it is a Magical Universe, then UFOs are quickly becoming an undeniable and essential part of it.

Ecologically we can be considered micro-organisms in the infinite consciousness of planet Gaia. My first awareness of the Magical Universe came during nature walks taken with my ever-inspiring mother. She would point out minute details and get very excited about them. I learned from her that we must stop killing and destroying and using nature all up. We must start being aware and realigning our economies in harmony with nature. We must love the Earth, and build societies which complement and work in harmony with nature. Education is not the only key. If we don't revolutionize the existing system, however, then mental and spiritual destruction will continue to dominate humanity. We must educate ourselves and our youth better.

Myth tells us the meanings behind the mysteries of life. We are a world in the process of writing new myths for our future descendants. This book contains many seeds for creating new myths about spiritual evolution: maps through the mine fields of modern lightning-fast change. Every aspect of experience redefines our shared knowledge, allowing us all to be involved in reading, creating and being touched by each other: to assume increasing personal responsibility for our lives, and, with a childlike willingness, to risk making mistakes in a world of unknowing and to view these mistakes as learning opportunities.

Humor is all important. Laughter gives life meaning. Taking everything lightly sets you free. Enjoying life is the only way to gain its true essence and power. Everything is miraculous.

We are becoming the masters of our minds. We can free ourselves from the traps of the material world to explore the indefinable and divine realms of the soul. The strange day-to-day setbacks, sidetrips, roadblocks and other all-consuming self-inhibiting things in our lives are just parts of the obstacle course upon which we grow and develop: just part of the lesson plan we agreed to before we were born into this life. We choose to work out our karma and to learn to evolve and reunite with our limitless Godself while facing the multi-faceted challenges of existing in a low-vibrational material world.

A mythical figure of my youth, Jack Kerouac, has been a motivating and inspiring force for every aspect of my life. His brother's death in Lowell, Massachusetts is what's pointed to by many as the factor that drove Jack to write so uniquely. That could be the force behind the Beatnik Era, The Hippie Era, and all the creativity that followed. I grew up in Methen and Lawrence, Massachusetts, both right near Lowell. My father, who was a great inspiration in my life on many levels, was great friends with the priest who baptized and buried Jack. I used to think I read Kerouac because he grew up nearby and became famous. I was wrong. In retrospect I see that I read Kerouac so I would be ready for what followed. Jack was an avatar. He gave his life as a beacon for others. His explorations of Buddhism and San Francisco led me to both. City Lights book store, where he and Ginsberg had their famous poetry readings, was one of the first stores to sell *Magical Blend* magazine when it was launched in San Francisco. We live in the Magical Universe, and a basic rule is: "Contradictions set us free." I wasn't a beatnik, but Jack Kerouac taught me how to think and write. Thanks Jack!

When I was young I dreamt of meeting and befriending and learning from famous accomplished people. *Magical Blend* has given me constant opportunities to do that. I have interviewed and become friends with best selling authors and artists and trend setters on a global scale. In my youthful dreams these famous people had it all together and emoted chic-ness, confidence and enlightenment. I am writing here to tell you that the Magical Universe most of us experience daily is a limited, less than perfect world. I often view it as a spiritual kindergarten. Most of the celebrities I have dealt with are just too cool, yet they all have feet of clay. They might be great writers or interviewers or musicians or artists, but some other aspects of their development have suffered.

At first this depressed me and disappointed me. Then I realized how freeing it is. We can be great, famous and inspiring to our world, and we don't have to be perfect! Then I was thrown again back onto wondering what is cool, happening, edge-cutting, meaningful. Is it Brian Eno's musical expression or Douglas Rushkoff's Techno insights? Dan Millman's Peaceful Warrior path or Jean Houston's Mystery School? If it's cool and edge-cutting and Now, is it more valid or less valid? Is the next two decades the time when edge-cutting and cool also become spiritual: inspiring consumers' creativity and transcendence? I think so. *A Magical Universe* has not only been a great opportunity, allowing me to personally interview and get to know many of the heroes of my youth, but it also has helped set the tone for what's happening in the future of all people!

We are a planet on the precipice of change, and it scares all of us. You have come to the first step. Remember Goethe, Hermann Hesse and Kahil Gibran? Roll them together and call them a hint. The 21st century is *not* Armageddon! It is not Nostradamus' worst nightmare by anyone's interpretation! It is not the end of the world. It is a time of major decision for each individual. Do you want slow spiritual growth or fast spiritual growth? Both are fine. Both are valid. Are you clear on who you were before you were born? Who you are when you dream? Where your moments of inspiration come from? Who you will be after you die? Do these things scare you or are you intrigued by them? That's the decision. You are unlimited potential in the Magical Universe. You hold all decisions and all the keys to growth and expression and freedom. What's it going to be, Bunkie? Stretch to spiritually limitless expression or stay with the world as it seems. Welcome to Quetzalcoatl's wild ride: the amusement park of the Magical Universe's version of spiritual evolution. This book is an invitation to the former, but the choice, as with everything, is yours.

This book is a threshold to the Magical Universe. Your perspective and your attitude unfold the nature of your experience. The world around us is a series of indefinable miracles and opportunities. Your thoughts, your goals, your willingness to keep your attention and belief in your highest possible expression is the key to your experience of each moment of your life in the Magical Universe.

In 1979 a group of creative and spiritual pilgrims sat on a windy dune by a beach in San Francisco. We used prayer, ritual, visualization, meditation and affirmations. We shared all our focused energy to help bring into existence a magazine that would be a huge commercial success and prove that true spirituality and creativity can function, even prosper, in the market place and newsstands of the world. All these years later this book is a hallmark in helping to continue to unfold that original vision and intention.

This book is hardly exhaustive. It is more of a sampler. If you liked a chapter or an article or an author or a musician, go find more. Immerse yourself in them and their creative works. Basically this is the best of *Magical Blend* magazine's first fifty issues. The magazine still is evolving. It has always had a life force of its own beyond the staffs' desires. We urge you if you liked this book to subscribe to the quarterly ongoing magazine. If part of this book touched you deeply please let us know. If some of this material was what you feel the world or you want more of communicate. *Magical Blend* is now on the Internet. The Internet is redefining publishing. This is the first of two books that will be published by *Magical Blend* in a six month period. The next is to be titled *Magical Blend*'s Solstice Shift. It will feature original writings by many of *Magical Blend*'s favorite authors on the evolving future and how to empower the individual while the winds of change howl around us. We will continue to evolve *Magical Blend* with each reader's feedback and input.

Magic, as defined by *Magical Blend* Magazine in *A Magical Universe*, is simply "change," the creative process, exploration into imagination and little-known aspects of reality, realizing more of our hidden potential. It is a Magical Universe. Magic can be as grand as using a spell to alter the path of a comet or as mundane as sitting on the back porch eating an apple.

As above, so below. All the secrets of the Magical Universe are inside each living thing: they are inside you as you read this. The secret is to first develop the desire to learn the secrets, then develop the ability to listen to your own inner voice. As you sit on your back porch, or wherever, eating an apple, you can just be eating an apple or you can be ingesting the secrets of the Magical Universe. Attitude and intentions are two important keys. Use this book to develop them.

And above all, have fun doing it!

Issue Thirty-One $8 Poetry and Passion • Cosmic Trigger II • John Cleese • Ken Carey • Miracle of Birth • Popular "Cult"ure • NLP Tapes • Christian Fundamentalism in Guatemala • Imagework

Issue Thirty-Two $8 Douglas Adams • Holographic Universe • Laurie Anderson • Russia's Religious Revolution • Shamanism • Tiny Tim • Peter Redgrove • Marina Raye

Issue Thirty-Three $8 Sexuality, Gender Politics and Personal Identity • The Third Wave of Feminism • Zuni Man/Woman • Jean Shinoda Bolen • Robert Bly • Marion Woodman • John Weir Perry • Robert Moore • Christopher Hyatt

Issue Thirty-Four $14 Photocopy Death, the Devil, UFOs and Other Dimensional Doorways • Jacques Vallee • Applied Demonology • Embracing Death • Angels and Aliens • Chemicals and Consciousness • Communicating with Compassion

Issue Thirty-Five $14 Photocopy Time and Space in the Aboriginal Dreamtime • Terence McKenna • Jean Houston • Political Dreamtime • Hyperreality • Florinda Donner • The Six Realms • American Dreamtime • The Joy of Spiritual Service

Issue Thirty-Six $8 John Lilly • Dark Moon Goddess • Jesus: In Search of a Misplaced Messiah • Feminism at the Crossroads • Barry Neil Kaufman's Six Short Cuts to Happiness • Entelechy • Dan Millman • Michael Murphy

Issue Thirty-Seven $8 Clarissa Pinkola Estés • Charles Bukowski • Susie Bright's Egg Sex • Raincheck on the End of Reality • Postmodern Zombies • Life Lived Backwards • Thomas Moore • White Boys Dancing

Issue Thirty-Eight $8 Laura Huxley • Allen Ginsberg • Huston Smith • Search for a Reincarnated Lama • Body As Music • Sexual Shaman • Nina Graboi • Baby Boomer Spirituality • Gabriel Cousens

Issue Thirty-Nine $8 Alice Walker, Isabel Allende and Jean Shinoda Bolen on Creative Inspiration • Joseph Chilton Pierce • Beginnings in Ritual • Vision Quest • Home Schooling • Bardos and Other Realities

Issue Forty $8 Terence McKenna • Taisha Abelar on Sorcery • Carlos Castaneda on Don Juan • Marija Gimbutas on the Goddess • Elder Leaders • An Alternative to the Madhouse • '50s Science Fiction and the Emerging Goddess • History and the Ego Death of "Man"

Issue Forty-One $8 Jerry Garcia • Starhawk on the Importance of Celebration • Jean Houston on Emily Dickinson • Rupert Sheldrake and Matthew Fox: The Sacred Universe • A Westerner's Walkabout • William Irwin Thompson • Lauren Artress on the Labyrinth • The Dynamics of Nurturing

Issue Forty-Two $8 Castaneda's Clan • Albert Gore, Jr. on Creating a New Relationship with the Earth • Riane Eisler on Birth, Sex and Death • Stephen King • Spalding Gray • Lucid Dreaming • Releasing Your Creative Potential • Macrobiotics • Larry Dossey on the Power of Prayer

Issue Forty-Three $8 Malidoma Somé • Clarissa Pinkola Estés: The Creative Fire, Part One • Fred Allen Wolf: The Dreaming Universe • Marina Raye: Sacred Sexuality • Reggae and Rastafarianism • Hoxey's Cancer Cure • Blade Runner Psychology • Michael Hutchison • Hyperspace • The UFOs of Ancient India

Issue Forty-Four $8 Terence McKenna, Part One • Ursula Le Guin • Timothy Leary • Jean Shinoda Bolen • Ambient Music • History of the Modern Ecological Movement • Merilyn Tunneshende: Carrying on the Castaneda Legacy • Q'ero Shamanism • New Hope for Cancer Sufferers • The Power of Silence

Issue Forty-Five $8 The Spirituality of Imperfection • Terence McKenna, Part Two • The Dreambody in Cyberspace • Tantric Sex • Clarissa Pinkola Estés: Part Two • Arrested Development • Axiom • Restoring the Environment • Dream Herbs • Marathon Monks

Issue Forty-Six $8 Whitley Strieber • Robert Anton Wilson • Douglas Rushkoff • Marlo Morgan • Star Trek • Jai Uttal • Paul Winters • Cult Behavior • Millenial Madness • The Herb That Ends Addiction

Issue Forty-Seven $8 Ken Eagle Feather on Don Juan • Merilyn Tunneshende on Toltec Sorcery • Keys to the Pyramids • Allen Ginsberg • Shakti Gawain • Jello Biafra • Nanotechnology • Native American Rappers • Druid Herbs • Castaneda-like Experiments

Issue Forty-Eight $8 Bob Weir • Jaron Lanier • James Redfield • Marsha Sinetar • UFOs and NDEs • Robert Bly • Eldridge Cleaver • Robert Anton Wilson • Smart Herbs • Castaneda Controversies • Raves

Issue Forty-Nine $8 Great Moments in Sex • Riane Eisler • Jimi Hendrix by Susie Bright • Stanislav Grof • Cannabis • The DNA of Pop • Sex, Drugs and Virtual Reality • Psychedelic Shamanism • Lisa Gerrard • Clarence Clemmons • Lynn Andrews

Issue Fifty $8 Transformative Secrets of Sex • Douglas Rushkoff on Cyberspace • Julian Cope • Feng Shui • Merilyn Tunneshende • Art of Manifestation • Barbara Marciniak • Melatonin Miracle • Dan Millman • Frank Black

Issue Fifty-One $8 Ray Bradbury • Moby • Disney and Gaia Consciousness • Nanotechnology • Donovan • Neal Stephenson • Free Energy • 10 Essential Herbs • Generation Treks

Issue Fifty-Two $8 Timothy Leary • Lucid Dreaming • Remote Viewing • Merilyn Tunneshende • Jon Anderson • Future Memory • Alien Prophesies • Spin Doctors • R. J. Stewart • Breaking the Silence About UFOs

---

Swan•Raven & Co.

A MAGICAL UNIVERSE
The Best of Magical Blend Magazine
Michael Langevin and Jerry Snider

PLANT SPIRIT MEDICINE
Healing with the Power of Plants
Eliot Cowan

TAROT OF THE SOUL
A guiding oracle that uses ordinary playing cards
Belinda Atkinson

CALLING THE CIRCLE
The First and Future Culture
Christina Baldwin

RITUAL
Power, Healing and Community
Malidoma Somé

WHEN SLEEPING BEAUTY WAKES UP
*A Woman's Tale of Healing the Immune System and
Awakening the Feminine*
Patt Lind-Kyle

For a complete catalog of Wild Flower Press or Swan•Raven books or information on additional books that we distribute,
call **800/366-0264** or write to

Blue Water Publishing
PO Box 2875
Rapid City, SD 57709

Internet URL: http://www.bluewaterp.com/~bcrissey/
e-mail address: BlueWaterP@aol.com